DICTIONARY OF E-BUSINESS

A Definitive Guide to Technology and Business Terms

DICTIONARY OF E-BUSINESS

A Definitive Guide to Technology and Business Terms

FRANCIS BOTTO

JOHN WILEY & SONS, LTD
Chichester • New York • Weinheim • Brisbane • Singapore • Toronto

Other Wiley Editorial Offices

John Wiley & Sons Inc., 605 Third Avenue,
New York, NY 10158-0012, USA

WILEY-VCH Verlag GmbH
Pappelallee 3, D-69469 Weinheim, Germany

Jacaranda Wiley Ltd, 33 Park Road, Milton,
Queensland 4064, Australia

John Wiley & Sons (Asia) Pte Ltd, 2 Clementi Loop #02-01,
Jin Xing Distripark, Singapore 129809

John Wiley & Sons (Canada) Ltd, 22 Worcester Road,
Rexdale, Ontario M9W 1L1, Canada

Library of Congress Cataloging-in-Publication Data

Botto, Francis.
    Dictionary of E-commerce: a definitive guide to technology
and business terms/ Francis Botto.
        p.   cm.
    ISBN 0-471-88145-7   (alk. paper)
    1. Electronic commerce—Dictionaries. I. Title.
    HF5548.32. B67 2000
    658.8′4—dc21   99-089915
                                                       CIP

British Library Cataloguing in Publication Data
A catalogue record for this book is available from the British Library

ISBN 0 471 88145 7

Typeset in 10/12pt Times by Footnote Graphics, Warminster, Wilts.
Printed and bound in Great Britain by Antony Rowe Ltd, Chippenham, Wiltshire
This book is printed on acid-free paper responsibly manufactured from sustainable forestry,
in which at least two trees are planted for each one used for paper production.

PREFACE

This dictionary defines important terms and phrases relating to e-business in the context of design, development and usage. It addresses the many milestone decisions, implementation processes and technologies along the migration paths that lead to e-business sites, as well as those along the paths that lead away from them. These deliverables via the Internet or World Wide Web provide a borderless world with geographically insensitive marketing, advertising and selling channels. Wall Street's response to this most contemporary of 'gold rushes' has seen company revenues sky rocket as Web sites make the transition from specialist entities to global successes. Virtual stores, search engines, information services and the many other Internet-related terms now grace the vernacular of Internet investors and analysts the world over.

At one level the World Wide Web is used in a point-of-information (POI) guise where products are described and displayed. The current goal is e-business embodying transaction processing with all its sub-processes, data stores and security measures. A myriad of migration paths to these Web architectures exist as the surrounding technologies develop at a pace, and as new and advancing methodologies dictate change. In spite of the seemingly singular medium that is the World Wide Web, CD-based applications continue to play a role with DVD variants offering high quality MPEG-2 video and an attractive medium for POI or e-catalogues. Hybrid CD-ROM and DVD-ROM multimedia productions may provide the local delivery of high quality video as well as present hyperlinks to e-business Web sites for on-line ordering and for transaction processing.

E-business promises another important chapter in the evolution of the role of technology in commerce. It is shrouded in a multiplicity of questions which this dictionary seeks to address through an in-depth study of the technologies, the services, their acquisition, migration paths, investment strategies and comparative advantages. More than a glossary or dictionary with scant definitions, it includes informative essays that address key issues.

It is hoped that you find this text a useful source of information.

Francis Botto

ABOUT THE AUTHOR

Francis Botto was born in Gorseinon, near Swansea, Wales, on 4 October 1962. A writer and researcher specialising in new technologies, in the mid 1980s he began a pioneering and prolific output of notable articles and enduring books that he wrote in the UK, and more recently in Australia. His continuing interest in IT has yielded a varied output of works addressing subjects like multimedia and Internet applications in contexts of usage and development, and more recently the development of new technologies such as SunSoft's Jini technology.

INTRODUCTION

E-business is an awesome, fast-changing subject, driving multiple paradigm shifts as radical as those that splintered from the Industrial Revolutions with all its recorded social, economic and technological impacts. For the first time virtual stores may provide POI (point-of-information) and POS (point-of-sale) functionality that provide advertising and selling channels leading to the global market. The benefits of e-business have been the focus of numerous papers, publications and conferences for some time, and far outweigh the much-publicised potential pitfalls that include the threat of larceny resulting from illegally obtained customer payment details, and the threat of an exodus of traders from the high street.

Industry's response to the security issue has proved technically complex with numerous cryptosystems being driven into obsolence. Standardisation and advancements in cryptography, which continue to exhibit minor flaws, see today's secure e-business sites win the confidence of consumers, banks and notable credit card companies including Visa and MasterCard. One catalyst is the SET (Secure Electronic Transactions) Consortium which specifies technologies and guidelines for secure, compliant applications initiated by Microsoft, Visa and MasterCard. The infrastructures, software components and technologies that combine to make the World Wide Web provide the key to modern e-business. They are being shaped by the following:

- updated developer's workbench which includes Microsoft Visual Studio
- programming languages such as Java, JavaScript, HTML, DHTML, VRML, C++, Visual Basic and VBScript
- Object Web with its standard components and building blocks
- modern standard client/server initiatives which include Sun Micro-systems' Java-based Jini technology which impacted in 1999
- updated mainstream Web site development tools from software publishers which include Microsoft, Asymetrix and Macromedia.

The aforementioned technologies are driving change, and are being driven themselves by underlying hardware advancements including:

- new processors, primarily from Intel (and other chip makers)

- client/server architectures that use server technologies like SMP, NUMA, and MPP
- advancing peripheral devices including modems
- the vast network that supports the Internet, including physical or wireless digital pathways and mobile networks
- more efficient protocols.

Access technologies like ISDN and cable are part of the English language, with many house purchasers wanting to know if they have been installed. To the vast audience currently benefiting from e-business, these are as transparent as the methodologies and the multiplicity of complex processes and sub-processes that constitute the development lifecycles of Web sites. The same may be said of the development lifecycle required to produce the tools and technologies themselves, where the levels of granularity and technical detail are incomprehensible to all but those directly involved with their creation.

Everyday E-business terms and phrases are entering the English language, and are beginning to frequent dictionaries of a general nature; terms that are prefixed by on-line are widespread, including on-line shopping, on-line banking, on-line share dealing, on-line travel agencies etc. E-business is yet another feature of modernity driven by the Internet and by technology as a whole, and is a new specialisation for analysts, and for industry professionals such as Web site designers, developers, researchers and technologists. Many new technologies, software enhancements and development tools are now prefixed by the term *e-business*, and it drives new global markets in the effort to capitalise on the swing of consumer shopping habits towards the Internet.

Coordination is a key feature pinned to that ubiquitous growing entity that has come to be known as the Internet or to some, the *Information Superhighway*. More than ever standards organisations including W3C, IETF, the Object Management Group (OMG), ITU, ISO and SET provide makers with the opportunity to develop compatible products and at the same time reduce wasted resources and expended energies while attempting to forge proprietary standards. Not that major manufactures will ever be relieved of this effort, but the growing transparency of hardware platforms from a Web-based e-business application viewpoint introduces stability and reassurance for those investing in such implementations and services.

E-business implementations used to address the mass market are at the heart of the current revolution, but more specialist impacts such as those in banking, stock markets, and money markets might be considered more significant as they are influential in determining the performance of an economy. A country's IT infrastructure, as well as those of its enterprises, drives trade at home and abroad. But the question mark which hangs over direct channel selling is echoed by e-business, namely will consumers buy products blind? Selling via the direct channel off the page, over the telephone or via TV shopping is meant to offer the consumer savings, but the theoretical price differential does not always favour the direct seller. Some of the consumer electronics giants favour high street and out-of-town stores with lower prices as they prefer to win consumer confidence by allowing them to experience their products at first hand. Furthermore, shopping in conventional stores is perceived as a leisurely experience to many consumers. Whatever arguments are presented, it seems that it is most probable that numerous sales channels will serve consumers, giving more choice, but those price differentials which exist between them will eventually subside as a slightly imperfect equilibrium takes hold.

SYMBOLS AND NUMERALS

& An ampersand symbol used as a prefix in the hexadecimal counting system.

? 1. A part of URL address which marks the beginning of data used by a CGI program which may be executed using a GET method. The URL defines the CGI program (such as `credit.cgi` for example) and the accompanying data used by the server that follows the question mark: `www.FrancisBotto.com/cgi-bin/credit. cgi?subject= transaction`
2. A wildcard that may be used as a substitute for a single undefined character in a search string.
(See CGI environment variables.)

* A wildcard that may be used as a substitute for an undefined series of characters in a search string.

/ A forward slash used as a separator in URL addresses such as *https:// www.FrancisBotto.com*, and to integrate comments in many languages.

/etc/password A Unix file used to store passwords.
(See Unix.)

1.2 Mbps A data transfer rate measured in Mbits/s, and one that the original MPEG-1 video standard was designed for. It is the approximate data transfer rate that is offered by single-speed CD variants like CD-ROM. 1.2 Mbps approximates 150 Kbyte/s.
(See CD-ROM.)

1.2 mm The thickness of a DVD or CD disk variant.
(See CD-ROM and DVD-ROM.)

1.44 Mbyte The formatted data capacity of a 3.5in high-density floppy disk for the PC.

1.544 Mbps   1. A data transfer rate offered by a single T1 line. *(See T1.)* 2. A data transfer rate of a primary rate multiplex of 255 channels of 64 Kbps ISDN channels.
(See ISDN.)

2B+D   Using the basic rate interface (BRI), this denotes two bearer (2B) channels and one (D) ISDN channel.
(See ISDN.)

2-D (two-dimensional)   An image that may be visualised from a 2-D vector coordinate data set, and is devoid of the Z dimension of depth. $[X, Y]$ vector coordinates may be used to store the image data in an array that may be held in memory, or on hard disk or on other DSMs like CD-ROM or DVD. Sets of 2-D coordinates are manipulated using a transformation matrix $[T]$, and in the case of ordinary coordinates this is a 2-row matrix:

```
[X, Y][T]=[X1, Y1]
```

To accommodate a three-row transformation matrix, the homogeneous coordinate representation is used where $[X, Y]$ becomes $[X, Y, H]$, and the resulting transformed coordinate set may be normalised so as it may be plotted.
(See 3-D.)

2-D curve   A curve that is devoid of the Z dimension, and may be generated or visualised using:

- A set of 2-D vector coordinates, or 3-D homogeneous coordinates stored in an array. This method may be considered an inefficient use of memory (if the coordinates are stored within the code itself) but improves the speed of drawing and transformation.
- Coordinates are generated using an equation (i.e. $x = \cos(y)$) and then written to an array, and used memory is reclaimed after plotting, it is regarded memory efficient but requires more processing.
- Coordinates loaded from a mass storage device such as CD-ROM, DVD or hard disk, or downloaded from a server.

(See 2-D and 3-D.)

2 MBps   A threshold bandwidth beyond which a network or access technology is described as broadband. 2 Mbits/s = 2//000//000 bits per second.
(See Access technology and B-ISDN.)

2-tier   A client/server architecture where the applications' logic, data and presentation elements are distributed between client systems and one or

more servers. Now regarded as old-fashioned, early implementations were based on 'dumb terminals' (or client systems) that did little more than send messages to, and receive messages from a server that was invariably a mainframe design. 2-tier architectures have been displaced by 3-tier implementations in most first world countries. The World Wide Web of the early 1990s was a 2-tier client/server model, with the Web server simply publishing HTML documents to the client via a largely uni-directional path. This changed in 1995 with the CGI (Common Gateway Interface). The partition that exists between the three application elements, thus indicating which are on the client and which are on the server, is a variable, and depends on the client/server architecture. The early static Web and many intranets were 2-tier, where the user simply received published information (or Web pages) from the Web server. There was no feedback from the client system, and the application elements were partitioned so that data and logic was on the server-side. The dynamic or active Web model that was initially driven by CGI impacted the partitioning of the application elements of data, logic and presentation. Client systems might be PCs, Macintosh computers, or NCs, while the server might be based on one or more of the latest generation of Intel processors and running the Windows NT Server OS. Equally, the server might be a powerful RISC platform running the Unix operating system. File servers, print servers and database servers may also be integrated in the design architecture to distribute processing and optimise performance. The connection or access technology between servers and clients is provided by a LAN variant.
(See 3-tier, Client/server and CGI.)

3-D (three-dimensional)   A 3-D computer image or animation stored and generated using absolute or relative coordinates that include X (horizontal), Y (vertical) and Z (depth) dimensions. Standard file formats and standard languages for developing 3-D animations for multimedia and virtual reality (VR) have emerged. The VRML (Virtual Reality Modeling Language) is suitable for the development of 3-D World Wide Web (WWW) pages. Web content development tools may be used to create 3-D graphics and animations for Web pages, and often do not require knowledge of VRML. Chips aimed at the acceleration of 3-D graphics include the Glint family that was developed by 3DLabs. Creative Labs licensed Glint technology from 3DLabs in 1994 following which they collaborated to develop the GLINT 3-D processor. This is used in the Creative 3D Blaster that was first shown at Creativity '95 in San Francisco, a milestone in the development of 3-D graphics cards. 3-D engines that may be used to generate 3-D animations include:

- Microsoft Direct3D
- Apple QuickDraw3D
- Silicon Graphics OpenGL

Authentic 3-D animations depend upon matrix multiplication where sets of coordinates are multiplied by a transformation matrix. 3-D vectors, or ordinary 3-D coordinates, $[X\ Y\ Z]$, may be exchanged for homogeneous vector coordinates $[X\ Y\ Z\ H]$. The homogeneous dimension (H) is added to accommodate a four-row transformation matrix, so increasing the number of possible 3-D transformations. The transformation of homogeneous coordinates is given by:

$$[X\ Y\ Z\ H] = [x\ y\ z\ 1]\mathbf{T}$$

The resulting transformed coordinates may be normalised to become ordinary coordinates:

$$[x^*\ y^*\ z^*\ 1] = [X/H\ Y/H\ Z/H\ 1]$$

Consider the 4×4 transformation matrix:

$$\begin{bmatrix} a & b & c & p \\ d & e & f & q \\ h & i & j & r \\ l & m & n & a \end{bmatrix} = \mathbf{T}$$

Scaling, shearing and rotation is achieved using the 3×3 matrix sector:

$$\begin{bmatrix} a & b & c \\ d & e & f \\ h & i & j \end{bmatrix}$$

The transformation matrix:

$$\begin{bmatrix} 1 & 0 & 0 & 0 \\ 0 & \cos\theta & \sin\theta & 0 \\ 0 & -\sin\theta & \cos\theta & 0 \\ 0 & 0 & 0 & 1 \end{bmatrix}$$

is used to rotate a 3-D object by the angle θ around the X-axis.
A rotation of an angle θ about the y-axis is achieved using the transformation matrix:

$$\begin{bmatrix} \cos\theta & 0 & -\sin\theta & 0 \\ 0 & 1 & 0 & 0 \\ \sin\theta & 0 & \cos\theta & 0 \\ 0 & 0 & 0 & 1 \end{bmatrix}$$

A rotation of an angle θ about the z-axis is achieved using the transformation matrix:

$$\begin{bmatrix} \cos\theta & \sin\theta & 0 & 0 \\ -\sin\theta & \cos\theta & 0 & 0 \\ 0 & 0 & 1 & 0 \\ 0 & 0 & 0 & 1 \end{bmatrix}$$

It is possible to concatenate the rotational transformation matrices so as to perform two rotations concurrently through one matrix multiplication. However, the rotations are noncommutative, so attention must be paid to the order of the transformation matrices during multiplication. To perform a rotation about the x-axis and the y-axis, the transformation matrix may be achieved as follows:

$$\begin{bmatrix} 1 & 0 & 0 & 0 \\ 0 & \cos\theta & \sin\theta & 0 \\ 0 & -\sin\theta & \cos\theta & 0 \\ 0 & 0 & 0 & 1 \end{bmatrix} \times \begin{bmatrix} \cos\theta & 0 & -\sin\theta & 0 \\ 0 & 1 & 0 & 0 \\ \sin\theta & 0 & \cos\theta & 0 \\ 0 & 0 & 0 & 1 \end{bmatrix}$$

$$= \begin{bmatrix} \cos\theta & 0 & -\sin\theta & 0 \\ \sin^2\theta & \cos\theta & \cos\theta\sin\theta & 0 \\ \cos\theta\sin\theta & -\sin\theta & \cos^2\theta & 0 \\ 0 & 0 & 0 & 1 \end{bmatrix}$$

Translation is achieved through the 1×3 matrix sector:

$$[l \quad m \quad n]$$

Perspective transformation is achieved using the 3×1 matrix sector:

$$\begin{bmatrix} P \\ Q \\ R \end{bmatrix}$$

The remaining element a produces overall scaling. For instance, overall scaling is achieved using the transformation matrix:

$$\begin{bmatrix} 1 & 0 & 0 & 0 \\ 0 & 1 & 0 & 0 \\ 0 & 0 & 1 & 0 \\ 0 & 0 & 0 & s \end{bmatrix}$$

Normalising the transformed coordinates drives the scaling effect:

$$[x^* \ y^* \ z^* \ 1] = [x/s \ y/s \ z/s \ 1]$$

It is important to note that 3-D images can also be stored using 2-D vector matrices that include X and Y dimensions only. Graphics transformation algorithms may be written in appropriate high level languages such as C++, Java and Visual Basic, and even in machine code or assembly language. Any high-level programming language that supports arrays may be used to develop graphics transformation software. However, APIs for popular 3-D engines such Microsoft Direct3D, Apple QuickDraw3D provide the necessary high-level programming statements to bypass the underlying mathematical elements. Intel MMX technology gives improved delivery of 3-D graphics and animations.

(See MMX technology and VRML.)

3-D modeler   An artist that creates 3-D animations.
(See Autodesk Animator Pro.)

3DO   A company engaged in the manufacture of multimedia related products including video capture hardware. It produces real-time MPEG-2 video encoding hardware used to capture, and to compress video in real time.
(See MPEG-2 and Video capture.)

3D now   A 3-D technology/ instruction set enhancement integrated in AMD processors.
(See 3-D.)

3-D surface   A surface that exists in three dimensions. APIs for popular 3-D engines such as Microsoft Direct3D, Apple QuickDraw3D provide the necessary high-level programming statements.
(See 3-D.)

3-D vector coordinate   Authentic 3-D animations depend upon matrix multiplication where sets of coordinates are multiplied by a transformation matrix. 3-D vectors, or ordinary 3-D coordinates are represented by $[X \ Y \ Z]$.
(See 3-D.)

3-tier   A client/server architecture where the elements presentation, application logic and data may be perceived as distributed across different platforms. The three tiers are separate and independent, and interact via appropriate glues or middleware and include:
- Tier 1: presentation that is the front-end and may be composed of view objects
- Tier 2: application logic that is the middle-tier
- Tier 3: data that is the back-end.

Tier 0 devices are those that connect with clients (at tier 1) and include devices such as printers, and DVD-ROM drives etc. The partition that separates these three entities, in terms of those that reside on the client and those that reside on the server, is a function of the client/server implementation, and the clients may be PCs, Macintosh computers, or NCs. If middleware is included, it may be based on an interface definition language (IDL) like CORBA.
*(See Client/Server, OMG, CORBA, IDL, JavaSpaces * and Jini *.)*

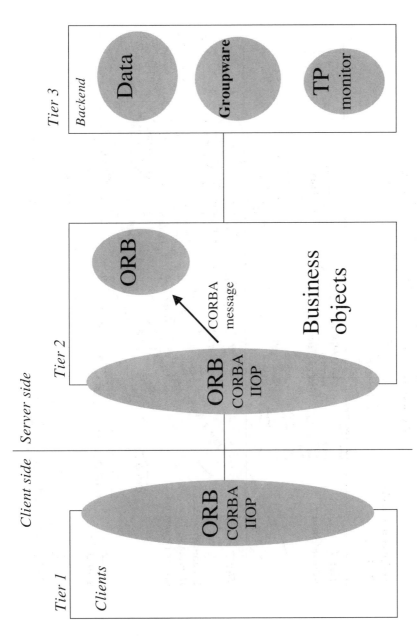

3-tier client/server CORBA-based OO architecture (simplified).

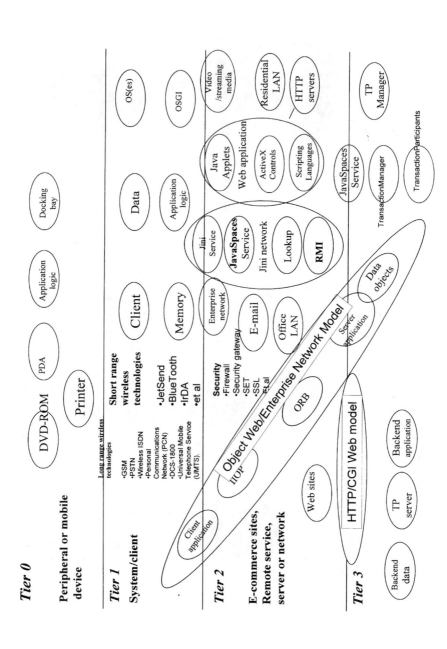

4GL (Fourth-Generation Language) A programming language/environment that does not require the programming of code on a line by line basis. One of the earliest 4GL programming tools for the PC was Sperry's Mapper. Sperry later became part of Unisys.
(See C++, Java, OOP and Visual Basic.)

4 kHz The bandwidth of POTs (plain old telephone services).

8 bit image depth An 8 bit image depth gives a maximum of 256 colours for digital video, and computer generated animations and images. The colour information for each pixel (or dot) is stored using eight bits giving a maximum of 256 (2^8) colours.The 8 bit colour information may be edited using a palette editor such as Microsoft PalEdit that is part of the complete implementation of Microsoft Video for Windows, and Asymetrix Multimedia ToolBook. A palette editor may be used to:
- alter the order of colour cells in a palette
- reduce the number of colours in a palette by deleting unwanted colour cells
- alter brightness
- alter colour contrast
- fade and tint colours
- copy colour cells from one palette to another
- merge two or more palettes into one
- develop common colour palettes that may be used with a number of different 8 bit video sequences to reduce any flicker that may occur as a result of palette switching that occurs when one image, animation or video sequence is exchanged for another. This operation may also be implemented using a palette optimiser.

(See AVI, MPEG*, Streaming *, and Video *.)

10base2 An industry name for thin-Ethernet or cheapernet LAN technology. It uses inexpensive coaxial cable, and is popular for small networks. Compliant network computers/devices are fitted with Ethernet cards (or chipsets) and are connected using coaxial cables.
(See Ethernet and LAN.)

10base5 An industry name for basic Ethernet LAN technology. Network computers/devices are fitted with Ethernet cards (or chipsets) and are connected using coaxial cables. It provides 10 Mbits/s data rates up to a distance of 500 m.
(See Ethernet and LAN.)

---

24 bit   A 24 bit digital video, computer-generated image or animation is generated and stored using 24 bits of colour information for each pixel (or dot). This results in a maximum of over 16.7 million (2^{24}) colours. 24 bit digital videos, animations and images are described as *truecolour*. Red, green and blue are each represented by eight bits, giving 256 tones of each, which in turn leads to over 16.7 million (256 × 256 × 256) colours. 24 bit graphics make possible near-photographic-quality images.
(See Computer graphics.)

30 bit   A 30 bit digital video, or computer-generated image or animation is generated and stored using 30 bits of colour information for each pixel (or dot). This results in a maximum of about one billion (or 2^{30}) colours.
(See 24 bit and 32 bit.)

32 bit   1. A program or operating system that uses 32 bit instructions. 32 bit operating systems include Windows 98, Windows NT and OS/2 Warp. 32 bit software is able to access memory more efficiently than 16 bit variants. It is capable of flat memory addressing where 4 Gbytes (2^{32}) memory segments may be addressed. A 32 bit segment register is used to point to addresses within a 4 Gbyte range. *(See Operating system and Windows.)* 2. A 32 bit processor uses 32 bit instructions. The earliest Intel 32 bit processor was the third generation 80386. 3. A data bus width (in terms of the number of its lines) connected to a device such as a processor, hard disk controller, memory card or graphics card. 4. An extension of the 24 bit image depth, an additional byte (or Alpha channel) provides control over the transparency of pixels. Red, green and blue are each represented by eight bits, giving 256 tones of each that in turn leads to over 16.7 million (256 × 256 × 256) colours. 32 bit graphics make possible photographic quality images. The Apple Macintosh is remembered as the first affordable platform upon which the 32 bit graphics capability became commercially available.

36 bit   An image depth.
(See 24 bit, 30 bit and 32 bit.)

44.1 kHz   A sampling rate required to produce CD-quality audio when using a 16 bit sample size. The resulting digital audio may be stored using media such as:
- CD
- CD-ROM
- Hard disk
- Zip disk
- Jaz disk

- Mini Disc
- CD-R
- DVD-ROM

(See Digital audio.)

48 kHz A sampling rate required to produce high quality digital audio that may be stored on Mini Disc, DAT, hard disk or another DSM that offers an appropriate data transfer rate.

(See Digital audio.)

56.6 Kbps A standard modem speed that is implemented using the standards x2 Technology and Rockwell K56flex. It exceeds the proven bandwidth limit calculated using Shannon's theorem by using PCM, and a digital link between the telephone company and the ISP. 56.6 Kbps modems are asymmetrical offering wider downstream bandwidths, so downloading times are shorter than those of uploading. The ITU has attempted to amalgamate two the industry standards:

- X2
- K56flex

The resulting V.90 standard was specified provisionally and finally released in 1998.

(See Access technology and Modem.)

64 Kbps A data transfer rate offered by a single ISDN channel.

(See ISDN.)

1000 The number of bits transferred in one second, using the unit Kbps.

1024 1. A kilobyte has 1024 bytes. 2. A megabyte has 1024 kilobytes. 3. A gigabyte has 1024 megabytes. 4. A terabyte has 1024 gigabytes.

1024 × 768 A standard display resolution sometimes referred to as XGA (eXtended Graphics Array).

1600 × 1200 pixels A standard graphics resolution used on many PCs, and its delivery requires an appropriate graphics card and display.

1995 A year when the World Wide Web became a 3-tier client/server architecture based on the HTTP/CGI model. *(See 3-tier, CGI* and HTTP.)* Also a year when SunSoft announced the Java programming language.

(See Java*.)

1999   A year when SunSoft launched its Jini technology and JavaSpaces. *(See Jini and JavaSpaces.)*

1 000 000   The number of bits transferred in one second using a 1 Mbps data transfer rate.

1 billion   A 30 bit digital video, animation or colour graphic may have up to (around) 1 billion (2^{30}) colours.

A

AAA server (Authentication, Access and Accounting)
(See Access profile.)

AAEI (American Association of Exporters and Importers.)

ABA (American Bankers Association.)

Absolute addressing A method of addressing stored information, where addresses are measured as offsets from a fixed address. CD-ROM block addresses include measurements of time and data blocks read. Minutes, seconds and blocks provide enough information to locate information. For example, a one-hour CD-ROM, would use the addressing scheme:

- Minutes (M): 0–59
- Seconds (S): 0–59
- Blocks (B): 0–74

A track beginning midway through the CD-ROM might be addressed 29:29:37 (M:S:B).
(See CD-ROM and DVD.)

Accelerator 1. A graphics card offering high-speed operation and optimised for GUIs like X Windows, Windows and OS/2. *(See 3-D and Graphics card.)* 2. A video accelerator is a graphics card that is able to speed up the playback frame rate of video sequences. The acceleration may be achieved by inserting duplicate frames, though today the challenge is to playback video at the capture frame rate rather than to artificially accelerate it. VideoLogic was one of the first companies to demonstrate the acceleration of Windows.AVI video files using this technique. *(See MPEG*.)*

Access   A process where users gain the rights to operate a local or remote system, application or program. The user may be required to enter an ID and one or more passwords. Access is also a database product.
(See Encryption and Security.)

Access profile   A log stored by an AAA (Authentication, Access and Accounting) server. It stores data that relates to users' access rights, accounting and authentication.

Access technology   A method used to connect a user/client to the Internet, or to a remote network or computer system. Access technologies may be physical or wireless and include:
- PSTN and analogue modem offering speeds up to 56.6 Kbps
- ISDN
- T1
- Cable
- DSL
- ADSL
- GSM
- DCS-1800
- DBS (Direct Broadcast Satellite)

(See 56.6 Kbps, ADSL, DSL, B-ISDN, ISDN, Cable modem, ATM, T1, Mobile network and Modem.)

Access time   An interval between a data request and the retrieval of that data. Hard disk and CD-ROM access times are measured in milliseconds (ms) (or thousandths of a second.) The length of access time depends largely on electromechanical architecture, but increasingly controllers play an important role. For instance, hard disk cache controllers may reduce a measured disk access time to tenths of a millisecond. In the perspective of DVD and CD-ROM average access time is a measure of the time taken for the laser head to locate and begin reading an appropriate region of disk. Access time tends to increase with turns of track that are farthest from the disk's centre.
(See CD-ROM, DVD and Hard disk.)

Account number   A unique number that identifies an account held at a financial institution such as a bank or credit card company. It reveals the financial institution, type of account, and even the branch or office that holds the account.

ACID (Atomicity, Consistency, Isolation, and Durability)   A series of properties that define the real-world requirements for transaction processing (TP).

Atomicity   A process of ensuring that each transaction is a single workload unit. If any subaction fails, the entire transaction is halted, and rolled back.

Consistency   A process of ensuring that the system is left in a stable state. If this is not possible the system is rolled back to the pre-transaction state.

Isolation   A process of ensuring that system state changes invoked by one running transaction do not influence another running transaction. Such changes must only affect other transactions, when they result from completed transactions.

Durability   A process of guaranteeing the system state changes of a transaction are involatile, and impervious to total or partial system failures.
(See Server and Transaction.)

Acknowledge   A message in an OO (Object Orientated) system that verifies a state, and may be passed between client and server objects that may perhaps confirm that a client is able to receive a series of packets or messages that may be data or events.

Acquirer   *(See Acquiring bank.)*

Acquiring bank   A bank whose clients are merchants who accept credit cards for customer payment transaction purposes. Each merchant is assigned an account into which is deposited the value of their card sales. Batches of sales slips are used to credit merchants' accounts. The bank submits charges destined for banks to the interchange network either directly or through third parties.

Acquiring financial institution   *(See Acquiring bank.)*

Acquiring processor   A company specialising in card processing, offering services which include:
- Billing
- Settlement
- Management Information Services (MIS)

Acrobat   An Adobe file format that permits formatted documents to be deployed efficiently over the Web. Adobe Acrobat Reader is required to read Acrobat files (that have the .PDF extension).
(See ActiveX control.)

ActionMedia II   An i750 chipset-based graphics card that can play video compressed according to the Intel Indeo video standard. It is an evolved

version of the original i750-based ActionMedia board developed to play and record video according to the Intel Digital Video Interactive (DVI) standard. Two ActionMedia DVI boards were required: one for playback and another for video capture and compression. DVI was a notable milestone in the development of the PC as a multimedia device, and in the evolution of digital video in the PC environment.
(See DVI and MPEG*.)

Active Channel A connection between a consumer and supplier, or between a client and server that adheres to the push or pull model for publishing digital information over networks such as the Internet. The channel variants exist in the CORBA/OMG NS as defined by the OMG (Object Management Group).
(See OMG*, CosNotification, Active Desktop, CORBA, Push and www. omg.com.)

Active Channels A connection to a Web site where information is pushed or pulled to the client.
(See Active Channel.)

Active Desktop A term used to describe the client side of an Active Web application that may use ActiveX scripting (with VBScript or JScript) in order to integrate and coordinate ActiveX controls and Java Applets.

Selected Active Channels invoke Explorer in full screen mode which provides standard Web Browser options. The Fullscreen button allows you to switch between the normal Microsoft Internet Browser application and the full screen view. Both views share many of the same user interface features. The application window view provides additional features, such as the ability to add Web addresses to a Favourites folder. These may then be visited without having to enter a Web address.

(See ASP, ActiveX control, Java*, Visual Basic, VBScript and JavaScript and OLE.)

Active Server Components   *(See ASP.)*

Active Server Page (ASP)   *(See ASP.)*

ATL (Active Template Library)   A development tool used to create Active Server Components that may be in-process or out-process.
(See ASP.)

Active Web Architecture   An architecture which provides bi-directional information flow between the HTTP server and HTTP client. The resulting interactivity on the client side permits data entry and the editing of HTML documents. It uses the Common Gateway Interface (CGI) between the HTTP server and its applications and databases. CGI is a protocol that provides the necessary communications. CGI scripts are created using a scripting language or programming tool.

Active window   A window is active or currently selected for use when the user:

- clicks on the window
- selects its related application button from the Taskbar
- selects the window from the Window menu
- selects the window using the keyboard by pressing Alt-Esc, or by pressing Alt-Tab.

(See Windows.)

ActiveMovie   A Microsoft streaming video technology which is integrated in the Microsoft Internet Explorer and supports the video formats Quick-Time, MPEG and AVI.
(See ASF and www.microsoft.com/imedia.)

ActiveX control   An object or component that adds functionality to an application that may be standalone, or deployed over the Web or a network. Microsoft ActiveX is an object architecture initially based on OLE 2.0, and intended for deployment over the Internet and compatible IP networks. More accurately, ActiveX is a reincarnation of OCX and may use COM and DCOM as glues. ActiveX controls may take the form of a streaming video player, or a streaming audio player that might be added to the Microsoft Internet Explorer, and are embedded in HTML pages performing various functions which may be the generation of a simple Marquee. ActiveX controls may be created using Visual C++, Visual Basic 5 Control Creation Edition, Java, Java 2 and other development tools. There are ActiveX controls in the public domain and in the shareware sector, as well as those that might be conventionally marketed and sold. ActiveX components running on the same system may interact using the COM protocol as a glue. Industry-wide support beyond Microsoft exists, and ActiveX compatible development tools include:

- Borland Delphi
- Powersoft PowerBuilder *(See www.powersoft.com)*
- Powersoft Optima++ *(See powersoft.com)*
- Symantec C++ *(See www.symantec.com)*
- MetroWerks Code Warrior *(See www.metrowerks.com)*.

(See Active Desktop, ASP, COM, DCOM, Glue, HTML, Java*, Middleware, CORBA and Visual Basic.)

ActiveX scripting   A process where ActiveX controls and Java applets are integrated in the underlying HTML code of an interactive Web application. Such scripting is generally used with Web applications, though standalone applications may also be built using the same. A basic HTML based application may be given functionality and responses to events through:

- JScript code
- VBScript code
- ActiveX controls such as Shockwave and multimedia streaming components
- Java applets.

Such a development strategy may be used to give the client-side a level of intelligence. Validations of user/customer data and interactions distribute processing to the client-side. This lessens the volume of data traffic, and serves to optimise application performance.

(See ASP, CGI, HTML, Java, Java applet, JavaScript, Shockwave, VBScript.)

ActiveX SDK (Software Development Kit)   A programming tool for creating ActiveX controls. ActiveX controls can also be created using:

- C++
- Java
- Visual Basic.

*(See ActiveX control, Java *, and Visual Basic.)*

ActiveX security A term used to describe the filtering of unwanted ActiveX controls or presenting the user with an option to do so.

(See Security gateway.)

ADC (analogue to digital converter) A device or electronic assembly used to convert continuously varying analogue signals into digital form. The accuracy achieved depends largely on the size of samples and on the sampling rate. Video capture boards and sound cards include analogue to digital (ADC) converters. Standard PC and Macintosh sound cards tend to record using 8 bit or 16 bit samples at sampling rates of 11.25 kHz, 22.05 kHz or 44.1 kHz. Highly specified sound cards may record using sampling rates of up to 48 kHz which equates to DAT quality. Video capture cards generally play a dual ADC role, converting audio as well as video into digital form. Normally audio is digitised using the same sample sizes and sampling frequencies available on most fully specified sound cards. Whether capturing from a VHS or S-VHS video source recording, the process of digitising a video signal requires a great deal more computation than that of an analogue audio signal. The maximum frame capture rate of a video capture card is a function of its maximum sampling rate, which is linked to the maximum data rate at which it can operate.

Address 1. *(See IP address.)* 2. CD-ROM addresses include measurements of time and data blocks read. Minutes, seconds and blocks provide enough information to locate information. For example, a one-hour CD-ROM, would use the addressing scheme:

- Minutes (M): 0–59
- Seconds (S): 0–59
- Blocks (B): 0–74

A track beginning midway through the CD-ROM might be addressed 29:29:37 (M:S:B). The length of a CD-ROM track in minutes may be used to calculate user data capacity. 3. A binary address of data or instructions, which are stored in memory. 32 bit software is able to access memory more efficiently than 16 bit variants. It is capable of flat memory addressing in which 4 Gbyte (2^{32}) memory segments may be addressed. A 32 bit segment register is used to point to addresses within a 4 Gbyte range. At a machine code level, the addresses of data and instructions are held in a register called a program counter. Typically its contents grow by increments of one, except when a conditional or unconditional jump occurs to a new memory location. This normally occurs when a subroutine is executed. At such times, the contents of the program counter are placed on a stack that is a portion of memory that operates according to the LIFO (last in first out) system. This ensures that the last address placed on the stack is the first to be retrieved. When the subroutine is completed (perhaps using the RET command), the return address is recovered from the stack, and placed back into the program counter register.

Address Book   A Windows NT-based server that is part of the Microsoft Commercial Internet System (MCIS). It allows users to query a database of users, which may include dynamic values such as IP addresses as well as static values, which might include names, addresses, age, interests, occupation etc. It is compatible with:

- NetMeeting which supports Internet telephony and conferencing
- Internet Locator server which may be used to query the database
- Microsoft SQL Server which may be used as the database.

(See Internet telephony, MCIS and Microsoft SQL Server.)

Address bus   A unidirectional address bus on a processor. It consists of a number of lines, and interfaces with memory devices and memory decoders.

Adobe After Effects   A 2-D/3-D animation program which permits various effects and enhancements.

Adobe Dimensions   A 3-D graphics program.

Adobe Illustrator   A graphics program used widely for Web and multimedia production and to originate images for print.

Adobe PageMill   A Web site development tool that may be used to develop Web applications.
(See ActiveX, Java *, CGI, Web server, MCIS.)*

Adobe PhotoShop   A program used widely for image manipulation, enhancement and editing.

Adobe Premier   A video editing tool.
(See Multimedia production, and Video capture.)

Adobe Streamline   A graphics package that provides a number of tools, and may convert images into line drawings
(See PaintShop Pro.)

ADPCM (Adaptive Delta Pulse Code Modulation)   A process where an analogue signal is converted into digital form and is a development of Pulse Code Modulation (PCM). The sampling rate influences how accurately sharply varying analogue signals are digitised. It is used in many digital audio, video and multimedia technologies.

ADSL (Asymmetric Digital Subscriber Line)   An access technology which uses the existing copper wire networks that are synonymous with POTS (Plain Old Telephone Services), though these may also include fibre optics. Its downstream bandwidth is considerably wider than its upstream bandwidth:

- Downstream bandwidth of between 1.5 Mbs and 8 Mbs. Typically it is 1.5 Mbs.
- Upstream bandwidth of the order of 16 to 640 Kbs that may be a function of the line length. Typically it is 384 Kbs.
- Line lengths of up to 5 km are quoted. Typically a repeater is required with distances greater than 1800 feet in order to overcome attenuation.

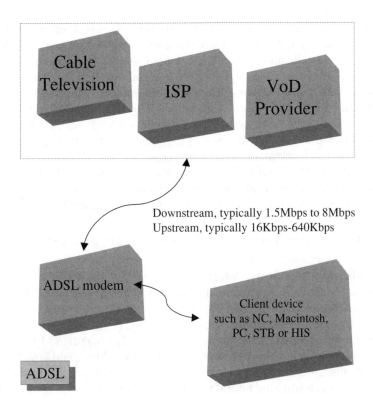

21

Applications include:

- high-speed Internet access
- VHS quality videoconferencing
- VoD (Video-on-demand)
- multimedia networks

Discrete multitone (DMT) modulation according to ANSI T1.413 separates upstream data from downstream data by separating the signal into separate 43 kHz carrier bands.

(See Access technology and DSL.)

Advisory Commission on Electronic Commerce   A commission that is part of the Internet Tax Freedom Act of 1998 and focuses on collecting tax revenues from Internet sales.

Affiliate program   Associate or commission-based advertising programs that route traffic to target sites. Referring sites that offer the appropriate links to the target sites are typically paid on a commission basis.

Agent   1. An Agent/manager architecture is used for system management in client/server systems. The agents represent managed subjects which are communicated with, and manipulated by managers. 2. A triggered agent is a program that responds to events with appropriate actions. The actions might be little more than answering a telephone call. More sophisticated agents may modify software, build databases or even data warehouses, or add items to a cache, in response to usage habits. Events such as changes to files or directories may also be used as triggers. 3. An habitual agent may be programmed to implement tasks at a precise frequency, such as hourly or daily. 4. A Microsoft ActiveX control intended to enhance the UI of local and Web applications. 5. In a telecommunications network, an agent interprets various commands, and responds to them appropriately.

Agent log   A log of Browsers used by visitors to an e-commerce site.

AI (artificial intelligence)   A term used to describe the use of a system to emulate human decision making and learning abilities. The founding father of artificial intelligence is Alan Mathison Turing, through his writings that include *Computing Machinery and Intelligence* (1950). Turing OBE, an English mathematician, Second World War code-breaker and computer scientist and inventor, also described the 'Turing machine', and how it could theoretically implement logical processes. Expert systems, or knowledge based systems (KBS), and neural networks are perceived as part of AI. It is believed that massively parallel processing (MPP) systems will unleash and emulate many human-like thought processes.

(See KBS.)

Algorithm 1. '*An algorithm is a set of rules for getting a specific output from a specific input. Each step must be so precisely defined that it may be translated into computer language and executed by machine*' (Donald E. Knuth). 2. A collective name describing the components of the problem solving process. It may be a program or series of steps defining a *modus operandi*, which yields what is regarded to be an acceptable solution. 3. A term used loosely to describe a program, or program segment. Algorithms for compression, and those that perform other operations, are often patented.

Alpha 1. A family of RISC processors manufactured by Digital. 2. A pre-release copy of an application that is distributed and tested in-house. It is the penultimate development stage that precedes beta testing. *(See Beta-copy.)* 3. An 8 bit data channel on 32 bit colour systems that provides control over the transparency of pixels, thus facilitating numerous video effects.

AltaVista A search engine.

`Alternate Style Sheet` A stylesheet used to define an *alternate* style to those declared as *persistent and/or preferred*. The persistent style is of course the default style and may be overridden by the alternate style.

Amazon An on-line trading entity that is synonymous with bookselling and is believed to be the first major implementation of an Internet-based e-commerce site. It is also collectively engaged in on-line auctions and the sale of music recordings. Its book listings feature sales ranks, editorial reviews, reader reviews and author reviews. Amazon is centralised mainly through the US site but also has European supporting entities in the UK and Germany.

AMD (Advanced Micro Devices) A chip manufacturer that produces PC processors. AMD came to prominence when it reverse engineered Intel's third generation 80386 processor and won the legal right to market and sell it.

(See Pentium.)

AMIS (Audio Messaging Interchange Specification.)

And   1. A logic gate which has two or more inputs and a single output. The output is one, or positive, when all inputs are set to one. 2. A logical operation in a search string that requires the presence of two or more words or phrases. 3. An operator in a program that tests for two or more conditions.

(See C++, Java, JavaScript, VBScript and Visual Basic.)

Andreeson, Marc   A computer scientist and entrepreneur, who created the Netscape Navigator Web Browser, and is the founder of Netscape. He also worked on one of the earliest Web Browsers, Mosaic, which was developed at the National Center for Supercomputing Applications at the University of Illinois.

(See Browser, Hypertext and Web.)

Animation   A series of frames used to create the illusion of movement. Animation types include:

- morphing, which dissolves one image into another, and may be created using dedicated morphing programs, or equivalent features in animation programs
- sprite, where one or more screen objects are moved
- cell-based, where entire frames are updated fully or partially to give the illusion of movement
- micons, where a continuous series of frames is repeated conditionally. The condition might be a mouse-click event.

(See Animation program.)

Animation program   A program designed for the production of 2-D and 3-D animations. Autodesk Animator Pro and Autodesk 3D Studio are popular off-the-shelf packages. Other 3-D animation development tools include NewTek's LightWave 3D, Strata Studio, and the Electric Image Animation System.

Annual company report   A document that addresses the previous financial performance of a company using balance sheets and profit and loss accounts, and may also make certain forecasts regarding growth. It is typically used by business analysts and investors and even by potential employees as they gauge the performance and current state of the enterprise.

(see Balance sheet and P&L.)

Anonymous class   An extension of the local class, and is declared and instantiated using a single Java expression.

Anonymous FTP (File Transfer Protocol)   An FTP server to which users may connect, browse its files, download files and possibly upload files also. *(See Archie and TCP/IP.)*

ANSI (American National Standards Institute)   A highly influential standards institution. The array of ANSI standards cover everything from character sets to programming languages such as C++.

AOL (America On line)   A large, international ISP that has POPs (points of presence) in many major cities. The Compuserve ISP is part of the AOL corporation.

Apache   A Web server that is free of charge and used with the Unix operating system. It may supersede the original NCSA Web server that is also available free of charge and runs on top of the Unix operating system.

API (Application Program Interface)   A set of interfaces and methods used by programmers that define operations specific to applications and hardware. For example, a development environment built using the CORBA-based Notification Services will have IDL modules or files as its collective API. Resulting client/consumer and server/supplier applications that may be in C++ or Java may be written line by line, or compiled from IDL code using an IDL2JAVA or IDL2CPP compiler.
(See CORBA.)

APM (Advanced Power Management)   A power management facility aimed at notebook and portable systems.

Apple Computer   A computer manufacturer founded by technologist and entrepreneur Steve Wozniak, and by entrepreneur Steve Jobs. Together they revolutionised computing by mass producing one of the world's most affordable PCs known simply as the Apple, and later the Apple II. It was designed by Steve Wozniak, whose dream was always to own a computer, once saying 'I don't care if I live in the smallest house, just so long as I have my very own computer'. Microsoft founders, Bill Gates and Paul Allen, had already written a Basic interpreter for the Altair personal computer, but had decided to focus on software as opposed to hardware. While Microsoft mined massive revenues from its DOS operating system for the IBM PC XT and AT, Apple Computer shook the computing world once again in 1984 with its Apple Macintosh or 'Mac' that changed the human-machine interface forever. It had a multi-tasking windows operating system exactly like that defined by Douglas Engelbart, and implemented at Xerox Palo Alto Research Center (PARC), and it also had a mouse, another Engelbart invention. A more subtle technical innovation was the use of an analogue graphics port in the Mac design that could theoretically drive an unlimited number of colours. Immediately it opened the door to affordable desktop publishing using such software packages as PageMaker that was then owned by Aldus, a company aptly named after the Italian inventor of the italic typeface. Microsoft responded with Windows, its own multitasking windows-based operating systems and GUI. This finally gained a respectable user base through the release of Windows 3.0. IBM's belated response to the 'Mac' was the Personal System/2 (PS/2) which was launched in the Summer of 1987, and offered 16-colour VGA and 256-colour MCGA colour graphics. This was significant for Microsoft because it was the driving technology which shaped the software it produced. It was a milestone in the evolution of the PC as a colour graphics system, and one that could theoretically become a multimedia appliance. Later Apple products include the Apple PowerBook, the Apple Newton PDA, and the more contemporary iMac series of personal computers.

(See Apple Macintosh and Windows.)

Apple Macintosh   A range of desktop computers produced by Apple Computer. When introduced in 1984 it pushed forward the boundaries of desktop computing through the:

- Graphical user interface (GUI or 'gooey')
- Mouse input device
- Analogue graphics port–PC users had to wait until 1987 before gaining analogue graphics.

It marked the beginning of affordable desktop publishing, with PageMaker becoming the chosen application, and was first advertised during the Super Bowl in January 1984. The advertisement was based on Orwell's novel *1984* where the Apple Macintosh was portrayed as saving society from the nightmare of Orwell's Big Brother scenario/theory. It became hugely successful and led Apple Computer to produce a series of Apple Macintosh computers.

(See GUI.)

Apple QuickTime   A digital video playback technology and standard developed by Apple Computer.

<APPLET>   An HTML tag that encloses a Java applet.

(See Applet and Java.)

Applet   A program which resides on a server and when requested it is downloaded and executed by the client browser. Applets deployed on the Web require machine independence and a virtual processor such as the

Java Virtual Machine installed on the client. The applet concept is not new, predating Java by a considerable margin.

Application development A process by which an application is created. The development lifecycle might include various standard stages such as:

- project planning
- design
- scripting
- prototyping a storyboard design
- production
- coding in a multimedia language such as OpenScript or Lingo
- coding in an Internet-related languages such as Java, VBScript, JavaScript, HTML, VRML and Perl.
- coding in general purpose languages such as Visual Basic and Visual C++
- alpha testing
- beta testing
- packaging the application for distribution on a CD variant, or for deployment on a network.

In the perspective of the Web or Internet, application development may require the use of:

- Content authoring programs, such as those that permit the generation of animations, and multimedia production tasks.
- Web site development tools that permit production tasks such as integrating media with navigation schemes etc.

(See C++, Java*, MCIS, VBScript and Visual Basic.)

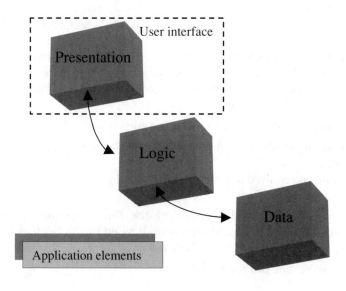

Application development tool/software A software package dedicated to the development of applications, with the most popular commercial example being Microsoft Visual Studio.

(See Microsoft Visual Studio.)

Application Message Queue A buffer used in Microsoft Windows to store messages posted by an application using the PostMessage routine. The size of the queue may be set using SetMessageQueue.

Application renovation An upgrade path used to modernise legacy systems that may be based on older mainframe computers, and essentially adds new client and connectivity components. The process may be viewed as an alternative to migrating from a mainframe-based solution to more modern client/server implementations. It offers the advantage of reduced costs, but relatively high maintenance costs associated with mainframe computers are seen as a key disadvantage.

(See Client/server.)

Application software A program or suite of programs designed to perform a particular task, or set of tasks. Mainstream business applications include word processors, spreadsheets, relational databases, and contact managers. These are generally included in integrated packages.
Examples include:

- integrated packages, such as Microsoft Office, Microsoft Works, and ClarisWorks
- word processors, such as Microsoft Word, WordPerfect, and Lotus Word Pro
- spreadsheets, such as Microsoft Excel, Lotus 123 and Quattro Pro
- databases, such as Microsoft Access, Paradox and DataEase
- contact managers, such as Outlook, Goldmine, and those supplied with many integrated packages.

The three staple elements of an application are:

- presentation, which is required by those applications that feature user interaction
- logic, which is required to process and manipulate data
- data, which may be of many different types.

The physical, or perceived, location of the three functional elements depends upon a series of logical topologies devised by the Gartner Group. This is explained under the entry *Client/server.*

(See Client/server and Microsoft Office.)

Application-level gateway   An application-level gateway is able to process store-and-forward traffic and provide security features. They may be programmed to maintain logs of application usage. Users must log in to the application gateway machine.

(See Firewall and Security gateway.)

Application Service Provider (ASP)

(See ASP.)

Archie   An on-line database of indexed words from FTP sites that was developed at Montreal's McGill University. The database may be searched using TelNet, or by sending e-mail messages that have simple instructions, to Archie servers.

For example, to find FTP sites and files that contain the word occam, the e-mail message would read:

```
set search sub
find occam
```

Archie would then return a listing of appropriate files and FTP sites. This information can be used to download the files using an FTP client program. Alternatively, e-mail messages with appropriate instructions can be sent to the relevant sites.

Architecture   1. A processor architecture refers to the internal design in terms of:

- whether it includes a CISC or RISC instruction set
- multimedia functionality such as MMX technology
- internal cache and internal cache size
- size of registers
- external and internal data bus size
- types of registers
- whether the processor is a von Neumann serial design (such as an Intel Pentium II), or a parallel variant.
- number of devices.

2. A system architecture generally refers to the type of operating system and the types of hardware it uses. For example, the hardware and software might be proprietary. 3. An underlying object architecture of an application in terms of the types of objects used that might be ActiveX controls or even OLE objects. Its glues, such as COM and DCOM, may also form part of an architectural description. *(See Glue.)* 4. An open system architecture is an attempt to standardise hardware and software. The rationalisation of hardware and software standards means that products from numerous manu-

facturers can be integrated into one system. 5. A firewall architecture includes component parts such as screening routers. *(See Firewall and Security gateway.)* 6. A general term that can be used to refer to the design of hardware and software, ranging from mainframes and networks, to applications programs and operating systems (OS).

Archive   A method of storing files for backup or long-term storage. Removable media that can be used for archiving purposes include 100MB Zip discs and 1Gbyte Jaz discs from Iomega, as well as media devices from SyQuest. Other media include conventional hard disk, and CD-R discs and DVD-RAM discs. Various file compression utilities may be used for backup purposes, including the popular WinZip program.
(See DVD.)

ARP (Address Resolution Protocol)   An IP protocol that can be used to convert logical IP addresses (such as 18.170.103.34) into physical addresses. An ARP request results in a node's physical address which might be used by Ethernet networks, Token Ring and FDDI (which may have a bandwidth of up to 100Mbps).
(See TCP/IP.)

ARPA (Advanced Research Projects Agency)   A US government agency formerly called DARPA (Defense Advanced Research Projects Agency).

ARPANET (Advanced Research Projects Agency NETwork)   An early network developed by the then DARPA (Defense Advanced Research Projects Agency) for researchers. Originally coined DARPANET its development was commissioned in 1969, resulting in a working network of four computers by 1970, growing to 37 computers by 1972, at which time it became ARPANET. Some assert that DARPANET was the technical and possibly, conceptual birth of the information superhighway or Internet. The key development resulting from ARPANET is the TCP/IP family of protocols. ARPANET ceased to exist in 1990.
(See TCP/IP.)

Array   1. A two- or three-dimensional matrix of data values which can be character, numeric, or even binary objects. All modern high-level programming languages support arrays, and the concept is similar to the use of tables in databases and data warehouses. *(See Data warehouse.)* 2. An uncommitted logic array (ULA) is an electronic package that has electronic devices (or gates) that are unconnected. By adding the connections in the form of a metalisation layer the ULA is given a specific functionality. 3. A transformation array is used to manipulate a 2-D or 3-D set of coordinates.

(See 3-D.)

As We May Think   A prophetic and momentous article published in July 1945 in *Atlantic Monthly*. Its author, Vannevar Bush, Science Adviser to President Roosevelt, put forward a new paradigm for information storage and retrieval. He foresaw the imminent miniaturisation of storage media, and described a central repository of published information accessible via multiple access points. Calling it Memex, its functionality approximated that of the evolving Internet, Infobahn, or information superhighway. As such, Memex may be considered the conceptual birth of the Internet. Vannevar's vision relates to hypertext. Hypertext set a familiar continuum in motion, first yielding hypermedia that introduced still images, and later modern multimedia that added computer animation, motion video, synthesised sound and digitally recorded waveform audio to hypermedia. Multimedia currently drives an ongoing re-evaluation of the way we store, retrieve and communicate information, as well as the way we generally think. It is reasonable to state that the near-term final stage in the continuum will be immersive virtual reality (VR), and a total integration of multimedia as an information communication medium within that environment. A noticeable underlying trend in the evolution of modern media is an increasing dependence upon concurrency; the growing number of human sensory channels interfaced concurrently renders tours within the medium more memorable.

ASCII (American Standard Code for Information Interchange)   A standard set of codes introduced to promote compatibility in terms of characters and symbols. Originally it consisted of 127 ASCII characters derived from seven bits. Eight bits were not used to preserve the sign bit. ASCII has since been extended into a larger highly standardised character set.

ASF (Advanced Streaming Format.)   A storage container data format (and standard) for streaming multimedia. The contents of the container are not defined, and neither is the communications protocol which may be:

- HTTP
- TCP
- RTP
- UDP.

The ASF container file contents are read by an appropriate media server, and transmitted to the client, where it may be stored or played.

(See MPEG * and Streaming*.)

ASN.1 (Abstract Syntax Notation One) A standard that defines the encoding, transmission and encoding of data and objects, which are architecture neutral.

ASP (Active Server Page) A technology included with IIS 3.0 which may be used to develop scalable, Browser-independent Web applications. DCOM and COM may be used as glues within ASP-based applications. Resulting Web applications may acquire information about the client browser, and act accordingly. This enables compatible HTML pages to be served to the Browser without error messages. The Microsoft Active Server provides the component parts to implement the aforementioned functionality, and includes the components:

- Browser capabilities, which acquires the connected browser's key features
- ActiveX Data Object (ADO), which provides access to back-end data (irrespective of its location), and is not limited to ODBC compliant data sources
- TextStream, which is used to create and open files.

Third-party and bespoke components can be integrated in an Active Web site and may be developed using an ActiveX control developer's workbench, including:

- Visual Basic
- Visual C++
- Visual C++ ControlWizard, which is used for OLE development
- ActiveX Software Development Kit.

Active Server Pages (ASPs) offer the advantages of:

- shorter Web application development life cycle, particularly with developers/development teams that have little CGI programming experience
- optimised server-side processing, because calls to CGI programs may invoke new processes on the server.

A server side software architecture that is Browser neutral. ASPs may be normal HTML that glues together scripts written Javascript, VBScript or other ActiveScript compliant language. The following ASP is compiled by the server and then the resulting HTML code downloaded to the browser

```
<% for a = 1 to 2 %>
        <font size= <% = a %> > Hello World </font> <br>
<% next %>
```

Downloaded HTML:

```
<font size= 1 > Hello World </font> <br>
<font size= 2 > Hello World </font> <br>
```

ASP applications may use ODBC databases, VBScript objects and ActiveX DLLs. ASP objects include Request that may be used to retrieve cookies using `request.cookies,` and to request information from forms using `request.form.` ASP pages also have a response object that is used to write to the HTML file using `response.write,` and to write to a cookie using `response.cookies.`
(See Active Desktop, ActiveX*, and CGI.)

ASP (Application Service Provider)   A resource that offers the hosting of applications and data held off-site. The terms and cost structures of such remote application hosting are variable, but they typically depend on elements such as leasing, time charges, traffic levels and multi-user scale.

Asymetrix   A company founded in 1985 by Paul Allen, who along with Bill Gates also founded Microsoft. Asymetrix is a leading developer and publisher of Windows-based multimedia and client/server application development tools. Its headquarters are in Bellevue, Washington and its European operation is in Paris with further subsidiaries in London and Munich. Its flagship product is Multimedia ToolBook, which was used to develop Microsoft Multimedia Beethoven: The Ninth Symphony.
(See OpenScript and ToolBook.)

Asymmetric compression   A compression/decompression algorithm where the processes that constitute compression are not reflected in decompression.
(See DCT, JPEG and MPEG*.)

Asymmetric key cryptography   A cryptosystem in which the keys used to encrypt and decrypt data are dissimilar.
(See Asymmetric*, Brute Force*, Ciphertext, Cryptosystem, Dictionary attack, Encryption, Plaintext, Public key encryption, RSA*, SET, and Transposition.)

Asynchronous   1. A data transmission technique where the sending device and receiver are not synchronised in real time. Each transmitted item, or packet, is encoded with start and stop bits, so the receiving device can decode it without ever receiving a timing signal from the sending device. Because the asynchronous data transmission technique makes good use of available bandwidth or data rates, it is particularly suitable for networked multimedia. 2. A mode of communications between running threads, where a call from one thread to another does not require a response before it can continue processing. Instead it proceeds processing, and receiving and sending messages.

33

Asynchronous messaging *(See Asynchronous.)*

AT&T (American Telephone and Telegraph) A telecommunications giant (or telco).

ATA An industry standard hard disk controller.

ATA-2 A disk interface technology.
(See Hard disk.)

ATM (Asynchronous Transfer Mode) An internationally agreed tele-communications standard that supports transmission line speeds of up to 622 Mbps. Other line speeds include 2 Mbps, 12 Mbps, 25 Mbps, 34 Mbps, 45 Mbps, 52 Mbps and 155 Mbps. The CCITT accepted ATM in 1990 as an internationally agreed standard for data, voice and multimedia networks. ATM bases itself on cell relay, which is a form of statistical multiplexing and is similar to packet switching. The data transmission consists of cells that have 53 octets or bytes, including a 5-octet header. Using 52 Mbps line speed, a single cell may be transmitted in:

```
53 × 8/52 Mbps =     8.15 × 10⁻⁶
               =     8.15 microseconds
```

The cells from different signals are interleaved, and the signal propagation delay and jitter, is a function of the transmission line speed. It is sufficiently low to give a stream of contiguous cells that is acceptable for real-time data, voice, audio and video transmission. Like packet headers, cell headers contain destination addresses.
(See Frame relay.)

ATMI (American Textile Manufacturers Institute.)

Attachment A file which is sent and received along with an e-mail message. The file may be binary or text, and is opened using an appropriate application.
(See E-mail.)

Attenuation *(See Digital audio.)*

Audio *(See Digital audio.)*

Audio compression A term used to describe the process of compressing audio data which can be decompressed and played using streaming audio technologies. In uncompressed form the large size of wave audio files occasionally place unreasonable demands on distribution media in terms of data capacity and/or bandwidth. Wave audio compression gives smaller file sizes, which are decompressed on playback using either dedicated hardware and software, or software alone such as an MP-3 player. Standard wave audio compression algorithms include MP-3, A-Law, IMA (Interactive Multimedia Association) ADPCM and MPEG-1. Whichever compression standard is used, the resultant file sizes, or the compression ratios achieved, depend on the compressor parameter settings chosen. As the compression ratio is increased, the resultant playback quality diminishes. High-quality wave audio therefore, tends to be compressed by a great deal less than a dialogue recording, for instance.

(See Streaming*.)

Audio Video Interleave   *(See AVI.)*

Authenticode   A technology supported by the Microsoft Internet Explorer, which permits components such as ActiveX Controls and Java applets to be digitally signed. When such a signed component is encountered, Explorer checks its signature status. An unsigned component causes Explorer to display an appropriate prompt, while a signed component causes Explorer to display a certificate. The certificate includes information about the component and its author. The user is given the option to download the component.

Authoring   A process of developing a multimedia e-commerce application, which can include the processes of:

- design
- scripting
- greeing on the content required in terms of images, video, text and sound
- developing an interactive design
- prototyping
- implementing the interactive design
- testing the interactive design
- multimedia production
- digitising text
- digitising images and retouching them in-house or using an appropriate bureau
- recording wave audio files
- composing midi files
- capturing video files
- application development
- implementing the interactive design

- production
- uniting acquired media files with the interactive design
- testing.

CD-based authoring requires an authoring station and authoring tool such as Icon Author, Macromedia Authorware Professional or Asymetrix ToolBook. For Multimedia production, or for the creation and gathering of all necessary media files, it may be necessary to use:

- video capture software and hardware such as VidCap and a Video-Blaster card
- video editing software such as VidEdit
- wave audio recording and editing software
- a midi sequencer such as CakeWalk.

Authoring consists of design, multimedia production, navigational scheme design, and production. For distribution purposes, disk pressing or deployment over a network may constitute a final stage.

(See Lingo, OpenScript and ToolBook.)

Authoring station   A hardware platform and software tool required to author a multimedia application. Normally it will have a video capture card and digital sound recording facility. It may also provide a means through which resultant material may be submitted to a replication company for mastering and manufacture.

Authoring tool   A program or program suite that permits the creation of multimedia e-commerce applications. Generally it is more complex than a presentation program, providing more advanced features such as indigenous or standard authoring/programming languages that are often visual in nature. *(See Authoring, Lingo and OpenScript.)* Occasionally, authoring tools are bundled with bitmap editors (graphics programs), palette editors, and video capture and editing programs. Modern authoring tools permit the deployment of applications over the Internet. Popular authoring tools include:

- Authorware Professional
- Asymetrix ToolBook Assistant/Instructor
- IconAuthor.

Modern authoring tools aimed at the production of CD-based multimedia may provide cost-effective migration paths to the Internet, and should also provide support for Java applets.

(See ToolBook and Authorware Professional.)

Authorisation   A formal clearance from a credit card or bank card issuer indicating that a transaction will be honoured.

Authorisation code   A code that indicates the willingness of the card issuer to honour a credit card or bank card transaction.

Authorware Professional   An authoring tool for Windows-based multimedia applications produced by Macromedia. The authoring process consists of dragging objects onto a flowline, which runs vertically in its own window. Authorware is considered to require no programming skills.
(See Lingo, OpenScript and ToolBook.)

Autodesk 3D Studio   A 3-D animation development program.

Autodesk Animator Pro   A 2-D animation development program.

Automated crime   A series of events that result in a computer fraud or crime automated by scripts or programs. Traces of the automated crime may be concealed by the executing software.

Availability   *(See Reliability, MTBF and MTTR.)*

AVI (Audio Video Interleave)   A Microsoft file format for storing interleaved audio and video. Using many video editing and video capture tools, the interleave ratio may be varied. The ratio may be specified as a single figure where, for instance, an interleave ratio of 7 indicates that seven video frames separate each audio chunk. Using Microsoft VidEdit, the statistics of a video file may be shown where the interleave ratio is displayed alongside the phrase Interleave Every. The interleave ratio is expressed as the number of video blocks which separate audio blocks. Generally high interleave ratios are applicable to video stored on hard disk, whereas .AVI video stored on a CD variant is optimised using lower interleave ratios which often equate to one video frame for every audio chunk. Sound track quality commonly found in AVI files ranges from mono 8 bit recordings digitised at 11 kHz, to 16 bit stereo recordings digitised at 44.1 kHz.
(See MPEG* and Video *.)

AWT Abstract Windows Toolkit   A set of Windows development tools focussing on GUI components like radio buttons, check boxes, data entry fields, dialogues and other similar widgets.

B

b2b   Business-to-business Internet commerce.

b2c   Business-to-consumer Internet commerce.

Backbone   A core high-speed transmission line, which serves a number of networks. Switches and bridges provide the physical connections between it and the multiple networks for which it provides bi-directional data traffic paths. A backbone is comparable to a main artery in anatomy, which divides into smaller veins and capillaries that might be thought of as switches and networks. A backbone might comprise ATM backbone switches, which comprise a number of ports for connection to networks. Enterprise backbones that have ATM backbone switches, offer scalability, fault tolerance, and are based on internationally agreed standards. A high-speed digital link that is part of the Internet and telecommunications infrastructure which supports the traffic levels required to unite disparate networks.
(See T1 and T3.)
(See ATM, Frame relay and Screening router.)

Backbone switch   A device that acts as a distribution point for data traffic flowing on a backbone. ATM backbone switches have a number of ports for connection to multiple networks and/or devices. ATM backbone switches are:

- scalable, because upsizing is possible through the replacement or addition of switches. Downsizing is also possible where switches are removed or replaced
- fault tolerant
- based on internationally agreed standards.

Specifications for ATM backbone switches include the:

- number of ports per switch
- number of calls that the switch can route per second

- speed of the backplane, or its data transfer rate in bits per second. The number of ports per switch.

Makers of ATM backbone switches include 3Com Corporation, Cabletron Systems, DEC, Cisco, Fore systems and NEC.

(See Screening router.)

Backdoor   A flaw in the security defences of a system or a network. For example, modern access either inbound or outbound, may bypass the network's collective security infrastructures.

(See Firewall and Security.)

Back-end   Another name for tier 3.

(See 3-tier.)

Background   1. Multi-tasking operating systems such as Windows 98, Windows NT and OS/2 Warp, are able to run applications in the background of others. Background applications and tasks generally receive less processing time, and run more slowly. 2. A background sound may be added to a Web page using FrontPage and other Web development tools. The sound technology used may be wave audio or MIDI.

(See Front Page, MIDI and Wave audio.)

Background mode   In Windows, Background mode permits the background colour to be toggled between opaque (on) and transparent (off).

Background task   A task that takes place in a multi-tasking operating environment and is allocated a specific and changing portion of processing time. The amount of time is less than allocated to tasks that are in the foreground.

Backtracking   A process of retracing a user's path of interaction. Using Windows Help systems the Back button provides a means of doing this. All fully specified authoring tools – such as Multimedia ToolBook – and Help System development tools allow the developer to integrate a backtracking feature in applications. Web browsers also feature backtracking controls.

(See Hypertext and Multimedia.)

backward-compatible   A hardware component, program object, language compiler, program or operating system that is compatible with an earlier version.

Balance sheet   A comparison between assets and liabilities of an enterprise that is normally published annually as part of a company's annual report. Assets may be intangible, tangible, or liquid, and may include buildings, profits, amounts due, intellectual property such as patents and copyrights, investments, shares, fixtures etc. Liabilities may include general running costs, leases, mortgage repayments, tax, amounts owed, materials, office supplies, miscellaneous operating expenses etc.

Bandwidth   A rate at which data is transferred to, or from, a computer or appliance, using a medium that might be physical or wireless. Media and their bandwidths include:

- A single-speed CD-ROM has a bandwidth of 1.2 Mbps (or 150 Kbytes/sec), and generally CD-ROM drives exhibit data transfer rates, which are broadly multiples of 150 Kbytes/s.
- A single ISDN line will provide a bandwidth of 64Kbps, whereas B-ISDN may offer multiples of that rate.
- The average bandwidth of a 24-speed CD-ROM drive is about 3600 Kbytes/s.
- ADSL has a downstream bandwidth of between 1.5 Mbps and 8 Mbps. Typically it is 1.5 Mbps.
- ADSL upstream bandwidth of the order of 16 to 640 Kbps, which can be a function of the line length. Typically it is 384 Kbps.

(See Access technology, ADSL, ATM, B-ISDN, CD-ROM, DBS and DVD.)

Bank card   A card that is linked to one or more bank accounts. It may have an assigned PIN in which case it may be used with cash dispensers, and it may perform transactions using international standards that include Switch, EFTPOS, and Cirrus.

Bankers EDI Council   A council formed by NACHA to help banks make the transition to EDI for corporate customers.

Banner advertisement   A graphic on a Web page that is usually animated or scrolling, it provides a link to the advertised Web site. The banner may be created using a scripting language such as JavaScript, or may even take the form of an applet or ActiveX control.

Barings   A merchant bank that collapsed in the 1990s owing to the irregular trading practices of a certain individual. A rescue package was put together by ING that now operate the bank under the name ING Barings.

Base case   A system that is specified as being a base case is the minimum implementation, or the bottom of a product range. A base case MPC-3 will have only the essential elements of the official specification, as will a base case NC.

(See NC.)

BASIC (Beginners All-purpose Symbolic Instructional Code)   A high-level language developed by Kemeny and Kurtz in the 1960s. Early implementations for personal computers include the BASIC interpreter developed by Microsoft founders Bill Gates and Paul Allen in the mid 1970s for the MITS Altair, the world's first affordable computer. Interpreted languages differ from compiled languages in that they are not compiled into object code (such as .EXE file) before execution. Instead the source code is interpreted in real-time when the program is run. In the late 1970s and early 1980s, almost every microcomputer (or personal computer) had its own BASIC interpreter stored in a ROM variant. Even the original IBM PC XT and a BASIC ROM. It was at this time that Acorn Computer (Cambridge, England) introduced Structured BASIC, advancing the language to structured programming. (*See Structured programming.*) Structured BBC BASIC gave procedures and routines names such as PROCfind, for instance, and were ended using commands like ENDPROC. BBC BASIC was also recursive in that procedures could be called from within procedures. Its most unusual feature, however, was the ability to include 6502 assembly language code within the high-level listing itself. This feature gave it flexibility, and helped programmers increase the speed of program execution by confining certain procedures to assembly language or machine code. This functionality evades many of the industry standard languages of today. The structure programming model adopted by BBC BASIC made the GOTO command redundant, and later did the same to line numbers, though BBC BASIC did include the GOTO command. Until the advent of structured programming, the flow of program execution was directed solely using the GOTO <line number> command. After structured programming, the next significant advancement of BASIC came when visual and object-oriented programming (OOP) arrived. Such Visual Basic development tools allowed programmers to draw objects in order to, perhaps, create a user interface. All the programmer then needed to do was to add code to the objects in order to define their behaviour in response to events such as mouse clicks. The BASIC syntax has changed dramatically, though it continues to be a procedural high-level language, and one that is considerably more than a language for novice programmers. It can be used to tackle demanding programming projects, and is considerably more portable than the early interpreted versions for popular microcomputers.

(See BBC BASIC and Visual Basic.)

Bastion host   A host that is critical to a network's security and Firewall architecture. This is the focus of network management, security monitoring, and is a network's principal defence against illegal usage. A dual-homed host may play the role of a bastion host.

(See Firewall.)

Batch file compression   A technique by which files may be compressed for distribution, archiving or backup purposes. It is appropriate for modem-based file transfer and DSM-based distribution. It can be used to compress any binary file. In the context of video distribution its main disadvantage is the fact that end-users have to decompress or unpack the files before they can be played. Decompression can be carried out using an installation program, a program such as PKUNZIP, or in the case of a self-extracting compressed file the user simply types the name of the compressed file. Standard batch file compression programs include WinZip.

Batch settlement   An accrued number of card transactions which may be processed.

Baud rate   A rate at which data is transferred from one point to the next, which broadly equates to bps. More precisely it is a measure of logic/bit changes per second over media which may be physical or wireless. It is the namesake of French telegraphic communications pioneer J. M. E. Baudot (1845–1903). It is a rarely used term nowadays, and is replaced by bits per second (bps), which is not quite the same thing.

(See Modem.)

BBC BASIC   A version of BASIC introduced with the BBC micro-computer in 1982. It supported structured programming where top-down analysis could be used design and develop software.

BBC procedures
BBC Procedures are defined using the syntax:

```
100 DEF PROCTRANSFORM
110 FOR X% = 1 TO 2
120 INPUT A% (X%)
130 NEXT
150 ENDPROC
```

BBC functions
BBC BASIC functions have the syntax:

```
100 DEF FUNCTION (X%)
110 INPUT X%
120 ENDFUNCTION
```

BBC variables
BBC BASIC support global and local variables, which may be

- integer

  ```
  100 A% = 100
  ```
- floating point

  ```
  100 X = 125.23
  ```
- string

  ```
  100 INPUTS = "Please enter the time."
  ```

BBC loop structures
A for . . . next loop:

```
100 FOR X% = 1 TO 2
120 INPUT A% (X%)
130 NEXT
```

A Repeat . . . until loop:

```
100 REPEAT
120 INPUT A% (X%)
130 UNTIL A% (X%) = 100
```

BBC arrays
Two-dimensional string and numeric arrays (with two rows and 1000 columns) are defined thus:

```
100 DIM A  (2,100)
110 DIM A% (2,100)
```

BBC comments
Program comments have the REM prefix

BBC reserved words
Built-in functions include ABC, SIN, COS etc.
(NB. Several BBC BASIC emulators for the PC may be found on the Internet.)

(See Visual Basic.)

BBS (Bulletin Board Service)   A dial-up service that is independent of the Internet. It can be used for publishing information, distributing files, and for electronic conferencing.

BCBSA   (Blue Cross Blue Shield Association.)

BCPL (Basic Combined Programming Language)   A high level programming language, BCPL was designed by Martin Richards in 1967, as a compiler writing and system programming tool. It was based on CPL (Combined Programming Language), which was developed jointly by Cambridge and London Universities. BCPL is perceived as a forerunner to C and C++.

Further reading: *BCPL the Language and its Compiler*, Martin Richards and Colin Whitby Stevens, Cambridge University Press, 1980.
(See C, C++, Java*, JavaScript, CBScript, and Visual Basic.)

Bend   A bend in an optical fibre results in increased attenuation. Such losses can be used to determine the degree to which a fibre is bent. This forms the basis of operation for many gloves and suits used in VR, where the fibres run along the lengths of fingers or limbs.
(See Led and Optic fibre.)

BER (bit error rate)   A measurement of how error-free the storage or transmission of data is. Typically expressed as the average number of bits in which one bit-error will occur. CD-ROM has appropriate error detection and correction codes. In Mode 1 CD-ROM data blocks, 4 bytes are reserved for error detection and 276 bytes are reserved for error correction. The three layers of error detection and correction integrated in the CD-ROM format include CIRC, EDC and ECC. Typically the bit error rate of CD-ROM equates to 10^{-18}, which amounts to one error for every 1 000 000 000 000 000 000 bits.

Berkeley sockets   *(See Socket.)*

Berners-Lee, Tim   The original architect of the World Wide Web, and inventor of its accompanying HYML (Hypertext Markup Language). The birthplace of HYML is considered to be CERN in Geneva. These origins led the original server to be referred to as the CERN server. The conceptual birth of the Web might be accredited to the visionary Vennevar Bush through his momentous article, 'As We May Think'. Theodore Nelson is also significant (but much more contemporary), through his work *Literary Machines*, and the project Xanadu. If Vannevar Bush and Ted Nelson were responsible for putting forward the concept of the Web, then Tim Berners-Lee must be considered its architect.
(See As We May Think, IP*, HTML, HTTP, Web and Xanadu.)

Beta copy   A test copy of a software product that has yet to be commercially released. Usually beta copies are distributed externally to beta test sites.
(See Alpha.)

BIAC   (Business Industry Advisory Council.)

Bi-directional   1. A highly compressed frame in an MPEG-1 data stream.
(See MPEG*.) 2. A link which offers upstream and downstream data trans-

mission. 3. A link in an information structure that can be following in either direction.

Big Blue   A nickname for IBM. It originates from the fact that early IBM mainframes were painted blue.

BIN (A Bank Identification Number)   A three or five-digit code that adheres to the ISO 8663 recommendation and dictates account numbers that are owned by card companies.

Binary   A counting system comprising only two states, either '1' or '0'. All electronic files are stored in binary form. Binary files generally contain executable programs and program data, and have the .EXE or .COM extension.

BIOS (Basic Input Output System)   A program stored in firmware on all PCs and includes low-level code for implementing I/O operations, startup code and the setup program. The setup program permits the system to be configured, and is invoked by pressing the Del key during the memory check, when the system is booting.

BISAC   (Book Industry Systems Advisory Committee.)

B-ISDN (Broadband ISDN)   An access technology that offers a wider bandwidth than conventional (narrow bandwidth) N-ISDN, which offers data transfer rates of 64 Kbps per single connection. Low-end B-ISDN implementations include multiple 64 Kbps channels. For instance video-conferencing architectures that feature FMFSV might include 6×64 Kbps channels, yielding a collective bandwidth of 384 Kbps.
(See Access technology and ISDN.)

Bit   A single, indivisible item of binary data that might be '1' or '0'.

Bit error rate   *(See BER.)*

BitBlt   1. BIT-BLock Transfer: a method of copying areas of an image from one point to the next. 2. BIT-boundary BLock Transfer: a Windows GDI (Graphics Device Interface) function that moves rectangular geometric shapes such as windows and dialogue boxes.

BitEdit   An 8 bit bitmap editor supplied with Video for Windows (VfW) and Asymetrix Multimedia ToolBook. Multiple instances of BitEdit program (which is supplied with VfW) may be run.

Bitmap   An image represented by pixel data which defines each pixel. The pixel data is referred to as bit map. Can provide intricate control over graphics resulting in high quality.
(See DCT and JPEG.)

Bitmapped display   Graphic controller and display partnership, where pixel data representing each pixel is stored in memory.
(See Bitmap.)

Black   An account or balance that is in credit.

Black box   A conceptual view of software or hardware, where the internal architecture and operation are ignored. All that is considered are input and output values.

BLOB (Binary Large OBject)   An item of binary data that is of no specific type, but is identified simply as containing some sort of digital data. It may be a graphic, a video file, a midi file, a wave audio file, a program file, or any type of digital data.
(See DBMS and OODBMS.)

Block   1. A segment of code that is enclosed within opening '{' and closing '}' braces. 2. A block of 2352 bytes on a CD/CD-ROM tack.
(See CD-ROM.)

Block address   *(See Absolute addressing.)*

Blue Book   A specification for multi-session CDs, and was announced by Sony, Philips, Apple and Microsoft.
(See CD-ROM.)

Bluetooth   A wireless and spontaneous networking and communication technology developed by the Bluetooth Special Interest Group. It operates at 2.4 GHz band and at up to 1 Mbps. Bluetooth creates multiple piconets (or small networks) by frequency hopping.

BMP   A graphics file format that tends to lead to larger files than more compressed variants such as CompuServe's GIF and JPEG.
(See JPEG.)

BNC   A connector consisting of round socket and plug which are locked together with a twist. It was invented by the engineers Neill and Concelman at Bell Laboratories.

Body suit   An item of clothing that provides a means of interfacing a user with a virtual or synthesised environment. It permits user-interaction to varying degrees that extend from giving simple hand signals, to grasping and manipulating virtual objects; it may also provide a means of stimulating the user's sensory organs through changes in temperature, pressure, moisture levels and so on. It may be used for:

- telepresence and telemanipulation
- computer-aided design
- computer games
- translating sign language into speech
- researching the effectiveness of manual or semi-automatic processes so as to refine ergonomic environments and minimise the risk of RSI (Repetitive Strain Injury)
- sports medicine.

Low-specification suits simply sense the flexing of limbs and fingers using silica fibres of the sort commonly used for data transmission and telephone networks. A silica or optic fibre is embedded along the length of jointed limbs. The operation hinges on the fact that the losses experienced by a beam of light propagated in a silica fibre increase when the fibre is physically bent. The resultant varying signal is referred to as bend information. The light sources used LEDS (light emitting diodes). More highly specified variants include a greater number of optic fibres or flex sensors to relay a greater number of movements. These will also contain a detection system that provides the spatial 3-D coordinates of the entire suit. The level of sophistication can extend to integrated transducers that sense angular rotation in three dimensions, temperature, pressure and moisture. Tactile feedback devices might also be included in the form of inflatable bladders.
(See LED, Optic fibre and VR.)

Bolt-on-application   An application that is coupled with another, like a SET implementation which is added to a Merchant Commerce Server.

Bookmark   A pointer to a Web page, it is usually stored in a Favorites folder and provides instant access to Internet resources and services. Document-based applications also support bookmarks that may provide instant navigation of bookmarked points.

Boolean   A variable type that has one of two states: either yes or no. Named after Irish mathematician George Boole who pioneered logic-based *Boolean algebra*, these variables feature in programming languages search engines and databases. AND, OR, NOR, NAND and NOT are Boolean operators. They are also logic gates used in electronics and in the architecture of digital components, and their behaviour can be described using a truth table. A truth table is a simple table which shows the output obtained for each and every combination of inputs.

Borland   A software company, whose name was changed to Inprise in 1998. It is best known for programming tools such as Delphi, Turbo Pascal and Turbo C++, as well as business applications. It is headquartered in Scotts Valley, CA. Its lesser known products include the Sprint word processor for DOS. The company was founded by Philippe Kahn, and its initial rapid growth can be attributed largely to its PC programming tools that include Turbo Pascal. Inprise (UK) International is headquartered in Twyford, and its European headquarters are considered to be in Amsterdam. Kahn is now the President of StarFish.
(See C++)

Borland JBuilder   *(See Jbuilder.)*

Borland Turbo ++   An implementation of C, based on the object-oriented programming (OOP) model.
(See C++, Java*, Object* and OO*.)

Bottom-up analysis   A design approach, where the process begins with the design of low-level components, and progresses to the design of higher level components.
(See Top-down analysis.)

Bps (Bits per second)   A measurement of data transfer rate. Modems are frequently specified in terms of their data transmission and reception speeds.
(See Modem and V standards.)

Brand certificate authority   A party authorised by a credit card company like Visa or MasterCard to carry out digital certificate management.

Branded payment card   A credit card or charge card that has the brand of a sufficiently large company like American Express, Visa or Mastercard.

BRI ISDN (Basic Rate Interface Integrated Services Digital Network)
An access technology that provides two 64 Kbps bearer (B) channels, and

one 16 Kbps data (D) channel for signalling. The B channels carry user data. ISDN drives improvements through voice telephony, Internet access, and videoconferencing. Internationally agreed ISDN standards are maintained by the ITU. International ISDN standards include:

- North America – National ISDN-1AT&T 5ESS
- Europe – Euro ISDN (CTR 4)
- Japan – INS-64
- France – VN-3
- Australia – AUSTEL TS013

(See ISDN.)

Broadband   A term used to describe access technologies and networks that typically offer bandwidths of 2 Mbps and more, though some narrow bandwidth networks and access technologies may also be described as broadband. Broadband offers high-speed data transfer and is useful for multimedia networks,.

(See Access technology, ATM and ISDN)

Broadcast quality   1. A video recording whose quality approximates that of broadcast television. *(See MPEG*.)* 2. A camcorder able to provide video recordings that are considered broadcast quality.

Brondmo, Hans Peter   A Norwegian computer specialist accredited with the invention of the motion icon (micon). He is believed to have invented it in 1989 at MIT (Massachusetts Institute of Technology).

(See Micon.)

Browse (browsing)   A process of following the intricate paths through a hypertext-based information structure. The user passes to and from nodes or objects. In the context of the Internet, it has come to be known as surfing. It normally takes place at the micro-level but can also exist at the macro-level also, where the user may be described as navigating as opposed to browsing. The line that divides navigating from browsing is made clearer by considering the difference between a walker and a motorist. The motorist gains a high level view of travel, and is thus navigating. The walker's experience of a journey is infinitely more detailed, hence the walker is browsing.

(See Browser, Client, and Netscape Navigator.)

Browser   An application that permits the user to browse the World Wide Web. The most popular Web browsers are Netscape Navigator and Microsoft

Favourites may be used to access, and to add to, your most frequently visited Web sites.

Current Web address

Links to Web addresses

History of selectable actions

Internet Explorer. Earlier implementations include Cello and Mosaic. A modern browser allows users to:

- add Web sites/pages to an address book
- navigate backwards and forwards through visited Web pages
- open a URL, which is entered using the keyboard
- playback streaming audio and video using a plug-in or ActiveX control
- playback streaming multimedia using an appropriate plug-in or ActiveX control
- send e-mail messages, though a browser is not an e-mail client/ application
- specify various preferences including the appearance of Web pages when displayed
- open HTML files that might be local or remote
- chat in real-time, using an appropriately enabled browser
- view Web pages that contain Java applets (using a Java enabled browser)
- download files
- make telephone calls over the Internet using an appropriate Web phone
- take part in videoconferences using appropriate hardware and software.

(See Active Desktop, Active X control, Client/server, Java*, Video-conferencing and Web.)

51

Stop - terminate download of HTML pages/information

Refresh - reload HTML pages/information

Home - go to the home page of the connected Web site

Search - connect with a search engine on the Web

Favourites - browse and choose selected Web sites

History - browse and select previously visited Web pages

Channels - browse and select Active Channels

Fullscreen - switch on or off the Fullscreen mode

Mail - send and receive e-mail

Print - print Web pages

Edit - edit Web pages

Back and *forward* browse buttons

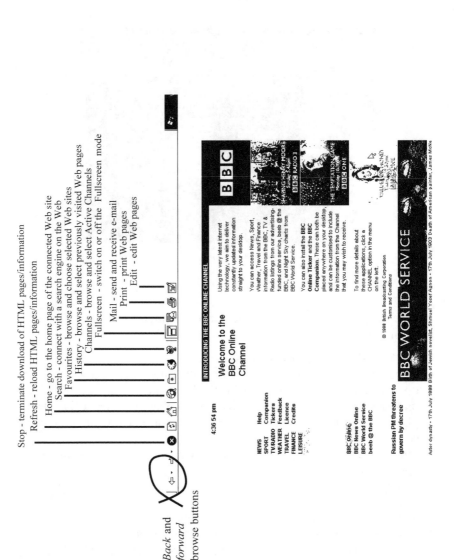

Brute Force Attack An attempt to crack a cryptosystem which uses exhaustive trial and error rather than privileged knowledge, Using public key cryptography, the attacker usually has the public key and attempts to gain the private key.

(See Brute Force RSA Factoring.)

Brute Force RSA Factoring A means of deciphering RSA. Attackers may be armed with the public-key (n,e), and then attempt to determine d in order to gain the private-key (n,d). This process begins by factorising n in order to yield the two large primes that is a common method of decypering RSA. Other methods, such as calculating $(p-1)(q-1)$, and attempting to determine d through iterative techniques are deemed equally difficult. Factoring may be carried using the algorithms of:

- Trial division which attempts to find all the prime numbers $<=sqrt(n)$
- Quadratic Sieve (QS), which is deemed fastest for numbers that are less than 110 digits
- Multiple Polynomial Quadratic Sieve (MPQS)
- Double Large Prime Variation of the MPQS
- Number Field Sieve (NFS), which is the fastest algorithm for numbers larger than 110 digits.

In 1977 Rivest asserted that it would take 40 quadrillion years to factor a 125-digit number. However, the 1994 factoring of RSA 129 took about 5000 MIPS-years. A MIPS-year equates to 1 000 000 instruction per second over a period of one year.

(See Cryptography and RSA.)

BSR (Board of Standards Review) – ANSI.

BS7799 A British Standard for information security management.

BT (British Telecom) A UK-based international telecommunications operator (or telco). It evolved as a state-owned enterprise, but was privatised in the 1980s.

BTLZ (British Telecom Lempel-Ziv) A data compression technique synonymous with modem-based data communications. It can be assumed to yield a compression ratio of around 4:1.

(See Compression.)

Buffer A quantity of RAM (Random Access Memory) that improves the rate at which data may be transferred between computers and peripheral devices.

(See Queue.)

Bug   A hardware or software fault. The first recorded case of an actual bug was witnessed by Grace Hopper, a computer pioneer who did much work in developing valve computers and high-level languages. Using the Harvard Mk 2 computer she discovered a hardware fault caused by a moth caught between the contacts of a relay. After debugging the system, the unfortunate moth was entered in the computer's log at 15:45, 9 September 1945. The process of authoring or developing multimedia often requires extensive testing and debugging.

Build   1. A version number which denotes the version of a program or operating system. It is interchangeable with the term *development build*. 2. A word used to describe the process of developing hardware or software.

Burst mode data transfer   1. A heightened volume of data traffic over a network. 2. A maximum, unsustainable data transfer rate from a CD-ROM drive. It is many times greater than the average data transfer rate, and is sustainable for a limited period only.

Bush, Vannevar   A science advisor to President Roosevelt. He put forward a paradigm for information storage and retrieval in the 1940s. He may be considered the originator of the Internet concept, and of the 'relational model' for storing and retrieving information. His name, therefore, is linked with standalone multimedia as well as with multimedia on the Internet. Principal facets of the Internet such as World Wide Web (WWW) and the many hypertext-based navigation and browsing tools have their origins in Bush's vision. His momentous article 'As We May Think' covering what he called Memex was published in *Atlantic Monthly*. Hypertext evangelist, Ted Nelson admitted publicly that he may have read this article.
(See Hypertext, Web and Xanadu.)

Business audio   A program that permits you to control a computer using voice commands. It is possible to do the same with dictation systems such as IBM ViaVoice. Depending upon which system is used they also have proof-reading and text-to-speech capabilities. Microsoft Windows Sound System is a typical example of a business audio system. Modern business audio tools are voice-independent.
(See Speech recognition, Wave audio and ViaVoice.)

Business system engineering   A collective term used to describe the processes of implementing business system, which fulfils an enterprise's requirements. The business system includes:

- business processes
- IS (Information Systems)
- personnel.

Button An active area on a screen, which may be an iconic representation of an option, feature or application. Windows buttons are labelled with appropriate identifying text such as Close or OK. Using visual programming tools buttons can be created simply by drawing them on screen. Once drawn they become objects that can be moved or copied. Their colour, frame thickness, fonts and other attributes can be altered usually by right-clicking them. As is the case with all event-driven applications development tools, the button is responsive to a mouse click. Its behaviour or response to such an event is determined by its method which usually takes the form of short segment of code. The method or code might run a video clip, for instance. Buttons can also be selected using the keyboard, usually by pressing the Alt key together with an appropriate letter that corresponds with a letter in the button's label. Using development tools such as MS Visual Basic, you simply draw buttons and then add methods (code) to them, thus determining their behaviour.

(See ToolBook and Visual Basic.)

Byte 1. A piece of digital information that is eight bits in length. 2. A computer magazine (*BYTE*) published by McGraw-Hill.

Bytecode A machine language used by virtual processors for interpretation and program execution. Such programming languages include the OO variants Java and SmallTalk. These languages are suited to heterogeneous environments, and may therefore be deployed effectively over the Web as applets. The virtual processor physically exists on the client, and is implemented in software, and is independent of hardware and accompanying operating systems. They may not be as responsive as native code components, where perhaps an ActiveX control is running on a Windows platform. However, any performance difference may be eradicated through the hardware implementation of the virtual processor on the client system, in which case it ceases to be virtual.

(See Java and OOP.)*

C

C++ An object-oriented version of the C programming language. Like modern programming languages such as Java, it provides the programmer with OO methodologies. Bjarne Stroustrup evolved C++ from C which has links with BCPL (Basic Combined Programming Language). It extends the C programming language through the inclusion of the OO concepts:

- inheritance
- polymorphism
- encapsulation
- data hiding.

(See Data hiding, Encapsulation, Polymorphism.)

ANSI C++ is an internationally agreed standard for the C++ programming language.

#include <file> When compiled the #include statement is implemented by the preprocessor which reads the contents of a named file.

main () A C11 program must have a main () function which begins and ends with open { and close } braces. This is the first function called when the program is run, and may be used to define variable types.

Comments Single-line comments in a C++ program must begin with //, and multiple line comments begin and end with /* and */.

Syntax (basic) All statements have a semi colon (;) as their suffix. White space may be included which is ignored by the compiler.

Compound statements such as those of a function or a subroutine begin with a single open brace "{", and end with a closing brace "}".

C++ variables C++ variable types may be defined as follows:

```
#include iostream ()
main ()
{
```

```
        char find;
        float prime;
        double prime_large;
        short int xx;
        long int xxxx;
        unsigned short int yy;
        yy = 35;            // assign the unsigned long int yyyy;
        }
        /* the character variable find, may store 256 character
        values */
        // the variable prime, may store signed 4Byte values
        /* the variable prime_large, may store signed 8Byte
        values*/
        // the variable xx, may store signed 2Byte values
        // the variable xxxx, may store signed 4Byte values
        // the variable yy, may store unsigned 2Byte values
        // the variable yyyy, may store unsigned 4Byte values
```

Defined variables may be equated to values using the statement:

```
    yy=35;
```

Variables may be defined, and assigned values using the statement:

```
    unsigned short int xx=45;
```

Multiple variables of the same type are defined using a comma as a separator:

```
    unsigned long int yyyy, yflow
```

Typedef   A C++ keyword that declares a name for a type, and not for a variable: typedef char* pchar. Using typedef, mnemonics may be assigned to the statements used to define variables and their types. The following statement assigns the word xxxx to the unsigned short int statement:

```
        #include <filename>
        typedef unsigned short int xxxx;
        int main ()
    {
    <   xxxx coordinate;
        // define coordinate as an unsigned short integer
        variable
    }
```

C++ literal constants   A variable may be assigned a value which is considered a literal constant:

```
    int yearsAfter=25;
```

A literal constant may also be used when performing arithmetic operations on variables. In the following statement where the time variable is assigned to the product of the variable present and 10, 10 is considered a literal constant:

```
    time=present*10
```

C++ symbolic constant A symbolic constant has a name, and is assigned an unchanging value. It may be used just like an integer constant. Symbolic constants improve program maintenance and updating; a single change made to a symbolic constant, is echoed at every point it may occur.

A symbolic constant *multiplier* may be assigned the value 10 using the statement:

```
#define multiplier 10
```

or

```
Const unsigned short int multiplier = 10
```

C++ enumerated constants Enumerated constants take the form of a type, and are a useful shorthand for defining a number of what might be related constants. The following code defines the constants back, forward, left, and right, where Move is the *enumeration*.

```
enum Move { back=4, forward, left=6, right=3};
```

The forward constant is assigned the value 5, an increment (of one) relative to the previously defined constant back.

C++ precedence In C++, arithmetic operators have a precedence value. These indicate the order in which such operators are implemented is significant with expressions such as:

```
dev = xx + yy * zz + yy;
```

Control over such arithmetic operations is obtained using parentheses, i.e:

```
dev = (xx + yy) * zz:
```

Parentheses may be nested.

C++ If statement The if statement determines whether or not the ensuing statement is executed, based on a single condition:

```
{
  if (xxx = yyy)
    transform = Scale;
}
```

C++ If . . . else statement The if . . .else statement is used to implement either one of two statements:

```
{
if    (xxx = yyy)
      transform = Scale;
else
      transform = Scale * adjust;
}
```

C++ logical operators Logical AND, OR and NOT are implemented using the syntax '&&', '||', and '!'.

(See Java*, Object*, and OOP.)

C++ to IDL language mapping   A mapping that equates C++ to the IDL equivalent.

Cabbing   A method of compressing objects such as ActiveX controls and Java objects into a single CAB file. This optimises their rate of transfer across networks.
(See ActiveX control.)

Cable modem   A modem that can operate over cable TV networks. The speed of operation is many times greater than the fastest analogue modems. Typically, a cable modem's data transfer rate is considerably greater downstream than it is upstream. For example, the Motorola CyberSurf cable modem offers an upstream rate of 768 Kbps and a downstream rate of 10 Mbps. Competing cable modems have downstream rates approaching 30 Mbps and faster. Cable modems offer high-speed access to the Internet, and are offered as extras by such ISPs as Telstra Big Pond (Australia).
(See Access technology, ADSL and ISDN.)

Cache   1. A segment of SRAm (Static Random Access Memory) that drives processor performance gains. Its rationale is to expedite the rate at which data may be read from and written to memory. It may be an integral part of the processor (internal), or external in the form of dedicated SRAM chips on the PC motherboard. The fast speed of SRAM overcomes the slower speed of DRAM (Dynamic Random Access Memory) making up the system memory. This significantly improves system performance. External memory cache sizes are relatively small, ranging from just 128 Kbyte to 1 Mbyte in size. An algorithm is used to estimate what portions of system memory should reside in the memory cache. The Pentium Pro has an internal cache accommodated on a single die or chip. 2. An area of memory or hard disk used as a temporary store for downloaded HTML files and data, including URLs. The size of the cache may be specified. *(See Browser.)* 3. A hard disk controller that expedites hard disk performance. A hard disk cache controller typically comprises a few megabytes of RAM, and is usually expandable. It speeds up read/write operations by using its on-board RAM as an intermediate data store between disk and system memory. Based upon which data is most often requested, a caching algorithm estimates which portions of hard disk should reside in on-board RAM, thus making it more readily available. The ingenuity of this technique simply takes advantage of the inescapable fact that a small percentage of disk data is rewritten and accessed most frequently. The decision making process which is insulated from the system processor fuels the view that it is an intelligent controller. Cache controllers are the most expensive of all variants, and in

terms of random access and data transfer rate they can be assumed to outperform all others. 4. A RAID often features a cache for improved performance.
(See RAID.)

Caffeine   A programming environment that has similarities with RMI. Produced by Netscape and Visigenic, caffeine requires VisiBroker for Java, and allows developers to create CORBA distributed objects without programming with CORBA IDL.

Capture reversal   An event that sees the reversal of a capture response when goods are returned after the completion of a sale.

Card association   A bank that supports franchise for shown card brands.

Card issuer   A card company or bank that has powers to grant credit or bank cards.

Cardholder   An authorised owner and user of a credit card or bank card.

Card-not-present   A card transaction where there is no physical evidence of the card, and typically exists in a MOTO (Mail Order/Telephone Order) situation.

Cardshield   A service proved by Shielded Technologies Inc. which can be applied in the development of a Web commerce solution that includes credit card transactions.

Carrier   A carrier signal is used to transport a signal over media that may be physical or wireless. The carrier might be encoded using frequency modulation (FM), amplitude modulation (AM), or another modulation technique.

CAS (China Association for Standardisation)

Casting   A process by which one data type is converted into another.

CBA (Canadian bankers Association)

CBEMA (Computer and Business Equipment Manufacturers Association)

CCC (Customs Cooperative Council)   An international organisation

CCIR 601   A standard for uncompressed digital video, also known as D1. Using CCIR 601 in order to digitise a 525-line NTSC signal running at 25 frames per second, its chrominance elements U and V, and its luminance Y elements are digitised individually. The Y element is digitised using 858 samples per line, and the U and V elements each are digitised using 429 samples per line. Each pixel is generated using 10 bits per sample. The digital video is coded at 270 Mbps which is derived as follows:

```
Y: 858 * 525 * 30 * 10 = 135Mbps
U: 429 * 525 * 30 * 10 = 67.5Mbps
V: 429 * 525 * 30 * 10 = 67.5Mbps
                          270Mbps
```

(See DCT, MPEG*, MPEG-1, MPEG-2, Multimedia and Video*.)

CCITT (Committée Consultatif Internationale Téléphonique et Télégraphic)   It has now been renamed ITU-T.

CD *(See CD-ROM.)*

CD-R (Cd-Recordable)   A drive capable of writing to blank Cd-R discs, usually in a variety of different formats including Video CD, Phot CD, CD-ROM XA, CD-I and CD-ROM. The mid 1990s saw the launch of more affordable CD-R drives, bringing low-volume CD-ROM publishing to the desktop. Important factors to consider when acquiring CD-R drives include:

- The maximum data capacities supported.
- The read rate of the drive, which may be single-speed, double-speed, triple-speed, quad-speed or faster.
- The disc recording speed, which may be single-speed, double-speed, triple-speed, quad-speed or even faster. High recording speeds yield saving in terms of person hours consumed.
- The disc formats supported, which might include audio CD, CD-ROM, CD-ROM XA, CD-I, Photo CD and Video CD.
- The interface type. Most operate over the SCSI bus variants.
- What type of interface software is provided? It is important that this should be user friendly.

(See CD-ROM and DVD.)

CD-ROM (Compact Disc – Read Only Memory)   A universal distribution medium based on compact disc. It was the first viable multimedia distribution medium. Announced in 1983 it is typically a 12 cm diameter optical disc offering data capacity in the hundreds of Mbyte range. It is available in

8 cm diameter form. The standard 12 cm diameter CD-ROM supports up to about 660 Mbyte (692 060 000 bytes) data capacity. A single disc is equivalent to between approximately 400 1.44 Mbyte. floppy disks or 1,500 360 Kbyte floppy disks. 8-cm-diameter CD-ROMs are also available.

A 12 cm CD-ROM can store up to 250 000 A4 pages of text or approximately 100 000 000 words. Note, these methods of quoting data capacity are rather vague and not likely to satisfy many people. Like audio CD, a CD-ROM disc physically consists of a metallic disc bonded to a polycarbonate base. This is coated with a transparent, protective lacquer. A track spiralling from its centre measures some 5 km long, and is arranged

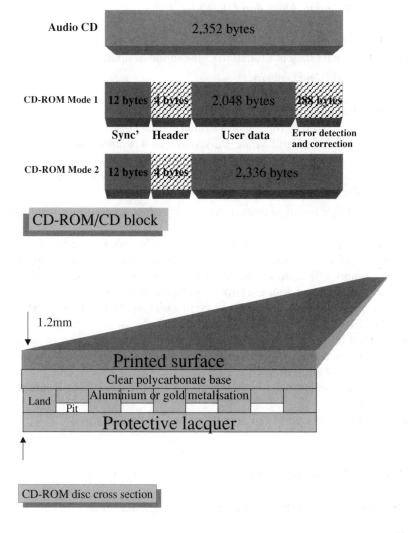

at a density of 16000 tracks per inch. The CD-ROM physical format includes:

- Mode 1 data blocks, which are used to store code and data where accuracy is critical.
- Mode 2 data blocks, which are used to store data that might be impervious to minor errors.

Data blocks are supported by all fully specified CD-ROM drives. One hour Mode 1 disc yields 527 Mbyte data capacity and Mode 2 gives 602 Mbyte data capacity. A Mode 1 data block will yield just 2048 bytes (2 Kbyte) user data, while Mode 2 holds 2.28 Kbyte user data.

(See CD-ROM data block and DVD.)

CD-ROM data block   A CD-ROM data block has 2352 bytes. User data yielded by each block is a function of the mode of operation.

(See CD-ROM data capacity.)

CD-ROM drive   A device for reading CD-ROM discs. It may be portable, external or integral to the computer/multimedia system. Modern drives are able to read Mode 1 and Mode 2 discs, as well as audio CDs. The principal factors which govern the performance of a CD-ROM drive include access time and data transfer rate. In general a CD-ROM drive may be specified in terms of the following information:

- Access time; highly specified drives may offer access times little longer than 100 ms.
- Average data transfer rate may be generally specified in terms of how fast the disc is rotated; a single-speed drive will give a data transfer rate of around 150 Kbte/s. This data rate is broadly doubled, tripled and quadrupled using double-, triple-, and quad-speed drives.
- The physical interface type may be proprietary, IDE, SCSI, SCSI-2 or a PCMCIA card or parallel port can be used.
- Compatibility in terms of disc formats that may be read is generally specified in terms of 8 cm diameter CD-ROM, CD-ROM XA, linear CD-I, Video CD and Photo CD.
- Physical characteristics include whether the drive is internal, external or portable.
- The maximum number of drives that may be daisychained.

(See DVD.)

Celeron   An Intel processor.

Certification Authority   *(See Digital Certificate Authority.)*

CGI (Common Gateway Interface)   A protocol that provides bi-directional information flow within the active or dynamic Web model, and may be perceived as permitting users to interact with remote applications such as E-commerce implementations. It is a protocol that provides bi-directional information flow between a HTTP server and HTTP client. The resulting interactivity on the client side, permits data entry and the editing of HTML documents. The Common Gateway Interface (CGI) may connect the HTTP server and its applications and databases. CGI scripts are created using a scripting language or programming tool.

CGI may be used to:

- query databases and post the output to HTML documents
- generate HTML forms for data entry
- interact with the indexes of on-line documents to produce searching and retrieval features
- interact with e-mail.

CGI programming is possible using Unix, Windows and Macintosh servers. CGI scripts may be created using:

- Perl
- Apple Script

CGI programs may be created using almost any high-level programming language including:

- C++
- Visual Basic

The CGI protocol is based on standard environment variables that are sometimes extended by the Web server used.

(See CGI environment variables.)

CGI environment variables   A set of variables which define the CGI (Common Gateway Interface), and are normally set when a CGI script or program is called by using the:

- GET method where the URL defines the CGI program (such as `credit.cgi` for example) and the accompanying data used by the server that follows the question mark:

  ```
  www.FrancisBotto.com/cgi-bin/credit.cgi?subject=
  transaction
  ```

- POST method in which the program is specified as part of the URL, passing data using the requester path: which is a uni-directional link from the client to the server.

  ```
  www.FrancisBotto.com/cgi-bin/credit.cgi
  ```

  HTTP_ACCEPT   Holds the "Accept:" headers from the client.

HTTP_COOKIE   Holds the contents of "Cookie:" headers from the client.

HTTP_FROM   Holds the contents of the "From:" header from the client that may be the client's:

- correct e-mail address if not withheld
- incorrect e-mail address which is simply false, or entered in error.

HTTP_REFERER   Holds the contents of the "Referer:" header from the client, containing a URL.

HTTP_USER_AGENT   Holds the contents of the "User-Agent:" header from the client, containing the Browser's name.

PATH_INFO   Holds the URKL's suffix or that data which follows the script's name.

QUERY_STRING   Holds the "query" part of an HTTP GET request that is the URL's suffix portion following '?'

REMOTE_ADDRESS   Holds the client's or proxy's IP address from where the request is being made.

REMOTE_HOST   Holds the host name of the client or proxy making the request, or its IP address only when NO_DNS_HOSTNAMES is defined in the config.h file.

SCRIPT_NAME   Holds the name and path of the CGI script being executed.

SERVER_SOFTWARE   Holds the name and perhaps version of the server software.

SERVER_NAME   Contains name of host on which server is running.

SERVER_PROTOCOL   Contains "CGI 1.1".

SERVER_PORT   Holds the port on which server is running.
(See CGI.)

CGI program   *(See CGI.)*

CGI Script   *(See CGI.)*

CGI scripting language   A language which may be used to create CGI programs or scripts.
(See CGI.)

Chat   1. A real-time, text-based communications medium, carried out over a network, or over the Internet. *(See IRC.)* 2, A Windows NT-based server, which is part of the MCIS. *(See MCIS.)* The Chat server provides real-time text-based communications. The communications may be private (one-to-one), one-to-many, or conferences. It has its own proprietary protocol and supports the IRC protocol. A Chat SDK and ActiveX control, permit the integration of Chat functionality, where a single server may support up to 48 000 users.

Checksum validation   A method of validating credit card numbers by using the *mod 10* check digit algorithm and is implemented by:
1. Doubling the value of alternative digits of the credit card number by beginning with the second digit:

1	3	6	5	8	9	7	6	2	4	2	7	6	0	8	7
	6		10		18		12		8		14		0		14

2. Adding the product values to the alternate digits beginning with the first:

$$7 \ + \ 16 \ + \ 26 \ + \ 17 \ + \ 10 \ + \ 16 \ + \ 6 \ + \ 22 = 120$$

In this instance the credit card number has passed the validity check because the result is evenly divisible by 10.

Ciphertext   An input into a decryption algorithm that sees it returned to plaintext.
(See Asymmetric*, Brute Force*, Cryptosystem, Dictionary attack. Encryption algorithm, Plaintext, Public key encryption, RSA*, SET* and Transposition.)

CISCO   A large international supplier of advanced network hardware products, including routers and bridges.

Class   A formal description of objects in terms of the methods and data they may use.
(See Class diagram.)

Class diagram   A pictorial representation of the class hierarchy, including links of inheritance, revealing sub-classes and their superclasses. It illustrates how interfaces and methods are inherited within the class hierarchy of an architecture.
(See C++ and Java*.)

Classpath   A path used by a Java program that points to folders containing classes, and it may be downloaded dynamically to a client using a codebase.

Clicks and mortar   A business that exists both physically, perhaps on the high street or in a shopping mall, but also has an e-commerce presence on the Internet.

Click-through rate   The percentage of visitors to a Web page or site that click on a particular link or area, perhaps an advertising banner.

Client   1. A collective portable or desktop system that provides the human-machine interface to a client/server architecture, including:

- e-mail client such as Microsoft Outlook for receiving and sending e-mail messages
- client software, for example Web browsers such as Netscape, Explorer or HotJava
- client operating system, which is typically Windows 95/98/2000/NT.

Between clients and servers there may be a number of hardware and software entities, including:

- Access technologies, such as ISDN or wireless media such as GSM
- Modems or NIC (Network Interface Cards)
- Protocols, such as TCP/IP at the transport layer, HTTP and UDP
- Middleware, such as those based on the IDLs of DCOM or CORBA NS, which provide a means of exchanging messages ORB (Object Request Broker).

(See HTTP, OSI, TCP/UIP and UDP.) 2. In the context of middleware based on the OMG Notification Services, such client applications are termed consumers, while the server applications become suppliers or publishers. In this context clients can operate according to the push and pull models within the client/server architecture. *(See CORBA*.)* 3. A device or appliance that is driven by remote server applications and data. It may be a portable device such as a PDA or palmtop appliance manufactured by enterprises such as Psion, Casio and 3Com.

(See Client/server and CORBA.)*

Client/server   A distributed system architecture where client systems are connected to server systems. The client provides an interface to applications and data that is stored on the server. The interface can be provided through a browser such as:

- Microsoft Explorer
- Netscape Navigator
- Sunsoft HotJava.

Client activity and processing is said to be on the client-side, while server activity and processing is on the server-side. The network that provides connection between clients and servers might be:

- a LAN
- a WAN
- an Internet
- an intranet.

Industry client/server standards for database manipulation include:

- ODBC (Open Database Connectivity) which is the most common
- IDAPI (Integrated Database Application Programming Interface).

Client/server network protocols include:

- IP/TCP
- IPX (Internet Packet eXchange).

Using the three-element representation of an application, the client/server model (which is observed by the Web) can be explained.

The five shown topologies are:

1. *Distributed presentation*, which distributes a portion of the user interface (UI), and may be equated to the inactive Web model, where the browser is used only to view documents. Remote presentation that distributes the entire UI to the client system.
2. *Remote presentation*, which distributes the entire UI to the client system.
3. *Distributed function*, which divides application logic between the server and the client. In the Web context this processing distribution may be achieved using appropriate plug-ins and ActiveX controls with Netscape navigator or Microsoft Explorer.
4. *Remote data access*, which is a model that sees the so-called fat client. This means that the client system is substantial (or 'fat') in terms of application logic.

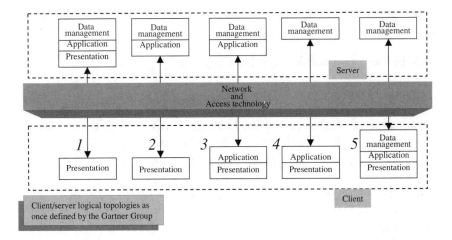

Client/server logical topologies as once defined by the Gartner Group

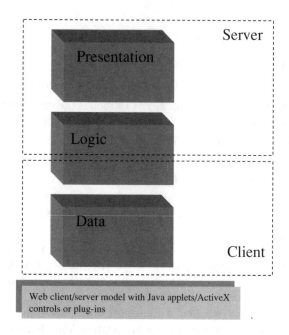

Web client/server model with Java applets/ActiveX controls or plug-ins

5. *Distributed database*, which distributes the data management functions between the client- and server-side. This configuration is used in Webcasting, where users are served information that matches their pre-defined criteria.

The distribution of the three key application elements (namely Presentation, Logic and Data or Data Management) can be used to explain the many client/server models.

(See 2-tier, 3-tier, N-tier, client/server architecture, Application*, Client*, Server and Webcasting.)

Cold Fusion　OO website development tool.

Commerce One　A large b2b supplier.

Client/server architecture　A hardware infrastructure used to platform client/server applications. It can be 2-tier, 3-tier or n-tier.
(See 2-tier, 3-tier and N-tier, client/server architecture.)

Client side　A term that indicates the presence of software or data on client systems. Synonym: local.
(See Client.)

Client system   A collective system with which users interact directly, and is physically located on users' desktops or in similarly close proximity.
(See Client.)

Codebase   An entity that may be downloaded dynamically to a client and contains a classpath to remote classes.
(See Classpath.)

COM (Component Object Model)   A software architecture based binary software components and is a glue used by OLE objects and software services. COM-based technologies include:

- Distributed COM (DCOM)
- COM+
- Microsoft Transaction Server (MTS)
- ActiveX controls.

COM+   A COM enhancement announced at the 1997 Professional Developers Conference in San Diego, CA. It provides developers with an improved workbench allowing them to program in almost any language, using many different tools and offers backward compatibility with COM.

Compaq   A large international computer manufacturer.

Compiled   A process by which the source code of a high-level language is translated into machine-executable form or machine code. Generally, compiled languages offer better run-time performance than interpreted languages.
(See C++, Java, Object*, and OOP.)*

Compiler   A program or program module able to convert source code into machine-executable code. Unlike an interpreter which attaches precise code to high-level statements each time a program is run, a compiler produces machine-executable object code once.

Compound document   A document which can integrate different document types and media types that emanate from different sources. The various documents may be OLE objects provided by an appropriate OLE 2.0 server. Alternatively, they can be objects of a similar architecture such as the more modern Microsoft ActiveX component architecture. Equally, they can be objects that comply with OpenDoc or JavaBeans component architectures.
(See ActiveX, JavaBeans and OLE.)

Compound object   An object that is constructed using multiple objects. *(See C++, Java*, OOP and OODBMS.)*

Compressed image   An image following compression through hardware and/or software means. *(See JPEG and MPEG*.)*

Compression   1. A method by which data of any sort (often image and video data) is scaled down in size, eventually consuming less storage space and requiring a narrower bandwidth. 2. Video compression optimises both the bandwidth and data storage capacity of media. Popular video compression schemes include Intel Indeo, MPEG-1, MPEG-2 and M-JPEG. *(See MPEG*.)* 3. Audio compression reduces the data storage requirements of wave audio files and optimises the bandwidth of distribution media. *(See Wave audio.)* 4. Disk compression increases the data storage capacity of hard disks. Commercial disk compression programs include Stacker (Stac Electronics), which is also available in hardware form that gives improved performance over software-only solutions. Stac Electronics made international news when it won a $100 000 000 lawsuit, resulting from Microsoft infringing its patents for compression algorithms. 5. Batch file compression is useful for archiving files and compressing them for distribution purposes. Compressed program files have to be unpacked or uncompressed before they can be run. Popular batch file compression programs include Pkzip and Lharc. 6. Data compression to reduce the size of data parcels transmitted and received using a modem. Standard data compression in this context include V.42bis.

Compression parameters   A video compressor setting can be used to optimise a video sequence for playback using a target system of a given bandwidth. MPEG compression parameters include the placement of I frames. More general compression parameters might include interleave ratio, frame playback speed, and compression ratio requirements. Generally the quality of video diminishes as the compression ratio increases. *(See MPEG*.)*

Compression ratio   A ratio that relates the size of a data file before and after compression. The video compression ratio using fully specified compressors can be altered. *(See MPEG*.)*

Compressor   A hardware and/or software solution used to compress motion video or still computer graphics. Using video compressors, it is possible to specify a number of compression settings.

Computer   A system or appliance that is able to process and store digital information. Its many components and subsystems may include:

- processor or CPU (Central Processing Unit)
- modem
- DVD-ROM drive
- graphics engine or card
- hard disk
- sound card
- electronic memory devices including RAM, SRAM, VRAM, ROM and NVRAM
- colour display
- video playback device such as MPEG-1 or MPEG-2 decoder
- QWERTY keyboard
- mouse
- microphone
- television tuner
- radio tuner
- set-top box decoder
- scanner.

(See Client, Thin client and Fat client.)

Computer graphics   A process of displayed images using a computer. The advancement of computer graphics has unleashed numerous computer applications ranging from computer-Aided design (CAD) to colour desktop publishing (DTP), VR, multimedia and 3-D graphics. Through the coupling of high-resolution colour monitors and high specification graphic controllers, truly photographic quality images are now possible. Built up of digitally defined pixel elements, computer images are invariably complex. For example, a 1024 × 768 pixel image yields 786 432 individual pixels. Digitising such a black and white image requires a corresponding number of bits, or 98 304 bytes (786 432/8), or 96 Kbyte (98 304/1024). Progressing to a grey-scale arrangement using bits per pixel to give 256 (2^8) grey shades, the same 1024 × 768 pixel image requires 768 Kbytes – eight times the storage capacity of its black-and-white equivalent. Such is the complexity of photographic quality images, a minimum of 24 bit colour graphics are required. Red, green and blue are each represented by eight bits, thus facilitating the selection of 256 tones of each. By combining each colour component, over 16.7 million (256 × 256 × 256) colours are made available. Yet higher quality results are achieved using 32 bit and 36 bit graphics. Such 24 bit graphics on a 1024 × 768 pixel resolution monitor means that a single frame consumes around 3072 Kbyte. Large image files of this sort are costly to process, transmit and store. They are also slow to transfer from computer to screen, as well as to and from hard disk. A solution to these problems lies in image compression. Many popular image file formats such as JPEG feature image compression.

(See JPEG.)

Computer name   A name of computer/system connected to a network. All Windows 98/NT systems have names when connected to a network. Additionally, their users are given passwords, which may be used to log on and retrieve their specified or default Windows configuration.

(See Windows.)

Concurrent computing   An environment in which processes, or program elements execute simultaneously.

(See MPP.)

Concurrent programming   A programming model where processes are implemented in parallel.

Concurrent programming language   A programming language that may be used to implement processes in parallel.

Confidence factor   A measure of the percentage probability of an event or circumstance being correct. In KBS (Knowledge Based Systems) it may be applied so as to weight facts and conclusions which exist in a knowledge base.

Constant   An unchanging entity.

Content authoring tool   A development tool that permits the creation of Web and multimedia content.

(See Multimedia authoring tool.)

Content provider   A company or individual that usually provides copyright material for inclusion in a multimedia production. Content providers typically include publishers, recording companies, photo libraries etc.

Controller   A generic name for a hardware component which controls a peripheral device, such as a disk drive, CD-ROM drive or monitor.

(See Graphics card and Hard disk.)

Cookie   A minor transaction that allows server-side components such as CGI scripts and programs, to store and retrieve data from the client system.

It gives Web applications the ability to write data to the client, which reflects usage habits. For example, the data may relieve the user from repetitive tasks, such as the re-entry of ID numbers or data each time a Web site is visited. Instead the server-side components may identify the user through cookies on the client system, extract them, and perform the necessary processes.

(See Security gateway and Shopping cart.)

CORBA (Common Object Request Broker Architecture) An object architecture featuring an IDL (Interface Definition Language) and is managed by the Object Management Group (OMG).

(See CORBA IDL and OMG NS.)

CORBA IDL (Common Object Request Broker Architecture Interface Definition Language) A language that is based on C++ and may be compiled in Java and C++ using appropriate compilers such as IDL2JAVA and IDL2CPP.

Corel Draw A popular graphics program used by many professional illustrators and graphics artists. Used widely in the production of graphics for multimedia applications/titles.

CosNotification An IDL module which defines the operations (or methods) used by the CORBA Notification Services which supports push and pull models on networks. The collective IDL modules might be referred to as the API of the implementation.

```
module CosNotification {

// The following two are the same, but serve
different purposes.
typedef CosTrading: :PropertySeq
OptionalHeaderFields;
typedef CosTrading: :PropertySeq
FilterableEventBody;
typedef CosTrading: :PropertySeq QoSProperties;
typedef CosTrading: :PropertySeq AdminProperties;

struct EventType {
   string domain_name;
   string type_name;
};

typedef sequence<EventType> EventTypeSeq;
```

75

```
struct PropertyRange {
   CosTrading: :PropertyName name;
   CosTrading: :PropertyValue low_val;
   CosTrading : :PropertyValue high_val;
};

typedef sequence<PropertyRange> PropertyRangeSeq;

enum QoSError_code {
   UNSUPPORTED_PROPERTY,
   UNAVAILABLE_PROPERTY,
   UNSUPPORTED_VALUE,
   UNAVAILABLE_VALUE,
   BAD_PROPERTY,
   BAD_TYPE,
   BAD_VALUE
};
struct PropertyError {
QoSError_code code;
PropertyRange available_range;
};

typedef sequence<PropertyError> PropertyErrorSeq;

exception UnsupportedQoS { PropertyErrorSeq
qos_err; };
typedef sequence<PropertyError> PropertyErrorSeq;

exception UnsupportedQoS { PropertyErrorSeq
qos_err; };
exception UnsupportedAdmin { PropertyErrorSeq
admin_err; };

// Define the Structured Event structure
struct FixedEventHeader {
EventType event_type;
string event_name;
};

struct EventHeader {
FixedEventHeader fixed_header;
OptionalHeaderFields variable_header;
};

struct StructuredEvent {

EventHeader header;
```

```
FilterableEventBody filterable_data;
any remainder_of_body;

}; // StructuredEvent

typedef sequence<StructuredEvent> EventBatch;
```

// The following constant declarations define the standard
// QoS property names and the associated values each property
// can take on. The name/value pairs for each standard property
// are grouped, beginning with a string constant defined for the
// property name, following by the values the property can take on.

```
const string EventReliability = "EventReliability";
const short BestEffort = 0;
const short Persistent = 1;

const string ConnectionReliability =
"ConnectionReliability";
// Can take on the same values as EventReliability

const string Priority = "Priority";
const short LowestPriority = -32767;
const short HighestPriority = 32767;
const short DefaultPriority = 0;

const string StartTime = "StartTime";
```
// StartTime takes a value of type TimeBase: :UtcT when placed
// in an event header. StartTime can also be set to either
// TRUE or FALSE at the Proxy level, indicating whether or not the
₄₅// Proxy supports the setting of per-message stop times.

```
const string StopTime = "StopTime";
```
// StopTime takes a value of type TimeBase: :UtcT when placed
// in an event header. StopTime can also be set to either

```
// TRUE or FALSE at the Proxy level, indicating
whether or not the
// Proxy supports the setting of per-message stop
times.

const string Timeout = "Timeout";
// Timeout takes on a value of type TimeBase:
:TimeT

const string OrderPolicy = "OrderPolicy";
const short AnyOrder = 0;
const short FifoOrder = 1;
const short PriorityOrder = 2;
const short DeadlineOrder = 3;

const string DiscardPolicy = "DiscardPolicy";
// DiscardPolicy takes on the same values as
OrderPolicy, plus const short LifoOrder = 4;

const string MaximumBatchSize = "MaximumBatchSize";
// MaximumBatchSize takes on a value of type long

const string PacingInterval = "PacingInterval";
// PacingInterval takes on a value of type
TimeBase: :TimeT

interface QoSAdmin {
QoSProperties get_qos ( );

void set_qos ( in QoSProperties qos)
raises ( UnsupportedQoS );

void validate_qos (
   in QoSProperties required_qos,
   out PropertyRangeSeq available_qos )
raises ( UnsupportedQos );

}; // QosAdmin

// Admin properties are defined in similar manner as
Qos
// properties. The only difference is that these
properties
// are related to channel administration policies,
as opposed
// message quality of service

const string MaxQueueLength = "MaxQueneLength";
```

```
// MaxQueueLength takes on a value of type long

const string MaxConsumers = "MaxConsumers";
// MaxConsumers takes on a value of type long

const string MaxSuppliers = "MaxSuppliers";
// MaxSuppliers takes on a value of type long
```

The Notification Module

Counter program   A program which records the number of occasions (or hits) a Web page or URL is opened. Such program variants may count Web pages that are opened and served to the client, and not merely count URLs. The program may be embedded in a HTML script.
(See CGI*.)

Coupling   A term used to describe efficiency of communication between network hardware and software components. *Tight* coupling between two network components indicates comparatively high-speed communication capabilities. *Loose* coupling indicates the exact opposite.

Cray, Seymour   A computer scientist made famous by his work in the field of MPP.
(See MPP.)

CRC (Cyclic reduncy check)   An error detection scheme used on CD variants as well as other devices.

Crawler   A program that automatically gathers metadata from Web sites and may be deployed to build index information for a search engine. It is sometimes called a robot or spider.
(See Search engine.)

Cyclic redundancy check   An error detection Scheme used on CD variants as well as other devices.

Creative Labs   A Singapore-based company specialising in sound cards and video capture cards. Its SoundBlaster card became an industry standard. Its video capture cards include the VideoBlaster range, which extends to video conferencing. It also marketed and sold the rather dated VideoSpigot video capture card, though it did not develop it.

Credit Card Merchant Account   A POS feature that enables an e-commerce Web site to process credit card transactions. Numerous companies offer such facilities over the World Wide Web where users are required to complete on-line forms, and produce relevant evidence of their on-line business. *(See POS.)*

Credit card number   A number assigned to a credit card.

Critical error   An error resulting from a hardware or software bug. Using DOS, the user will be prompted by R(etry), I(gnore), F(ail), or A(bort).

Cropping   A process of trimming an image or frame. In terms of video or picture editing, an image or video data is cropped as you would snip a photograph using a pair of scissors. Most editing programs provide an Undo Crop command (on the Edit menu) in order to cancel a previous cropping operation.

Cross-platform   A software program, module or object that may be run on more than one platform. Java applications are cross-platform. Such applications may be described as platform or hardware independent. For instance, a platform-independent program might run on Windows, OS/2 and 386 Unix.
(See Java*.)

CRT (Cathode Ray Tube)   A display device used in desktop colour monitors, consisting of a screen area covered with phosphor deposits (or pixels) each consisting of red, blue and green phosphors. the CRT was the first optronic device. The distance between the phosphors is termed the dot pitc. Most monitors feature a dot pitch of .26, while more highly specified versions offer a smaller dot pitch. An electron beam is projected from the back of the CRT on to the inner screen, using an electron gun. To help focus the electron beam a fine mask is included behind the screen phosphors. This fine gauze separates the three-colour phosphors allowing the elecron beam to shine more accurately upon them while improving picture definition in the process. The electron beam scans each of the phosphor-lines horizontally. The rate at which the electron gun scans a single line is termed the horizontal frequency, or the line frequency. There are two methods of scanning the lines:

- interlaced.
- non-interlaced.

In a non-interlaced arrangement all the lines are scanned one after another. The rate at which all lines are scanned is termed the refresh rate or the vertical frequency. Using an interlaced configuration the lines making up the screen are scanned in two separate fields. One field is used to scan even numbered lines and the other to scan odd numbered lines. This interlaced technique was introduced in television broadcasting specifically to reduce screen flicker. Today, however, a monitor that operates at high resolutions in a interlaced mode is thought to be one that will flicker. Non-interlaced monitors with sufficiently high screen refresh rates are preferred. These provide flicker-free images, with improved stability, and are least likely to cause eye strain. The minimum acceptable refresh rate, or vertical frequency, for a non-interlaced monitor is around 70 Hz.

Cryptoanalysis A subject/science which addresses attacks on crypto-systems.

(See Brute Force*, Cryptosystem, RSA, Public key encryption, Asymmetric* and Dictionary attack.)

Cryptography A process that ensures data or information is read or used only by its intended readers or users. This is achieved through:

- encryption, which disguises inputted information or data, so it may not be read or used. Resulting encrypted information or data may only be read or used following decryption
- decryption, which returns the decrypted data or information to its original usable and readable form.

Implementations of cryptography are called cryptosystems, and take the form of algorithms. Cryptosystems may be categorised in two main groups including:

- secret-key, where the processes of encryption and decryption each require the use of a single key which is the same for each process. The key is a number, and preferably a large one, hence the phrase 56 bit key etc. Unless the recipient of the encrypted data already knows the key, it may be left to the sender to transmit its details unencrypted. This is a notable flaw of secret-key encryption, because it exposes the key to unintended users such as eavesdroppers. A remedy is found in public-key encryption described next.
- public-key, where the sender need only know the recipient's public key. This may be obtained in unencrypted form, because it may not be used to decrypt data, rather all it may do is encrypt data. In order to decrypt data, the recipient uses a private key, which is the mathematical inverse of the public key. It may be considered impossible to determine the private key from the public key in so far as most security requirements are concerned.

The mathematics that underline public-key encryption have a simple goal: namely, to make difficult the derivation of the private key from the public key. This is achieved through a one-way function, which describes the difficulty of determining input values when given a result. RSA is among the best-known cryptosystems or algorithms. This was developed by MIT professors Ronald L. Rivest, Adi Shamir, and Leonard M. Adleman.

(See RSA and www.rsa.com.)

Cryptology   A subject/science that addresses cryptography and crypto-analysis.

(See Asymmetric*, Brute Force*, Cryptosystem, Dictionary attack, Public key encryption, RSA* and SET*.)

Cryptosystem   A means of securing data so as it can be read only by its intended users.

(See Asymmetric*, Cryptography, RSA and SET*.)

Cryptosystem Operation   *(See Symmetric Cryptosystem Operation.)*

Crystal Reports   A reporting engine.

CSS (Cascading Style Sheets language)   A styling language used to create style sheets that may be attached to HTML documents, and declares the appearance of entities/properties that include margins, positioning, color or size. Such stylesheets may be included in HTML using:

- <LINK>
- <STYLE>
- the CSS @import syntax
- <STYLE>

```
<HTML>
  <HEAD>
    <TITLE>title</TITLE>
    <LINK REL=STYLESHEET TYPE="text/css"
      HREF="http://botto.com/cool" TITLE="Cool">
    <STYLE TYPE="text/css">
      @import url (gttp://botto.com/basic);
      H1 { color: blue }
    </STYLE>
  </HEAD>
  <BODY>
    <H1>Headline is blue</H1>
    <P STYLE="color: green">While the paragraph is
green.
  </BODY>
</HTML>
```

CTI (Computer Telephony Integration) A convergence between tele-communications and computer systems, it provides a computer-to-telephone link and includes applications like:

- banking by telephone
- predictive dialers
- operator/attendant consoles
- interactive fax applications.

(See TAPI.)

Current directory An active directory whose files may be listed or executed directly. Using DOS current directory files can be listed by entering DIR at the command prompt. Directories may be changed by entering CD followed by the directory name. Using Windows dialogue boxes it is possible to change directories by double-clicking the directory name shown in the Directories box; a root directory is indicated as "..".

Cursor A visible bitmap that indicates the point of data entry or user-interaction on screen. It may take the form of a pointer, hand, or even hour-glass when the underlying software is busily computing.

CU-SeeMe An enterprise within Cornell University, which produces an Internet videoconferencing solution.

Cut A technique where video footage is switched from one sequence to another.

Cut and paste A process by which a section of a screen image or video sequence is removed (cut) and implanted (pasted) elsewhere.

Cybercafé A café which provides customers with access to the Internet usually via coin (or card) operated computers.

Cybercash A secure electronic payment solution from CyberCash, Inc., Reston VA. CyberCash is recognised as the world's leading provider of multiple secure electronic commerce payment solutions, including credit and cheque.

(See http://www.cybercash.com)

Cybermall A virtual or Internet equivalent of the conventional shopping mall.

Cyberspace A term used to describe the Internet (or Net).

Cyrix A chip maker, and manufacturer of PC processors.

D

D channel   A 16 Kbps signalling channel that supports two 64 Kbps data channels, according to the ISDN standard.
(See ISDN.)

D1   *(See CCIR 601.)*

DAC

Daemons   A program or process dedicated to perform what is usually a singular given task, such as sending mail. TCP/IP daemons include those added by third parties that include SCO.
(See TCP/IP.)

Daisychain   A method of uniting a number of CD-ROM drives or other connected devices.

Data compression   *(See Compression.)*

Data cube   An information storage model. In the context of a data warehouse, data cubes are evolved as a result of extractions from operational data. They can be assumed to be static entities that do not change, and may not be altered or even built from query data. A cube cache is used to store them in memory. If grown beyond three dimensions, the cube becomes a hypercube.
(See Data warehouse.)

Data dictionary   A type of metadata which defines stored data along with its relationships. Typically the database dictionary is dynamic, updating its contents as data structural changes occur.
(See Data warehouse and DBMS.)

Data extraction   A process that abstracts data from one or more sources in order to build a static database of unchanging data.
(See Data warehouse.)

Data hiding   A means of making the underlying workings of types or classes transparent to the programmer. The programmer merely has to understand the behaviour and functionality of the class.
(See C++, Java and OOP.)

Data link   A direct serial connection between two nodes or devices, it is devoid of intermediate switches or devices.
(See MPP.)

Data mart   A single-subject (and generally small-scale) data warehouse, which provides DSS for a limited number of users.
(See Data warehouse.)

Data mining   A data analysis technique sometimes referred to as data or knowledge discovery, which is implemented using an appropriate tool that may be used to generate summaries and information overviews which place data in the perspective to time, usage, geographical location, or places it in another category. It is a useful technique for analysing patterns of business operations, and the use of enterprise data, as well as data derived from external sources and entities which may be monitored for behaviour and cyclic patterns that influence the decision-making process. A practical revelation discovered by data mining may be as simple as the realisation that cutting trading hours in the evening of a chain of stores results in significant savings.

Data partitioning   A method of segregating data, so that it is distributed across different systems. It can serve to store selected records in more secure (and often expensive) mass storage (such as SRAM or an appropriate level of RAID), while storing less important data in conventional storage media, namely hard disks.
(See RAID.)

Data Protection Act (DPA)   A UK Act created in 1984 to deal with privacy of information and the need for companies and organisations to register with the DPA bureau as 'data users' or storers of personal information. The DPA provided the mechanism for people to retrieve their personal information held by registered data users. However, it falls a long way short of America's freedom of information because access to many data users remains prohibited.

Data replication   A dynamic and changeable, verbatim copy of data. A multiplicity of such replicas may exist.

Data schema   A term which describes a database structure, such as the entity relationship (E-R) diagram of an RDBMS. The E-R diagram shows the links that unite the database tables.
(See Data warehouse, Database, and RDBMS.)

Data sonification   A general term used to describe the process of enhancing data through the addition of audio.

Data transfer rate   A rate at which data is transferred from a mass storage device, such as hard disk, or from removable media, or over a physical or wireless medium,
(See Hard disk and RAID.)

Data warehouse   'An integrated, subject-oriented, time-variant, non-volatile database that provides support for decision making' (Bill Inman). A unified data repository extracted from multiple data storage structures that may emanate from various data sources. It provides a single interface with relational and/or multi-dimensional data. It is the rebirth of what IBM termed the *Information Warehouse* in the 1980s. Data warehouses form the information storage methodology in modern decision support systems (DSS). Collectively these systems provide a means of querying data that emanates from disparate information storage models. On-Line Analytical Processing (OLAP) is a crucial facet of the data warehouse architecture, providing a means of abstracting and analysing data in a manner that makes transparent the multiple data sources and data storage models used. The data mining system (DMS) is also a key DSS component. Data mining is an attempt to embed intelligence into the interrogation of stored data, and may automate the querying of data, and provide user access to new data structures whose information is in close proximity in terms of related subject matter, and assist in solving defined problems. the underlying storage metaphors of a data warehouse may be:

- two-dimensional, where values are stored using the table metaphor, adhering to the established formal RDBMS model for information storage
- multi-dimensional, where data is perceived as a three-dimensional cube or a data cube, where values have x, y and z coordinates.

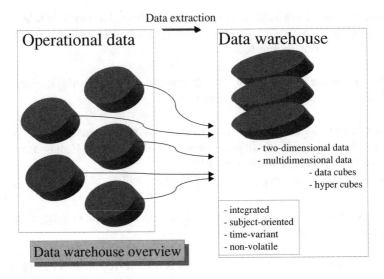

Data extraction

Operational data

Data warehouse

- two-dimensional data
- multidimensional data
   - data cubes
   - hyper cubes

- integrated
- subject-oriented
- time-variant
- non-volatile

Data warehouse overview

Data cubes are evolved as a result of extractions from operational data. They may be assumed to be static entities which do not change, and may not be altered or even built from query data. A cube cache is used to store them in memory. If grown beyond three dimensions, the cube becomes a hyper-cube. According to Inman's definition, a data warehouse is characterised as:

- *integrated*, providing a unified interface to multiple data sources that may use disparate information storage models
- *subject-orientated*, revealing data which is in close proximity in terms of subject matter, providing related information, that may be dedicated to specific analysis.
- a time-variant, permitting data retrieval and analysis using the dimension of time.
- *non-volatile*, making the collective data entities static in definition, except during the periodic instances where updates are driven through the data by the integrated operational systems. On-line updates are impermissible, and the data warehouse may be considered as being read-only.

Further reading: Inman, Bill and Kelley, (1994), The 12 Rules of Data Warehouse for A Client/Server World, *Data Management Review*, **Vol 4**, May, pp. 6–16.

(See Database, DBMS and DSS.)

Database   An electronic information storage system offering data storage and retrieval. A generic term that describes the storage of information on a

record by record basis. Records are divided into fields of different types including text, numeric, data, graphic, and even BLOB (Binary Large OBject). The records are stored in tables or files. Databases types include flat file and relational. The flat file database model embodies no links between different files or tables. A relational database is quite different in that records from one file may be linked to records stored in a separate file or table. Codd's standard text about relational databases published in the 1960s specified different types of relational links. Types of link include one-to-one, one-to-many, and many-to-many. There are many commercial examples of the relational database that base their design on the original writings of Codd. Relational databases are formally referred to as RDBMS (Relational Database Management Systems) which flat file databases are termed simple DBMS (Database Management Systems). Commercial examples of software products that permit the development of RDBMS include Paradox for Windows, dBase, Microsoft Access, Oracle and Ingres. Relational databases are used to store tabular information in the form of records, and useful versions are able to generate graphs. Popular PC relational databases include Microsoft Access, Borland Paradox, dBase, Q & A and DataEase. Because they are relational, an invoice can extract information from a number of different tables or files. Flat file databases are used to store isolated records, and cannot be used to link files or tables. They are used for simple applications such as card files. Text databases are used to store documents such as articles and even complete books. Documents may be indexed where the user interface simply allows users to search for documents which contain target words, phrases or sentences.
(See Data warehouse and DBMS.)

Database middleware   *(See Glue and Middleware.)*

Database server   *(See Server.)*

Data type   A classification for data. Modern relational databases commonly store the following different data types including currency, numeric, data, alphanumeric, Boolean, graphical and BLOB (Binary Large Object).
(See OODBMS, Data warehouse and BLOB.)

DBMS (Database Management System)   A system that provides the operations necessary to manage stored data which may be two-dimensional or multi-dimensional. A DBMS:

- Requires a data dictionary, which defines stored data along with relationships. The database dictionary is dynamic, updating its contents as data structural changes occur.

- Ensures that entered data undergoes pre-defined validity checks.
- Transforms entered data so it can be stored by the underlying data structure.
- Provides storage for data, its relationships, forms, reports, queries and miscellaneous files.
- Includes security features, such as the password protection of files, allocated user access rights, prohibit certain users from accessing certain files and from making data changes.
- May maintain data integrity in a multi-user environment.
- May provide a database communications interface, which might permit users to submit forms-based queries through Web browsers, publish reports and data using various media that include the Web, e-mail and Lotus Notes.
- Provides features pertaining to backup and recovery.
- Provides access to data using a query language (such as SQL or a variant thereof), or a querying mechanism which might involve the completion of tables using defined query statements (such as the Borland Query By Example (QBE) technique).

(See Data warehouse.)

DBS (Direct Broadcast Satellite)   A communication and broadcasting technology, where information is transmitted (from a geostationary satellite) and received by a satellite dish, which is typically 18 in to three ft in diameter. It can also be applied as an access technology which offers downstream bandwidths or perhaps 400 Kbps. Hughes Network Systems (US) offer such service and implementation. Up to 200 television channels may be chosen using many DBS or Direct To Home (DTH) services. MPEG-2 encoding is used for many DBS services.
(See MPEG-2 and Satellite system.)

DCOM (Distributed Component Object Model)   A protocol which glues software components on networks such as those that use HTTP, and is based on the Open Software Foundation's DCE-RPC specification. It is compatible with Java applets and Active X components and was formerly called 'Network OLE' though it has since been evolved.

DCT (Discrete Cosine Transfer   A widely used mathematical technique for image compression. It provides the basis for lossy image compression where redundant image data is omitted. It is part of the JPEG algorithm, and is also used in videotex. *(See JPEG and Videotex.)* The DCT process operates by converting image data from the *spatial* to the *transform* domain. The complex underlying mathematics are transcribed to matrix manipulations. The resulting intensive arithmetic operations are best implemented using dedicated image processors or general purpose processors that have multimedia capabilities such as those integrated into Intel MMX. Image energy in the *spatial* domain is defined as the square of the pixel values. This energy is spread evenly over pixel blocks and resulting coefficients. Following the transformation, the energy is confined to a fewer coefficients.

DDE (Dynamic Data Exchange)   A standard technique by which data may be exchanged between running Windows applications. For example, a database tool might have a DDE interaction with a spreadsheet in order to draw graphs based on spreadsheet data. A DDE interaction is occasionally called a conversation. Nowadays most Windows users harness OLE (Object Linking and Embedding) rather than DDE. OLE 2.0 compatible applications can be assumed to be considerably less difficult to link.
(See ActiveX* and OLE.)

Debugger   A program or feature which permits program code to be corrected or debugged. It assists the process through appropriate prompts and indications as to where the bugs exist in the source code listing.

Decode   A process by which encoded data, which may be compressed, is interpreted and delivered to the receiving system or device. For example, the process may involve the decoding of MPEG video.
(See MPEG*.)

Decoder   1. A device which is able to interpret an encoded signal. An MPEG decoder is able to uncompress digital video, as is an MPEG-2 STB. *(See DCT and MPEG.)* 2. An electronic device, which is able to decode digital addresses. A simple two-input device may set up to four digital outputs. Such devices may form part of the address decoding between the processor and connected electronic devices.

Decryption   A process by which encrypted data is unlocked to become readable.
(See Encryption.)

Defragmentation program   A program used to defragment a hard disk. It ensures that used data blocks are arranged in a contiguous stream.

Dell   A large multinational computer maker that uses the direct selling channel.

Delta channel   *(See D channel and ISDN.)*

De-militarised zone   A public access area that lies outside a network's security boundaries.
(See Firewall.)

Denial of service attack   A concentration of traffic directed at a server or system that is so intense it renders it inoperative.

Density   A measure of how densely packed data bits are on a storage medium.

DES (Data Encryption Standard)   An encryption technique; a symmetric cryptosystem. Both senders and receivers use a common 56 bit key to encrypt and decrypt messages and data. The US government backed DES in 1977, and has since recertified every five years.
(See Encryption.)

Design   A cryptosystem, which uses symmetric key cryptography.
See Asymmetric*, Brute Force*, Ciphertext, Cryptosystem, Dictionary attack, Encryption, Plaintext, Public key encryption, RSA*, SET* and Transposition.)

Design pattern   A software pattern may be a vocabulary of methods and guidelines, or a reusable element, or a set of elements that reveal themselves as common denominators when developing E-commerce applications. A resulting reuse strategy may involve the use of pre-built components at the micro level that include methods and functions, and those at the macro level that include complete objects and interfaces. It follows then that a design pattern is a consistency, or an unchanging software component or code fragment that may require little or no modification to be applied in a different client or service implementation, though this interchangeability may be reliant upon the client or service application context. The pattern may obviously bring together one or more classes, interfaces, methods, functions, modules or objects that may:

- compress the development lifecycle,
- permit non-Jini experts to bypass coding the reuse elements,
- introduce a consistency in the design of clients and services,
- help adhere to official or naturally evolved, unoffical software standards,
- simplify maintenance procedures,
- provide efficiencies in terms of shared source in a team collaborative environment.

A replicated worker pattern deals with the implementation of processes through concurrent processes, and therefore has application in the domain of parallel computing. It is a distributed computing concept and may consists of a *master* process that executes in control of a number of *workers*, and this terminology is key to the synonym *master-worker* pattern. The origins of software patterns are traced reliably to notable texts like *Design Patterns: Elements of Reusable Object-Oriented Software* by Richard Helm, Erich Gamma, Ralph Johnson, and John Vlissides, and more recently to *Pattern-Oriented Software Architecture: A System of Patterns* by Frank Buschmann, Regine Meunier, Hans Rohnert, Peter Sommerlad, and Michael Stal. These and the many other texts have a link with the pattern language concept put forward by Christopher Alexander that address architectural design. His works include *Notes on the Synthesis of Form*, Harvard University Press, 1964 and *A Pattern Language: Towns, Buildings, Construction*, Oxford University Press, 1977.

DES X   A version of DES encryption.

DHTML (Dynamic HyperText Markup Language)   A version of HYML where changes can be made to running HYML objects. The resulting object array may undergo dynamic changes on the client-side that result from user interactions. It was released jointly by Microsoft and the World Wide Web Consortium (W3C).
(See HTML and OODL.)

Dial-up password file   A file used to store passwords, authenticating access to networks via dial-up links.
(See TCP/IP.)

Dictionary attack   An attack on a cryptosystem using the iterative technique of comparing the key with a dictionary of possibilities, usually beginning with those that are most likely to match the key.
(See Brute Force* and Cryptosystem.)

Digital   A device such as a computer that processes and stores data in the form of ones and zeros. In a positive logic representation, 'one' might be '−5' volts and zero '0' volts. This lowest of levels at which computers operate is known as machine code. Binary arithmetic and Boolean algebra (named after Irish mathematician George Boole) permit mathematical representation. Boolean algebra and Karnaugh maps used widely for minimisation of logic algebraic expressions. Though digital signals exist at two levels (one or zero), an indeterminate state is possible.

Digital audio   An audio signal recorded in digital form. The most common standard digital format is that defined in the CD-DA Specification. Digital audio is used widely in modern multimedia through wave audio files. Audio may be digitised using either video capture boards or sound cards. Audio sources can take the form of a microphone, CD player, audio tape, audio cassette, and even electronic musical instruments. Audio cards may be regarded as analogue to digital convertors (ADCs) where the accuracy of digitisation and subsequent quality achieved largely depends upon the sample rate and number of bits used per sample. the audio quality required can also be present from within many authoring programs. The memory capacity consumed by a sequence is a function of quality. If it is necessary to calculate the exact memory/data capacity consumed, then the following simple formula can be applied: Memory capacity required (bits) = Sequence duration (secs) * Sampling rate (Hz) * bits per sample

For example, if an 8 bit sound digitiser with a sample rate of 11 kHz were used to digitise a 15 second sequence, then:

```
Data capacity required (bits) = 15 * 11 000 * 8
                              = 1 320 000 bits
                              = 165 000 bytes
                              = 161.13 Kbytes
```

The memory or disk data capacity required naturally increases linearly with increased sample rates.

(See Wave audio.)

Digital camera   A camera able to store pictures in digital form. A popular range of digital cameras is the Kodak DC series.

Digital cash   A virtual equivalent to cash and credit held in a wallet, bank card, credit card or charge card. Debits from digital cash repositories are credited to merchant's wallets or repositories.

Digital certificate   A means of linking an entity's identity with a public key and carried out by a trusted party.

Digital Certificate Authority   A business that has the authority to issue digital certificates, and public and private RSA cryptography keys.

(See http://www.versign.com)

Digital signature   A digital signature may be applied to an encrypted message. A message digest is ciphered using the sender's private key and then appended to the message, resulting in a digital signature.

Digital video   A video sequence that is stored and played in digital form. Digital motion video is the most animating feature of modern multimedia. Using videodisc players it has been possible to incorporate colour full-motion, full-screen video (FMFSV) in a computer environment for some time. Because ultimedia is a blend of concurrent processes, its storage on a single optical disc required various elements to be interleaved on the same track. Before this concept could be addressed, the inability of conventional (serial) desktop computers to play motion video stored on CD-ROM, represented a significant hurdle. Reasons as to why this is not possible lie in the inadequate rate at which data is transferred from CD-ROM to computer, and in inadequate data storage capacity. A blanket solution to both problems lies in image-compression. For example, if frames of video are compressed significantly, then the need for large data storage capacity and, more importantly, high rates of data transfer is reduced. Intel refined such a technology that it acquired from General Electric in October 1988. Called Digital Video Interactive (DVI) its home was the Intel Princeton Operation that is part of the Microcomputer Components Group. It originally began in the David Sarnoff Research Center, New Jersey, the former RCA laboratories. Using DVI up to 72 minutes of FMFSV (at 30 fps) can be stored on a single 12 cm diameter CD-ROM disc.
(See MPEG*, M-JPEG, Video* and Streaming*.)

Digital watermark   A virtual equivalent of a watermark, it indicates ownership of digital images or documents.

Direct Broadcast Satellite   *(See DBS and Satellite system.)*

Direct channel   A sales channel where the consumer purchases products off the page, or uses another medium such as television. It usually involves payment using a credit card or bankcard.

Direct connection   A modem connection without error connection, compression and overflow control. It may be assumed that in such a situation the modem rate equates precisely to the connection rate.

Direct3D   A data stream that encapsulates the user's public key and Certificate Authority's (CA) endorsement.
(See SET.)

Director   A tool used to create interactive movies, produced by Macromedia. Resulting productions can include Lingo scripts, and may be deployed over the Web using Macromedia Shockwave technology.
(See Lingo, Shockwave and Streaming*.)

Disintermediation   Refers to the Web in terms of providing users with direct access to information sources, services and commerce.
(See E-commerce.)*

Display   *(See Monitor.)*

Dissolve   A cut from one image or video sequence to another. More precisely, it is the fading of an image into a background colour or image, or the fading of an image while one image is faded up.

Distributed computing   An OO system that sees concurrent processes interact with shared resources, and inter-component communications implemented in an efficient and co-ordinated way. It involves leasing, distributed events such as those of store and forward agents, and protocols that define processes and sub-processes required to make the collective system operational, and reliable using persistent stores of states that are recoverable following failure.
(See JavaSpaces and Jini*.)*

Distributed debugging   A methodology for debugging client/servers, where the collective distributed system is perceived as a single system.
(See Distributed computing.)

Distributed glue   A name given to the collective entities that bind together (dynamically) running components that are on the client and on the server. As is the case with local glues, standard OO component architectures use different distributed glues.

Distributed events
(See ActiveX, Glue, JavaBeans, OLE, and OpenDoc.)*

Dithering   A process by which the image-depth of a graphic is altered. Programs such as PaintShop Pro are able to dither images, and may be useful for:

- targeting a system that may be limited to simple 8 bit graphics
- improving the quality of displayed graphics (particularly where a machine will attempt to display 24 bit images at a 16 bit image depth)
- reducing the size of image files, so improving the response of a Web application.

Djinn (Gin)   A community of users, devices and resources that are held together with Jini software infrastructure, and have agreed policies of trust and administration.

DLL (Dynamic Link Library)   A file that contains a number of functions that may be called by different applications. The Windows architecture is itself based on DLLs. DLLs may be:
- dynamic, where programs interacts with it a run-time
- static, where the DLL is embedded into the application when compiled.

Static libraries tend to make applications fat, requiring more memory that their dynamic counterparts.

A DLL has a:
- file which contains its source code, and entry and exit functions.
- module definition file
- resource definition file.

Typically DLLs offer:
- leverage program investment through improved reusability
- better code compatibility
- easier migration paths
- cost-effective system renovations
- better program performance
- improved memory management.

(See C++ and Java.)

DNS (Domain Name Service)   A server that converts domain names (such as www.digital.com) into IP addresses.

(See TCP/IP.)

DNS negotiation   A process by which the DNS address is determined by the PPP server and passed to the PPP client.

(See TCP/IP.)

Docking station   A bay that provides a notebook computer with additional connectivity and resources typically associated with desktop computers.

Domain category   A collection of servers on the Internet that share the same suffix in their URLs. For example, http://www.cia.com.au is in the domain com/au (which is a mnemonic for a commercial site in Australia). Other domains include .edu (educational), .gov (government), .mil (military) and .net (network).

(See Domain name, E-mail, TCP/IP and URL.)

Domain name   A name of a domain. For example, in the URL www.microsoft.com, Microsoft is a domain name.

(See E-mail, TCP/IP and URL.)

Domino An applications and messaging server program for Lotus Corporation's Lotus Notes.

Dot pitch A measurement of the distance between addressable pixels on a monitor screen, indicating the clarity of picture and maximum resolution supported.

Doule double An item of data that consists of 64 contiguous bits. It is twice as long as a double word.
(See C++.)

Double word An item of data that contains 32 contiguous bits. It is twice as long as a 16 bit word.
(See C++

DoubleSpace A real-time disk compression program built into MS-DOS 6.0 to MS-DOS 6.2. Depending upon the file types stored on a hard disk it theoretically doubles disk data capacity. There are numerous other so-called on-the-fly data compression programs on the market for both the PC and Apple Macintosh. Foremost among these is Stacker from Stac Electronics. *(See Compression and DriveSpace.)*

Dow Jones A share index that moves upward or downward, the averages the top US companies' share performance throughout trading.

Downloading A process of copying files from a remote server to a local computer. The reverse process is called uploading.
(See Browser and FTP.)

Downsizing A process of reducing the complexity of software so that it can be ported to a less powerful system. For instance, a client/server database application could be simplified to run on a PC-based LAN. Equally, an operating system originally developed for a mainframe or workstation may be downsized to run on a PC.

Dr Solomon A large international software company specialising in anti-virus software.

Dreamweaver A Web authoring tool.

DriveSpace A Microsoft, real-time disk compression utility, which is integrated in Windows 98. It increase the data capacity of a hard disk, and of removable magnetic media, by around two-fold.

The compression ratio attained is a variable, and:

- increases with data files that are largely uncompressed such as BMP and text files
- diminishes with pre-compressed files such as JPEG and WinZip.

Dropped   1. A packet which does not reach its destination. 2. A frame in a video source recording which does not appear in a captured digital video file is said to be dropped.
(See Video capture.)*

DSA   An encryption technique.
(See Encryption.)

DSL (Digital Subscriber Line)   A digital access technology that can be wireless or physical based on twisted pair, or modern media.
(See Access technology.)

DSM (Digital Storage Medium/Media)   A medium used to store digital data. Commercial examples include audio CD, CD-ROM, CD-ROM XA, CD-I, Digital Versatile Disc (DVD), floppy disk, Sony Mini disc, Philips DCC (Digital Compact Cassette) and DAT (Digital Audio Tape).
(See CD-ROM and DVD.)

DSN (Data Source Name)   A means of identifying and connecting to a database. A DSN is required for many Web applications that interact with, and query databases that are typically ODBC compliant.
(See ODBC.)

DSS (Decision Support System)
(See Data warehouse.)

DTP (Desktop publishing)   A term used to describe the use of a desktop computer to design and produce documents of the sort distributed by the publishing sector. Fully specified DTP packages provide the user with a choice of fonts, formatting tools, page make-up features, drawing tools, and a means to import pictures into documents. Professional DTP packages include PageMaker and Ventura.

Dual-homed host   *(See Firewall.)*

Dumb terminal   A client device which is restricted to the presentation element of the application. It has no more application logic than that which is required to send requests, and receive visual information. Physically it consists of a keyboard, display, and a network interface.

(See Client/server.)

DUN (Dial-up Networking) A connection to a remote computer or network.

DVD An optical disc technology that provides a sufficiently wide bandwidth to play MPEG-2 video. DVD was once an acronym for Digital Video Disc and Digital Versatile Disc. It offers maximum data capacities of 4.7 Gbyte, 8.5 Gbyte and 17 Gbyte, and exists in three forms:

- DVD-ROM that provides the same functionality as CD-ROM, but with a wider bandwidth and considerably more data capacity
- DVD that is aimed at the consumer market as a replacement for VideoCD and VHS video
- DVD-RAM that is a rewritable format able to support data capacity of 2.6 Gbytes
- DVD+RW that is rewritable format offering a data capacity of 3.0 Gbytes.

The general DVD specification includes a:

- 1.2 mm thick, 120 mm diameter disc
- 4.7 Gbytes for a single layered, single side
- track pitch of .74 micrometers
- 650/635 nanometre laser
- RS-PC (Reed Solomon Product Code) error correction scheme
- variable data transfer rate yielding an average of 4.69 Mbps.

DVD-ROM drives offer backward compatibility with CD-ROM, and the important factors that apply to the performance of a dedicated CD-ROM drive are applicable. Features which drive the DVD-ROM specification include the:

- supported data capacities, i.e. 4.7 Gbytes, 8.5 Gbytes and 17 Gbytes
- interface type
- ability to record CD-R discs
- burst transfer rate
- MTBF (Mean Time Between Failures)
- DVD disc average access time
- CD-ROM disc average access time
- average CD-ROM data transfer rate, i.e. 16-speed, 24 speed, 32-speed etc.
- CD-ROM burst transfer rate
- disc spin modes that may be either CAV and CLV

- MPC3 requirements are met
- installation may be vertical or horizontal.

(See CD-ROM and LED.)

DVD video   An alternative term of MPEG-2 video stored on DVD disc. *(See MPEG*.)*

DVD-ROM   *(See DVD.)*

DVI (Digital Video Interactive)   A largely obsolete, but nonetheless pioneering, video compression and decompression technology for the AT and MCA bus, thus aimed at PC ATs and PS/2 systems (beginning with model 50). Intel Indeo superseded DVI. It is specified as being able to generate full-colour full-screen, full-motion video (FSFMV). The original specification embodied 8 bit digital video. The MPEG were presented with the DVI compression algorithm but it was rejected. However, the compression techniques used in DVI were influential in the development of the MPEG compression schemes. Digital Video Interactive (DVI) was demonstrated at the second Microsoft CD-ROM conference of 1987. An image-compression technology, DVI permits full-screen, full-motion video in the PC environment. DVI offered full-colour FMFSV at 10 to 30 fps and a frame size of 512×480 pixels resolution.

(See MPEG and MMX.)

Dynamic   A language that may accept a class while running, and Java has this capability.

Dynamic class handling   A name given to the ability of the Java Application Environment (JAE) to download classes from a HTTP serer at runtime.

Dynamic Data Exchange   *(See DDE.)*

Dyamic HTML   *(See DHTML.)*

Dynamic language   A programming language that supports an incremental compiler where code changes may be made to running programs.

Dynamic Link Library   *(See DLL.)*

Dynamic load balancing   *(See MPP.)*

E

Ebay.com   An on-line auction.

E-business   A generic term used to describe business processes implemented in electronic or virtual environments like the World Wide Web.

E-cash   *(See Digital cash.)*

ECML (Electronic Commerce Markup Language   An open standard and set of guidelines for Web merchants that enable digital wallets from multiple vendors to exchange information between customers and merchants; ECML may be used with any payment mechanism. It is supported by wallet software vendors, e-commerce software vendors, merchants and payment card organisations. ECML will be submitted to the (IETF) and the World Wide Web consortium (W3C) P3P committee.

E-commerce   An application of the Internet that sees it used in a point-of-sale (POS) guise. One of the earliest e-commerce Web sites was the Amazon on-line book store. A key concern of companies contemplating e-commerce solutions on the Web, and of users also, is the security of transactions using credit cards and other electronic funds transfer systems such as Switch. Encryption plays an important role in maintaining the privacy of customer details. SET is seen as the internationally agreed standard solution for providing such confidentiality.
(See Encryption an SET.)

E-commerce hybrid CD-ROM   A CD-ROM production that features hyperlinks to e-commerce Web site for transaction processing, and has POI applications that may include video.

E-commerce hybrid DVD-ROM   A DVD-ROM production that features hyperlinks to e-commerce Web site for transaction processing, and has POI applications that may include video.

E-commerce site development lifecycle   A collection of processes and sub-processes required to create an e-commerce Web site. A Web server facility is required, and may be:

- An acquired, leased or rented in-house Web server solution featuring an ISDN or T1 connection, necessitating personnel to maintain and run the server. It may be chosen for security reasons, or when it is important to evolve the Web server in house.
- Platformed on a Web host, or a company dedicated to providing turnkey Web server solutions. The Web server is hosted on a remote site.
- Platformed on a public server such as those offered to its subscribers by AOL, Compuserve, Prodigy and the many others. Other public servers include Geocities and Angelfire offering businesses with a low-cost migration path to architecting a low-cost e-commerce presence on the World Wide Web.
- Co-located on a server farm, where ISDN or T1 connection technologies, maintenance and day-to-day running take place off-site.

Dell, Hewlett-Packard, IBM, Olivetti, Compaq and the many other computer manufacturers produce server implementations, many of which are turnkey solutions. Such servers are specified in terms of processor types, number of processors, mass storage capacity, bundled operating systems and server software, as well as the many other such common features. Generally it may be assumed that much of the low-level technical descriptions of servers may be ignored when purchasing from the major producers such as those mentioned earlier. It may also be assumed that they will always bring the latest technologies to market – at a time when perhaps budget computer makers are not,. Web servers run either the Windows NT or Unix operating systems (OS), and there are many differentiating features that separate them *(See Operating system)*. A Web server hosted off-site should allow you to include a domain name of your choice and, for security purposes, to restrict user access to directories or files. It must also allow transactions to be conducted in a secure mode using mainstream encryption techniques such as SHTTP. This may be verified by adding the 'S' prefix to the collective Web address, and then by opening the site using a Web browser. You may also need a site certificate, confirming your ownership rights. It may also be necessary to run your own programs and scripts, including CGI variants, as well as accommodate any additional requirements imposed by the Web site authoring software you may have used such as the FrontPage extensions. More complex E-commerce sites require programming in languages such as Perl, C++, Java Visual Basic etc. Such languages may be used to create feedback forms etc. An e-commerce site typically comprises many components like CGI scripts, counters and applets. Many of these may be gathered from public domain resources on the World Wide Web, or shareware versions may be used. An e-commerce site may be secured using many different technologies including SSL, RSA and the many products that offer everything from password protection to firewalling.

(See Application development, Security and Firewall.)

E-commerce site domain name   A name of a domain. For example, in the URL www.microsoft.com, Microsoft is a domain name.

(See E-mail, TCP/IP and URL.)

E-commerce site map   A map of an e-commerce site.

E-commerce site security   (See Security*.)

EDI (Electronic Data Interchange)   A standard set of formats and proto-cols for exchanging business information over networks and systems. Translation programs may play the role of converting extracted database information into the EDI format so that it can be transmitted to appropriate entities such as banks that have appropriate EDI-capable IT implementa-tions.

EDI Trading Partner   An EDI entity/establishment able to receive or transmit EDI data.

EDI Transaction Set   A message or block of EDI information that relates to a business transaction.

EDi Transaction Set Standards   A formal standard that dedicates syntax, data elements, and transaction sets or messages.

EDI Translation   An EDI conversion to and from the X12 format.

EDI Translator   An entity that converts between the flat file to EDI formats.

EDIFACT (Electronic Data Interchange For Administration, Commerce and Transportation)   A standard for electronic data interchange that is approved by the UN.

EFT (Electronic Funds Transfer)   A transfer of funds from one account to another using an EFT implementation.

EIGRP (Extended Interior Gateway Routing Protocol)   A protocol developed by Cisco for routers.

EJB (Enterprise JavaBeans) A server-side implementation of the JavaBean component model, and EJBs may be used to build applications using appropriate tools, and are CORBA compliant.

EJB to CORBA mapping A mapping that equates EJB to the CORBA equivalent.

Electronic cash *(See Digital cash.)*

Electronic mail *(See E-mail.)*

Electronic publishing A term used to describe information made available through electronic means. Through the Internet, hypermedia and hypertext marked the beginning of a renaissance in electronic publishing, radically altering the manner in which information is presented and used. Other media for electronic publishing include CD-ROM and DVD-ROM. *(See Web.)*

Electronic signature *(See Digital signature.)*

E-mail A method of communicating documents and digital files electronically; a computer-based equivalent of a latter. E-mail addresses generally conform to name@domain.domain_category.country:

- name – might be a login name
- domain – might be a company name such as Microsoft
- domain category – is the type of domain *(See domain category)*
- country – is the geographic location of the server that might be uk (United Kingdom), nz (New Zealand), au (Australia) etc.

For instance, subscribers to Compuserve have e-mail addresses that have the syntax: 123456.7654@compuserve.com. Other ISPs (Internet Service Providers) allow users to use their name as an ID. Examples include F_Botto@compulink.co.uk, or fbotto@cia.com/au. E-mail messages may be sent using browsers (such as Netscape Navigator and Microsoft Explorer), though these are not e-mail applications or clients such as Microsoft Outlook or Endora Mail. The latter offer folders such as inbox, outbox and sent messages, and are dedicated applications that support such e-mail protocols as SMTP and POP3. Compuserve (owned by AOL) offers e-mail functions and features, as well as options dedicated to its own services. The MIME (Multipurpose Internet Mail Extensions) are applicable to such transmission, permitting the integration of program and video files within e-mail documents and communications. Typically, a computer fitted with a modem (Modulator Demodulator) is used for transmission and reception of e-mail, though within organisations NICs are more common. E-mail messages may be sent over LANs, intranets and the Internet. Users generally read their e-mail messages by downloading them from a server, and there is often an option within the e-mail program which allows them to choose whether or not leave a copy of the e-mail message on the mail server.

(See POP3.)

E-mail autoreply   A reply to an e-mail message which is created automatically using an e-mail autoresponder such as MReply. In an e-commerce context, such responses are useful for conveying the receipt of orders, advertising related products and promotions, publicising trading hours, and so on.

E-mail responder   A program that replies automatically to received e-mail messages.

Embedded style   A style attached to one specific document using the form:

```
<HEAD>
<STYLE TYPE="text/css">
<!—
P {text-indent: 10pt}
—>
</STYLE>
</HEAD>
```

Encapsulation   A term which describes hiding the internal workings of an object. The resulting object encapsulates code and data that is hidden from the user and the remaining collective OO system. Essentially it becomes a black box, and all that matters are its responses to stimuli, such as defined events that are intercepted and processed by the object's public interface.

(See C++, Java and OOP.)

Encode   A process of converting data, or an analogue signal, into another form in terms of data representation. For example, Video-on-Demand services often use MPEG-2 video that is encoded using uncompressed source recordings that may be analogue or digital. Equally, streaming video/multimedia sites store video encoded according to the MPEG-1 specification.

(See MPEG.)*

Encryption   A process of ciphering messages or data so that it can be deciphered and read only by intended recipient(s). Encryption techniques include:

- DES
- Triple DES
- DES X
- RSA
- DSS.

(See Decryption, DES, DES X, DSS, RSA and Triple DES.)

Enterprise computing   A general term used to describe the application of computers and Information Technology (IT) in medium-size to large businesses. Only larger small businesses are considered to be enterprises.

Enterprise JavaBeans   *(See EJB.)*

Entity relationship diagram   A diagram that illustrates the design structure of a relational database, together with all its data tables and links. Programs that may be used to draft such diagrams include EasyCase. Entity relationship diagrams rarely included reports and query information, though some relevant notes might be included.

(See Database.)

Entry   A group of object references in a class package such as the `net.jini.core.entry.Entry` interface.

Enumerated constants   A type of constant that is supported by C++. Enumerated constants take the form of a type, and are a useful shorthand for defining a number of what might be related constants. The following statement defines the constants back, forward, left, and right, where Move is the enumeration.

enum Move { back=4, forward, left=6, right=3};

The forward constant is assigned the value 5, an increment (of one) relative to the previously defined constant back.

(See C++.)

E-procurement   An on-line system for an organisation's buyers to make purchases.

E-purse   A value that may be stored on a SmartCard and represents an amount that may be used to make small purchases.

108

Error log   A log of errors experienced by a server.

Escrow   A transaction where a person delivers an entity of value to a third party (or escrow holder) that is held until a condition occurs; the entity is finally delivered by the third party to an intended recipient. The escrow holder transfers the legal papers and funds when closing the escrow.
(See Key escrow agent.)

Ethernet   A Local Area Network (LAN) standard. Ethernet adapters included on computers may comprise thin-Ethernet or more expensive thick-Ethernet connectors and cables. Ethernet may be considered as being put forward in 1974 by Robert Metcalfe through his Harvard PhD thesis.

Event   A change in state, which may invoke a response or a series of processes and sub-processes that may be implemented by objects. The event may a simple message sent from one object to another and its origins may be anything from another message from an agent to a physical mouse click or key press. Applications and operating system environments that respond to such events are termed event-driven.

Event-driven   A concept where state changes of entities such as objects may be relayed to other listeners or objects in what might be a collective OO system. Almost all modern software implementations and systems, and environments are event-driven.

Event generator   An object whose state changes are relevant to another object, and may send notification messages to compliant objects when events are generated.

Event listener   An object that responds to events, or more specifically responds to one or more event types.

E-wallet   A virtual equivalent to the wallet.
(See Digital cash.)

Expanded memory   *(See EMS.)*

Expansion bus   A bus used to provide a means of expanding a PC to include various peripheral devices that might range from graphics cards to MPEG players. Standard expansion buses include 16 bit ISA (Industry Standard Architecture), IBM MCA (Micro Chanel Architecture) and EISA (Enhanced Industry Standard Architecture).
(See EMS.)

Expert system *(See KBS.)*

Explorer A program which is part of Windows 95 and Windows NT, and is used to peruse files, open files, launch programs, and perform file management functions. It shows file details such as their size in bytes, the date and time they were last modified, and their attributes including whether they have read, write or read/write status. It is commonly used to move, rename, copy and delete files and even complete directories. The move, copy and delete commands work with multiple selected files, so you can copy and move batches of files without having to go through the monotony of dealing with one file at a time. Windows applications can be run from Explorer by double-clicking them, or by double-clicking files that were created with them. Explorer can be used to:

- connect to shared directories on other network users' drives
- declare directories as shared
- give shared directories password protection
- monitor who on the network is using shared directories
- stop sharing shared directories.

(See Windows.)

External Style Sheet A template/document/file containing style information that may link with one of a number of HTML documents, permitting a site to be re-styled by editing one file. They may be linked to a HTML document using the form:

```
<HEAD>
<LINK REL=STYLESHEET HREF="style.css" TYPE="text/css">
</HEAD>
```

Extranet A private network based on Internet technologies, it may use telecommunication networks to securely share enterprise and corporate data with partners, suppliers, vendors, customers and businesses. An extranet can be viewed as part of a company's intranet that is extended to users outside the company. Extranets require firewalls, use of digital certificates or similar means of user authentication, encryption and virtual private networks (VPNs) that provide access via public networks. An extranet may typically:

- communicate data using Electronic Data Interchange (EDI)
- publish catalogues for wholesalers and trade partners
- provide team collaboration environments
- share training programs
- share services such as on-line banking
- provide news publishing.

Products like Lotus Notes are applied as the basis of extranet solutions. Netscape, Oracle and Sun Microsystems have an alliance to ensure compatibility between their extranet products that use JavaScript and CORBA. Microsoft has offered support for the Point-to-Point Tunneling Protocol (PPTP) and has developed an Open Buying on the Internet (OBI) standard.

E-zine   A virtual equivalent of a magazine publication, it is typically distributed using the Internet.

F

Failover A contingency measure that provides an alternative service provider, should a failure occur.

FAQs (Frequently Asked Questions) A list of questions asked most often by users and developers.

Fatbrains An on-line entity that is engaged in bookselling.

FAT32 (File Allocation Table) A filing system used by the Windows 98 operating system. It is an advancement of the FAT16 implementation, and is able to address hard disks with up to a 2 Gbyte formatted data capacity. It is more efficient than FAT16, because it uses smaller clusters of 4 Kbyte that are used to store files. Clusters are used to store data from a single file. The larger 32 Kbytes-clusters of FAT16 are comparatively inefficient. For example, when a 34 Kbyte file is written to the hard disk, two 32 Kbyte clusters are used. The second cluster has some 30 Kbyte of unused payload. So even though the file is just 34 Kbytes, it consumed 64 Kbytes of hard disk, which equates to two of its 32 Kbyte clusters. Clearly, FAT32's dependence on 4 Kbyte clusters helps eradicate the unused data capacity of clusters. This yields considerable storage capacity gains.
(See Hard disk.)

Fat client A system within a client/server architecture (such as that of the Web) that features:

- presentation, which is typically in the form of a Web browser
- complete application(s)
- a data cache, which is used to stored information from a server-side database, or back-end database.

Many systems connected to the Web may be described as thin clients. Fat clients depend heavily on client-side processing and resources, while thin

113

clients do not. This higher demand for hardware results in higher client system costs.

Generally fat clients may integrate:

- improved intelligence, because the user's interaction can be personalised through the local customisation of the application. Additionally, intelligence features such as those associated with KBSs are more feasible.
- additional local applications, such as industry standard products from companies such as Microsoft, Lotus and Inprise.
- data verification, prior to sending messages to the client-side, thus improving system responsiveness, while reducing network traffic
- security on the client-side, through password checks, and restricted access to documents, data, and applications.

(See Application*, Client/server, KBS, Thin client and NC.)

FDDI (Fibre Distributed Data Interface)   A computer-to-computer fibre link technology, and an internationally agreed ANSI standard. The topology comprises a dual multi-mode optic fibre, LED (or laser) and Token Ring network. Data rates of up to 100 Mbps are possible. Without repeaters, transmission distances up to 2 km are attainable, at a data transfer rate of 40 Mbps.

(See LED and Optic fibre.)

Feedback form   A form that may be used to gather information about visitors to e-commerce sites and may be created simply by using HYML.

Field   A column in a database table or a container for data entry in a form. Entries within fields are termed field values.

(See Data warehouse.)

Field value   A data item in a database.

FIFO (First In First Out)   A queue whose operation hinges on regurgitating items in the order in which they were deposited. An analogy is that of a vending machine used to sell chocolate bars that are stored in a vertical dispensing tube.

Fifth-Generation Language   A fifth generation language is non-procedural. They are declarative in that actions are not implemented through fixed procedures. They are also known as AI languages and include PROLOG (PROgramming LOGic).

(See AI.)

Financial EDI An exchange of payment information in standard formats between business partners.

Find and Replace A phrase used to describe the automated process of replacing a specified word or phrase with another. The phrases find and replace and search and replace are interchangeable.

Firewall A software/hardware implementation that partitions a network or system, so restricting access to selected users; it appropriately isolates a network.

A firewall may be perceived as physically existing

- between the Web server(s) and the ISP's physical site, or
- between the network and the Internet, or
- between one or more networks.

It may perform the simple functions of checking client connections and requests, securing server-side applications and data. The firewall's collective components may intercept inbound data packets, and perform a number of security checks. These may revolve around the origins of the packet, checking such packet information as its:

- source IP address
- source IP port that identifies the originating application.

Firewalls are key to many organisation's security strategy. Other adopted security facets include:

- passwords for logging on to networks
- client-side password checks for connecting to Web sites
- client-side password checks for connecting to e-mail applications and services
- password protected compressed hard disks, made possible using Stac Electronics disk compression programs.

Firewalls may also include the ability to virus check and to screen incoming documents and executables such as ActiveX controls, plug-ins, Java applets and any other code that is downloaded and intended to be processed. Cookies may also be filtered. Firewalls may be at the network level that harness packet filtering techniques using routers. The routers are intelligent in that they may be programmed to behave as a selective barrier to unwanted network traffic.

Dual-homed host firewall A dual-homed host has two network interfaces that connect with disparate networks, while a multi-homed host typically interfaces with two or more networks. The term *gateway* was used to describe the routing functions of such dual-homed hosts. Nowadays the term *gateway* is replaced by *router*. A dual-homed host may be used to isolate a network, because it acts as

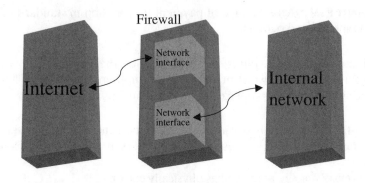

Firewall - in the form of a dual-homed host

barrier to the flow of TCP/IP traffic. The implementation of a Unix dual-homed firewall requires (among other things) that:

- IP forwarding is disabled, thus yielding a protective barrier
- unrequired network services are removed
- programming tools are uninstalled.

Bastion host   A host that is critical to a network's security. This is the focus of network management, security monitoring, and is a network's principal defence against illegal usage. A dual-homed host may play the role of a bastion host.

Screened subnets   A subnet which restricts TCP/IP traffic from entering a secured network. The screening function may be implemented by screening routers.

Commercial firewall products include

- *Firewall-1*, which is a commercial gateway product, from the Internet Security Corporation, and uses:
  – application gateway
  – packet filtering.
- *ANS Interlock*, which is a commercial gateway product from Advanced Network Services.
- *Gauntlet*, which is a firewall product from Trusted Information Systems.

(See ATM, Cookie, Encryption, Packet filtering, Risk exposure, Screening router, security, Security gateway, SET and Subnet.)

Firewire   A high-performance interface which permits the connection of peripheral devices such as mass storage devices, modems and printers. It is otherwise known as IEEE1394, and as such it is an internationally agreed standard.

Firmware   A program or data stored using a ROM variant. Firmware is thus involatile and permanent.

Flash   A multimedia Web technology developed by Macromedia, it is used widely to deliver graphics, video and animations using Web applications. The quality levels achieved are considerably higher than those attainable without Flash installed on the browser.

Flash RAM card   A PCMCIA card offering removable disk functionality.

Flatbed scanner   *(See Scanner.)*

Flat-screen display   A display which is not based on a CRT (Cathode Ray Tube), but on a flat-screen technologies that include:

• TFT (Thin Film Transistor) or active matrix, which currently offers the best response and performance. The response time is the lowest of all current flat-screen displays and the performance level approximates CRT-based designs most closely. Screen sizes and screen resolutions vary, as do the number of colours offered at various resolutions. The latter is a function of the video chipset implementation. Notebook and Subnotebook screen sizes vary from about 10.3 in upwards, though larger screen sizes are desirable.

• HPA (High Performance Addressing), which is an enhanced implementation of passive display technology, offers slightly lower response times, though the number of colours and resolution is the same. The lower response time results in slight shadows and trails in the case of moving screen images and sprites. Low-end notebooks are most likely to be:
  – DSTN or a passive display
  – CSTN (Colour Super-Twist Nematic), which is a passive display technology.

Flat-screen technologies are currently displacing CRT-based desktop monitors at the upper end of the desktop monitor market, and are the standard display technology used in notebooks.

Floating-Point Data types   A data type that may represent fractional numbers which be the:

• float type which is allocated a 32 bit single-precision number
• double type, which is allocated a 64 bit double-precision number.

Such data types are implemented using the statements:

```
float altitude;
double angle, OpenRoad;
```

Flowchart   A symbolic representation of the flow of program execution. Flowcharts can also be applied to objective decision making, such as choosing a computer, sound card, monitor or anything in fact. Windows programs capable of generating flowcharts including Visio, ABC Flowchart and AllClear.

FMFSV (Flow Motion Full-Screen Video)   A term used to describe video which can be assumed to fill the entire screen, or a greater part of it, and which provides the illusion of a frame rate of not less than 25 frames per second (fps) without the use of duplicated frames. MPEG-2 or DVD video is FMFSV. 25 fps is the frame rate delivered by PAL and SECAM broadcast standards. The American NTSC broadcast standard provides 30 fps. Ideally the frame rate should be greater than 25–30 fps. The frames that make up an FMFSV may be full frames as in the case of an M-JPEG video stream or a combination of full frames and partial frames as is the case with MPEG video. The full frames or reference frames occur at regular intervals, and dictate the number of authentic random access points provided by an encoded MPEG video sequence. The frame resolution of what can be described as FMFSV varies, but it should not fall below 720 × 360 pixels. Larger standard frame resolutions may broadly equate to 640 × 480 pixels, 800 × 600 pixels, 1024 × 768 pixels, 1240 × 1024 pixels and 1600 × 1240 pixels.
(See MPEG* and Video*.)

Folder
A metaphor for a directory. Folders are used to store files, which are usually of a specific type.

Form   1. A metaphor for a paper form that is used by client browsers in order to interact with programs and data that may be on the client- or server-side. Typically forms permit users to enter:
- signup details with Web sites
- contact details
- password details
- credit or debit card details for purchase from E-commerce sites.

(See MCIS.) 2. A metaphor for a paper form, used for data entry and viewing data in a database. RDBMS development tools, such as Excel, DataEase for Windows, Paradox for Windows, may be used to create table-based applications. *(See Data warehouse and DBMS.)* 3. A data sector type on a CD-I disc. Like CD-ROM blocks, CDI sectors are 2352 bytes long, including headers, sync information, error detection and correction data. Like Mode 1 block, Form 1 sector yields 2048 bytes user data. Unlike Mode 2 block, however, Form 2 sector yields 2324 bytes user data.

Form method   A method for customer information and for taking orders. Forms may be created using HTML and by using scripting languages:

```
<FORM> NAME="Customer" ACTION=
"http://botto.com/cgibin/form/cgi METHOD=get>

</FORM>
```

The <FORM< tag may have the attributes:

- NAME, which is the form's name.
- ACTION, which indicates the URL where the form is sent to.
- METHOD, indicates the submission method that may be POST or GET.
- TARGET, which indicates the windows or frame where the output from the CGI program is shown.

Fortune 100   A league table of the top 100 American companies.

Fortune 1000   A league table of the top 1000 American companies.

Fps (Frames per second)   A measure of the speed at which frames making up a video sequence are played or captured.

Frame   1. A tiled area of a browser's window. A frame provides an efficient method of presenting information without using a separate Web page. For example, a frame might be used to play a video sequence or animation. A frame-enabled Web application reduces the complexity of designing multiple pages at design time, and is toured more easily by users. Frames are supported by many Web page design, and Web application development tools such as Microsoft FrontPage. *(See FrontPage and Visual InterDev.)* 2. A single image making up a video sequence. Digital video sequences may consists predominantly of partial frames called interframes, or full frames called intraframes. *(See MPEG* and Video*.)* 3. A single item of transmitted data using the frame relay protocol, that is designed for modern digital networks, and does not integrate the demanding error detection and correction schemes prevalent in older protocols. *(See Frame relay.)*

Frame relay   A protocol designed for modern communications networks. Typically it may be operated at speeds between 9600 bps and 2 Mbps, though higher speeds are possible. Compared to X.25 it makes better use of network bandwidth as it does not integrate the same level of intense error detection and correction. That is not to say that frame relay is unreliable; it is simply optimised for modern networks which do not impose the same level of error on transmitted data, which is the case with older network

technologies for which X.25 was designed. The frame relay protocol may be applied in WAN and backbone implementations, and integrated into solutions that require high data transfer speeds.
Each frame consists of:

- a flag, which separates contiguous frames
- an address field, which stores the data link connection identifier (DLCI) and other information
- a control field, which contains the frame size, and receiver ready (RR) and receiver not ready (RNR) information
- an information field, which contains up to 65 536 bytes
- a frame check sequence, which is a CRC for error correction.

(See Cyclic redundancy check and X.25.)

Framework   A suite of interfaces, and code, which define the behaviour of objects or components in an application. The application may be local, or a client/server implementation.

Freeserve   A UK-based free ISP that was created by the Dixons group. It obtains revenues through advertising and telephone usage.

Freeware   Software that is free of charge and may be freely included in e-commerce sites, and include entities like ActiveX controls, CGI scripts and various programs.

Fremont   A Hewlett-Packard e-commerce development environment that requires Java programming.

Front-end   A name given to the client application or system, which may be served by a server-side or back-end application. Between the back- and front-end applications is middleware or *glues*, which exist at a number of levels. These may bind together and coordinate application logic, data and presentation distributed across the back- and front-ends.
(See Application software, Black-end, Client/server and Glue.)

FrontPage   A Web page development package marketed and sold by Microsoft. It offers the following:

- includes Explorer, which is used to display the navigation scheme integrated in your Web pages
- includes Editor, which is used to design Web pages
- includes Web Server, which is used to publish and test Web pages before their deployment over the Internet or compatible IP network
- can be used to integrate ActiveX controls and Java applets in Web pages

- does not require programming skills
- can be used to create Web pages that interact with ODBC compliant databases.

FrontPage includes:

- the Personal Web Server, which provides a testbed for Web applications before deploying them on the Web
- the Server Extensions, which are building blocks for driving predefined functionality gains through your Web site implementation
- the Explorer and Editor, which permits the developed Web design to be navigated, browsed and edited.

FrontPage is bundled with Windows NT Server, and is available separately.

(See PWS, ToolBook, Visual InterDev and Web server.)

FTP (File Transfer Protocol)   A protocol used to transfer files between FTP servers and client systems. It is a standard method for distributing files across IP/TCP networks. When using an FTP client program, users are able to link with FTP sites, and browse the remote directories and files as if they were on a local hard disk. Users can then download and upload files typically using ratio FTP sites.

(See Anonymous FTP.)

FTSE 100   A share index that moves upward or downward, and averages the top 100 companies' share performance throughout trading. It is the equivalent of the American Dow Jones.

Full duplex   A simultaneous bi-directional transmission of different data streams.

Full frame updates   A video sequence that is composed of full frames. Any such frame can provide a valid entry point for non-linear playback or editing. Such video sequences are also to as intraframe sequences.

(See M-JPEG and MPEG.)

G

Garbage collection   A memory management feature. Garbage collection reclaims the space occupied by an object at such times when there are no references to.

(See C++, Java and OOP.)

Gates, Bill   An entrepreneurial technologist who along with Paul Allen co-founded of Microsoft. Microsoft's most significant milestone product in its early development was MS-DOS, an operating system for the IBM PC and compatible computers, based on Digital Research's CP/M operating systems. Prior to this, he and Paul Allen had written a BASIC interpreter for the Altair, one of the world's first affordable microcomputers. The Windows family of products has proved the most successful of all Microsoft products.

(See Windows.)

Gateway   A gateway provides a link between disparate networks so they may communicate. The Internet has host nodes that are clients and servers. Systems that direct traffic in a network or at an ISP are gateway nodes. A server that is a gateway node in an enterprise may also be a proxy server and a firewall.

(See Portal site.)

Gateway page   A page that helps determine how effectively it is retrieved by search engines, and includes appropriate metadata. It also known as a jump, a doorway and a bridge.

GCC   A compiler program.

Geocities   A resource on the World Wide Web that offers among other things hosting services for Web sites.

123

GET method   A means of running a CGI script or program where the URL defines the CGI program (such as credit.cgi for example) and the accompanying data used by the server that follows the question mark: `www.FrancisBotto.com/cgi-bin/credit.cgi?subject=` `transaction`
(See CGI environment variables.)

GIF (Graphics Interchange Format)   A standard graphics file format that produces relatively compact files.

Gigabit Ethernet   An upscaled version of the Fast Ethernet network standard. It may deliver up to 1000 Mbps access speeds, and is backwardly compatible with 10BaseT and 100 BaseT Ethernet standards.
It can be used over the following media:

- multimode fibre optic cables over a maximum distance of 500 metres
- single- or mono-mode fibre optic cables over a maximum distance of 2 kilometres
- coaxial cable over a maximum distance of 25 metres.

(See Optic fibre.)

GIOP (General Inter-ORB Protocol)   A protocol or set of message formats and data structures for communications between ORBs.
(See IIOP.)

Global roaming   A term used to describe the process of reading e-mail messages other than by using your local ISP's point-of-presence. The ability to access e-mail for subscribers for international ISPs such as Compuserve is unimportant, due to the availability of worldwide points of presence. Web-based, global roaming e-mail services are available which simply provide users with a PIN. Mail may then be read using any Internet access device, such as those available in so-called cybercafés. The term global roaming is also applicable to mobile telephony that major digital carriers offering the ability to use services in specified countries which can be assumed to include all first-world countries.
(See E-mail, POP3, and GSM.)

Glue   A term given to the entities that provide communications between distributed and local application components. In a client/server context, is an alternative name for middleware. The underlying client/server system architecture may be that of the Web. Object-oriented glues include all the collective entities that provide the communications between distributed components. Glues in the Web architectural model include the protocols:

- TCP/IP
- HTTP
- SMTP
- miscellaneous low-level protocols including UDP.

Glues in LANs might include Ethernet and even proprietary protocols. Protocols are the lowest level glues in both traditional and modern OO systems. The next level is the programming models that is of concern to systems programmers, systems architects and programmers. This dictates the method of communications between components that include:

- remote procedure call (RPC)
- message queuing, where messages are exchange between components normally using queues, buffers or even pipes which interface more loosely coupled components, perhaps via a WAN.
- peer-to-peer, where either component may be the server (sending a message) or the client (receiving the message) remote procedure call (RPC).

Local glue   A collection of entities that unite client components, so as they may operate collectively. OLE, OpenDoc, ActiveX, JavaBeans components require local glues so that their running operations may be coordinated. These common OO component architectures use different local glues, where:

- OLE uses ODL (Object Definition Language)
- ActiveX uses COM
- OpenDoc uses CORBA IDL (Interface Definition Language)
- JavaBeans uses a subset of the Java programming language.

(See Active*, Java, OLE, and OpenDoc.)

Scripting   A scripting language such as VBScript or JavaScript may also be perceived as a glue, as may HTML.

(See JavaScript and VBScript.)

Distributed glues   A name given to the collective entities which bind together (dynamically) running components that are on the client and on the server. As is the case with local glues, standard OO component architectures use different distributed glues.

(See ActiveX*, JavaBeans, OLE, and OpenDoc.)

Gold code   A final build of a program, which is released for end users. It is the final stage of development, and will have been alpha and beta tested. Programs that are sold conventionally, such as those from Microsoft, and those that are shareware or freeware are termed *gold code.*

GPRS (General Packet Radio Service)   A packet-switched mobile network.

Graphical user interface   *(See GUI.)*

Graphics card

An electronic assembly used to generate graphics and text. Occasionally it is referred to as a graphics engine or graphics controller. A VGA card is a graphics engine, but is more commonly referred to as a graphics adapter or card. Standard IBM graphics cards include Monochrome Display Adapter (MDA), Colour Graphics Adapter (CGA), Enhanced Graphics Adapter (EGA), Video Graphics Array (VGA), Multi-Colour Graphics Array (MCGA, used on PS/230) and 8514/A. The fastest graphics controllers are of the local bus variety. These connect more directly to the processor's data bus. The graphics card specification of a PC is influential in determining the quality of digital video playback attainable. A video card comprising dedicated hardware for decoding and playing MPEG, VideoCD or Intel Indeo will generally yield improved video playback. The many areas that separate graphics cards include the following:

- the expansion bus type
- 3-D graphics capability
- screen resolutions supported
- screen refresh rates at each resolution: particularly important at higher resolutions and should not fall below 70 Hz
- the number of colours possible
- speed of operation
- does it require the presence of another graphics card? If yes, what type of connector does it require? A special features connector or Vesa Media Channel connector?
- what refresh rates can it deliver at the desired resolutions and will these be supported by the attached monitor?
- does it accelerate Video for Windows playback?
- does it scale up Video for Windows video?
- does it have the ability to play Intel Indeo video at high speed?
- does it accelerate 3-D graphics?
- does it have the ability to play video compressed according to one or more standards, which might include MPEG1 or MPEG2?
- obvious factors that drive a graphics card's performance include the bus width of the graphics processor used, the amount of VRAM (Video RAM) it has, and its interface type.

Graphics engine   An alternative name for a graphics card, or for the chipsets responsible for generating graphics.

Graphics format   An image file may be produced and stored according to a number of different graphics file formats that include CompuServe GIF,

PCX, Windows BMP, PIC, TIFF, IMG, EPS and others. The efficiency of various image file formats in terms of the data capacity they consume tends to vary significantly.

Groupware A name given to a software implementation which provides collaboration and communication across an enterprise's (business's) network solution, or even over the Web. Orfali, Harkey and Edwards define groupware as: 'Software that supports the creation, flow, and tracking of non-structured information in direct support of collaborative group activity.' Conventional modern groupware integrates:

- e-mail
- conferencing such as whiteboards
- telephony including voice mail
- scheduling
- workflow
- shared document databases
- Internet access.

The best known groupware product is Lotus Notes.

GSM (Global System for Mobile Communications) GSM networks include multiple BTSs (Base Transmitter Stations) that provide the final free-space radio communications to and from cell phones and devices. Typically they each serve geographical sectors with a radius of between 5 and 8 km. These naturally determine the coverage of the network and as you drive the receiving device seamlessly switches between BTSs. It operates in the uplink band between 890 MHz and 915 MHz, and provides a data transfer rate of 9.6 Kbps, which is very slow compared with even analogue land services. The speed restriction on the mobile station (or phone, or GSM modem-based Jini device) is 250 Km/hour, which imposes limitations on the modes of transport that GSM can be used from. Personal Communications Network (PCN) or DCS-1800 is used by the operators One-to-One and Orange in the UK, and is comparable with the GSM networks operated by Cellnet and Vodaphone in the UK. It operates in the uplink radio band between 1710 MHz and 1785 MHz, and like GSM provides a data transfer rate of 9.6 Kbps. Also like GSM the speed of the mobile station (or phone, or GSM modem-based Jini device) is 250 Km/hour, which imposes limitations on the modes of transport that DCS-800 may be used from.

GUI (Graphical User Interface – 'gooey') A user interface consisting of icons, usually facilitating interaction via a mouse, resulting in minimal keyboard use. Sometimes referred to as the graphical front-end. The most widespread commercial examples include those of the Microsoft Windows continuum, though others exist in the form of Apple System, OS/2 Warp, and X Windows. Originally when the Windows concept was originated at Xerox PARC (Palo Alto Research Center), the UI was called a WIMP (Windows, Icons Mouse and Pointer) environment.

H

Hacking An illegal intrusion into a system where its services, programs and data are used without authority. It may involve:

- eavesdropping or sniffing where the hacker taps into a connection
- brute force factoring of a public key in a cryptosystem
- dictionary attacks.

(See Asymmetric*, Brute Force*, Cryptosystem, Dictionary attack, RSA and Public key encryption.)

Hard disk A magnetic mass storage device consisting of fixed disks. Removable versions are available but most are fixed. Storage capacities are increasing all the time. The usefulness of a standalone PC is greatly enhanced following the installation of a magnetic hard disk drive. This presents a practical solution to rewritable mass storage for the present, yielding data capacities many orders of magnitude greater than may be held on floppy disk. All hard disks must be paired with an appropriate controller, with which they must be 100 per cent compatible. Popular commercial variants include IDE, E-IDE or ATA-2, SCSI, SCSI-2, Fast Wide SCSI, and Ultra SCSI. There are basically three ways in which a controller may be supported. First, it is included on the motherboard itself. Second, it is combined with a hard drive in the form of a hard card where the complete assembly is plugged into an expansion slot. Third, it represents a single card which plugs into an expansion slot. Controllers capable of accepting multiple devices provide an economical path to vast data storage capacity in the future. An inexpensive array of drives may be built up, thus lowering the considerable cost of a single high capacity drive bought at the outset. Where a number of drives in an array exhibit comparatively lengthy access times, it may be more practical to replace them with a single large disk, or several larger ones. More expensive controllers are often expandable in terms of additional daughter boards. For example, SCSI daughter boards can increase the number of drives in standard multiples of seven. Such controllers can easily

yield tens of gigabytes using inexpensive drives. Some controllers are also capable of mirroring, i.e. writing the same data to two disk drives simultaneously, thus making the data more secure. Controller technology and performance has advanced considerably in recent years, giving rise to an array of commercial devices ranging from scant MFM implementations to caching variants comprising on-board processors. The main thrust of advancement bases itself on the need to expand data capacities, lower access times and increase data transfer rates. In addition, the emergence of multiple device controllers reveals a secondary aim. Cache controllers speed up read/write operations by using on-board RAM as an intermediate data store between disk and system memory. Based upon which data is requested most often, a caching algorithm estimates which portions of hard disk should reside in on-board RAM. The ingenuity of this technique simply takes advantage of the inescapable fact that a small percentage of disk data is rewritten and accessed most frequently. The decision making process regarding which data should reside in RAM may suggest that they are 'intelligent controllers'. Cache controllers are the most expensive of all variants and will outperform standard implementations. It is most often these types of controllers which are able to support increasing multiples of drives through the addition of daughter boards. High-performance cache controllers can offer access times as low as a fraction of 1 ms.
(See RAID.)

Hard disk controller A device that interfaces a hard disk with a computer. Numerous commercial variants exist including IDE, E-IDE, SCSI, SCSI-2, Fast Wide SCSI, and Ultra SCSI.
(See Hard disk, RAID and SCSI.)

Hardware event queue A Windows buffer used to store keyboard and mouse events.

Hash An element that reduces the number of possible values using a hashing function such as the Secure Hashing Algorithm (SHA-1).

Hash signature A hash signature is generated by scrambling data blocks sequentially and producing a unique value for a given message or a file's contents. The signature:

- uses a hash function to create a hash value from a file
- concatenates a user's secret key with the file
- concatenates a user's secret key with the file
- creates a hash file which can be sent to the receiver who can decrypt the file with a copy of the secret key.

HDSL (high bit rate DSL)   A data transmission line that uses two pairs of copper wire as its medium. It offers T1 data speeds of up to 2 Mbps (in the UK).
(See ADSL.)

HDTV (high-definition television)   An emerging television broadcast technology that produces superior quality images using advanced high resolution digital video technologies like MPEG-2.
(See MPEG-2)

Help system   An on-line information system that provides guidance on software usage through hypertext, hypermedia or multimedia. Such systems are usually context-sensitive, so that information regarding a current program operation may be produced immediately. Windows Help systems are essentially hypermedia applications. They may be authored using a word processor that is able to produce standard RTF (Rich Text Format) files together with a Help compiler such as that supplied with Borland programming tools. Numerous other Help compilers exist.

Hertz   A unit representing the number of cycles or pulses per second. The alternating current (AC) supply in the UK is distributed at 50 Hz or cycles per second.

Hexadecimal   A base 16 counting system that is used widely in computing. Four binary digits represented by a single number or letter: 0, 1, 2, 3, 4, 5, 6, 7, 8, 9, A, B, C, D, E, F.

Hierarchical   A hypertext structure in which objects are only accessible through a parent object. Hierarchical or tree structures are well known and are normally represented using unidirectional links. Strict hierarchy demands that objects are only accessible through a parent. Compromised hierarchy, however, is less formal, permitting links to bypass children objects.

High-level language   *(See HLL.)*

HIPPI (High Performance Parallel Interface)

Hit   1. An event when a Web site is visited by a user. 2. In terms of processor cache memory, the hit rate is the percentage of memory requests that can be satisfied by the cache memory.

HLL (High Level Language)   A programming language consisting of easily remembered commands, constructs and statements. OOP (Object

Oriented Programming) languages and visual programming languages are highly evolved HLLs.

(See C++, Java and Visual Basic.)

Home page   A highest level page in the hierarchy of Web pages at a Web site. It has a URL such as www.homepage.com. A home page may consist of a single page or a number of linked pages. It may include links to other sites, graphics, sound bites, video, an e-mail address and various forms for user feedback; it may also include a counter that records the number of hits or times it is visited.

(See ActiveX*, DHTML, HTML, HTTP, Java*, Visual InterDev and Web.)

Host name   A name designated to a network device, which permits it to be addressed without using its full IP address. The Internet Request for Comments (RFC) N0. 1178 provides guidelines for naming hosts. Using host names there is a requirement to perform translations between host names and their respective IP addresses, using a lookup file containing host names and related IP addresses, or the Domain Network Service (DNS).

(See IP address and TCP/IP address.)

Host-based Processing   An architecture where a host computer is connected to dumb terminals. Typically the terminals do not have GUIs such as Windows, but are text-based. They are sometimes termed green screens, because many earlier terminals had screens bearing green phosphor. The terminals are said to be dumb, because they lack processing capabilities. They merely accept user commands, pass requests to the host, and receive information from the host. Many host-based processing architectures are being renovated or migrated to client/server architectures. A coexistence strategy is also being adopted, using mainframe and client/server-based architectures to form collection IT solutions.

(See Application renovation, Client/server and Mainframe.)

Hot metal   A Web authoring tool.

HotDog Pro   A Web site development tool.

(See CGI, HTML and Web server.)

HotJava   A Web browser produced by Sun Microsystems. It does not enjoy the popularity of Netscape Navigator or Microsoft Internet Explorer, but is nonetheless equally sophisticated.

(See Browser.)

Hotmail   A popular Webmail system.

HP Fremont   *(See Fremont.)*

HP-UX   A Unix operating system variant.

HSCSD (High-Speed Circuit-Switched Data)   A mobile network technology used by Orange.

HTML (HyperText Markup Language)   A standard language consisting of formatting commands and statements that may be used to create Web pages. HTML may be used to include hyperlinks leading to Web pages, frames or sites, and many other functions including visitor counters. HTML has its roots in SGML, and is the standard language of the World Wide Web. When the Web was first introduced, almost all Web sites depended heavily on HTML. Today, however, HTML is almost a framework used to hang other components such as:

- ActiveX controls
- Java applets
- JScript programs
- VBScript programs.

The HTML syntax is similar to old word processor formatting languages such as LaTex and even that which was included in the Borland Sprint word processor. the Web browser interprets the HTML first by reading the *tags*:

```
<HTML>
<HEAD>
<BODY>

</BODY>
</HEAD>
</HTML>
```

These basic tags form the basis of all HTML listings, and encapsulate such entities as VBScript code, JavaScript code, ActiveX controls and Java applets. Such components are enclosed between the <BODY> tags.
(See DHTML and Web.)

HTML 3.2   'The HyperText Markup Language (HTMl) is a simple markup language used to create *hypertext* documents that are *portable* from one platform to another.' (World Wide Web Consortium (W3C)(Raggett, 1997) HTML 3.2 replaced HTML 2.0 (RFC 1866) and is a variation of

SGML Standard Generalised Markup Language. (ISO 8879), and we now have HTML 4.0.

Raggett, D. *HTML 3.2 Reference Specification W3C Recommendation 14-Jan-1997* Raggett D., Le Hors, A. and Jacobs, I. HTML 4.0 Specification W3C Recommendation, revised on 24-Apr-1998.

(See HTML.)

HTML Help   An on-line Help development tool for Microsoft.

HTML template   A template file that a Web server uses to display information. The information may originate from a query submitted to a database.

(See HTML.)

HTML validator   A testing program used to validate HTML documents at various levels, including 2.0, 3.2 and future versions of HTML as specified by the W3C.

HTTP HyperText Transfer protocol)   A standard protocol that allows Web browsers to communicate with Web servers. The transport protocol is provided by TCP.

(See HTML, TCP and Web.)

HTTP_ACCEPT   A CGI variable that holds the "Accept:" headers from the client.

HTTP_COOKIE   A CGI variable that holds the contents of "Cookie:" headers from the client.

HTTP_REFERER   A CGI variable that holds the contents of the "Referer:" header from the client, containing a URL.

HTTP_USER_AGENT   A CGI variable that holds the contents of the "User-Agent:" header from the client, containing the browser's name.

Hybrid CD-ROM/DVD-ROM   A CD-ROM or DVD-ROM which posses hyperlinks to Web pages, as well as having its own data and media files. For example, MPEG-2 video might be stored on the DVD-ROM for improved video quality, while test, graphics and other less dynamic content may be stored on the Web.

(See CD-ROM and DVD.)

Hyperlink   A link in a hypertext-based navigational scheme that permits the user to browse from one document to another, or from one Web site to the next.

Hypermedia   An extension of the hypertext concept where text is combined with images. The terms hypermedia and multimedia are often regarded as interchangeable but they are *not*. In French media circles the ludicrous and ridiculously extravagant term hypermediatisation was coined in 1991. It was used to describe the immediacy with which news began to be transmitted, brought about by satellite broadcasting technology. With the time normally required by the reporter to prepare an informed report sacrificed, the concept of resulting, often confused, reports became known as hypermediatisation. Available to Macintosh users through HyperCard since 1987, hypermedia is a relatively mature area of multimedia. HyperCard for the Apple Macintosh may be considered as the earliest commercially successful hypermedia authoring tool that combined text, graphics, animated sequences and sound. It made the Macintosh an effective personal computer for multimedia. A plethora of hypermedia authoring tools has since emerged, including ToolBook for the Microsoft Windows environment on the IBM PC and compatible machines. Hypermedia applications developed using such tools can be thought of as interactive books that combine images, text and sound.

Hypertext   *'It seemed so clear to me right from the very beginning that writing should not be sequential . . . the problems we all have in writing sequential prose derives from the fact that we are trying to make it all lie down in one long string . . . if we could only break it up into different chunks that readers could choose . . . '* (Ted Nelson)

A term coined in the Sixties by Ted Nelson to describe the concept of linking textual information and presenting it in a non-linear fashion so as it may be navigated and browsed. The Web is synonymous with hypertext. Just as modern multimedia led to a re-evaluation of the way we communicate information in the 1980s and 1990s, hypertext had a similar impact in the 1960s. In a few cases, the birth of what is now known as hypertext also had a similar effect in the 1940s. The rationale behind the development of hypertext was a simple one: to optimise the processes of writing, storing textual information, and accessing that information. It improves accessibility of stored information by eliminating the need to follow rigorous set sequences. It allows the user to reference masses of related material through the pursuit of *ad hoc* paths. Advantages of this are easily understood when considering traditional methods. A word unknown to the reader of a book first leads to the index being searched. Failing this, the reader naturally attempts to find reference to the word in another book. The many references required to research a subject or satisfy curiosity is time consuming. With information linked, indexed and stored on computer, hypertext expedites this process, and gives users the opportunity to take regular excursions to satisfy references. It also makes information available that would not otherwise occur to the casual reader. The word 'car'. for instance, might be linked to numerous options such as: combustion engine, Henry J. Ford, Detroit, Rolls-Royce, catalytic converter, and a whole host of relevant texts. Hypertext is equally useful when writing or simply arranging gathered information. An appropriate hypertext tool, can be used to implant and manifest links between related items of text automatically.

(See Multimedia* and Web*.)

I

Idempotency   An attribute of a message that sees repetition yield a constant result.

IDL (Interface Definition Language)   A language that can map to others and is neutral in terms of providing interfaces and operations to applications written in compliant languages. Examples include CORBA IDL that is used widely to create middleware implementations.

IDL to C++ language mapping   A mapping that equates IDL to the C++ equivalent.

IDL to Java language mapping   A mapping that equates IDL to the Java equivalent.

Idl2java   A compiler which converts IDL programs into Java.

IEEE 1394   *(See Firewire.)*

IETF (Internet Engineering Task Force)   An international standards organisation dedicated to the maintenance, ratification and publication of Internet related technologies.

IIOP (Internat Inter-ORB Protocol)   A standard specification for transmitting GIOP messages over TCP/IP networks such as the Internet. *(See GIOP.)*

IIS   *(See Microsoft IIS.)*

Imported style sheet   A style sheet which can be imported to (combine with) another sheet, combining:

- main sheet, which apply to the whole site
- partial sheets, which apply to specific documents.

Form:

```
<LINK REL=STYLESHEET HREF="main.css" TYPE="text/css">
<STYLE TYPE="text=css">
<!--
@import url (http://www.botto.com/fast.css);
@import url (http://www.botto.com/fast.css);
....other statements
-->
</STYLE>
```

Inline style   An attached style, which affects one element and is specified in the start tag as a value of the STYLE attribute:

```
<P STYLE="text-indent: 14pt">Indented paragraph</P>
```

Inner class   A class that is local to a given block of Java code.

<INPUT TYPE   An HTML tag used to define input components such as radio buttons. For example using HTML you may add radio buttons using the following form that merely displays four radio buttons labelled £30, £40, £50 and £60:

```
FORM> NAME="Customer" ACTION="http://botto.com/
cgibin/form/cgi METHOD=get>

<INPUT TYPE= "radio" NAME="rad" VALUE="1">
£30
<INPUT TYPE="radio" NAME="rad" VALUE="2">
£40
<INPUT TYPE="radio" NAME="rad" VALUE="3">
£50
<INPUT TYPE="radio" NAME="rad" VALUE="4">
£60
</FORM>
```
(See HTML, <META>, <TITLE>, Search engine and Web page description.)

Instantiate   A process of creating an object using an object-oriented programming language such as Java or C++ or a development tool.
(See Object.)*

Instant messaging   A real-time communications facility used on networks and over the Internet. AOL offers Instant Messenger that:

- provides real-time news and financial reports
- receives alerts
- sends messages

- shares photos, pictures and sounds
- provides chat functions.

Interactive television A form of television broadcasting where the user is presented with a non-linear medium. The user can select content using on-screen options to control what screened matter is shown. Depending on the implementation the viewer may be able to select camera angles and replay selected footage and scenes. Interactive television services may offer TV shopping services also, and Internet related facilities, which include e-mail.

Interchange A banker's interchange exchanges data and money between banks to which it is connected and are managed by such organisations as Visa and Mastercard.

Internet A global network of computer networks based on the TCP/IP protocol. Internet has the World Wide Web as its foundation.

Internet investor An investor specialising in Internet related businesses.

Internet telephony A method of making telephone calls using packet-switched IP networks. In 1997, low-cost Internet telephony began to change the face of telcos, Internet Service Providers (ISPs), and corporations; the

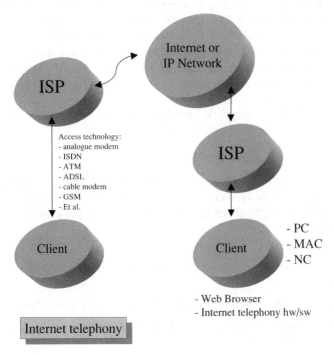

largely unregulated Internet became interwoven with telephony. For the first time ISPs could mine revenue-rich long-distance and international call businesses, which were once the preserve of telcos like BT and Mercury. Corporations and government departments may also 'toll bypass' the telcos by using Internet telephony over their own networks such as intranets, and significantly reduce their operating costs in the process. Similarly since VocalTec launched the Internet Phone in 1995, growing numbers of ISP subscribers have been making long distance and international calls for the cost of a local phone call. Internet telephony theoretically means that an ISP could become an international telco. The domestic long-distance calls business presents ISPs with one opportunity to compete with Telcos, as does the international calls business. The technology is also being embedded into existing switched network, where it will become transparent to the user. The successful proliferation of Internet telephony also hinges on emerging internationally agreed standards, such as H.323, which collectively will unify ISP services globally.

Interoperability   A software or hardware attribute that indicates compatibility between products from different vendors. It is normally based on a standard specification.

Interpreted   A programming language in which resulting programs are converted into an executable form each time they are run. For example, Java is interpreted at run-time from byte codes that are the result of compilation. Java then is both compiled and interpreted, but as it does not result in native machine code in the case of execution using JVMs, it is often considered an interpreted language.

Intranet   A localised network based on Internet technologies, featuring the same client/server architectures and technologies.
(See Extranet.)

IP Address   A physical IP address consisting of 32 bits, which identifies networks and its connected computers. The syntax for such addresses consists of four bytes each written in decimal form, and separated by a full stop: 118.234.98.87

The three types of IP address include:

IP Address Class A   A networks may have between 2^{16} (65 536) and 2^{24} (16.7 million) hosts.

IP Address Class B   B networks may have between 2^8 (256) and 2^{16} (65 536) hosts.

IP Address Class C   C networks may have up to 253 hosts, and not 255 because two values are reserved.

The addresses consists of a network address (netID) and a host address (hostID). The leftmost digits represent the netID address. This is set to zero when addressing hosts within the network.

(See Subnet.)

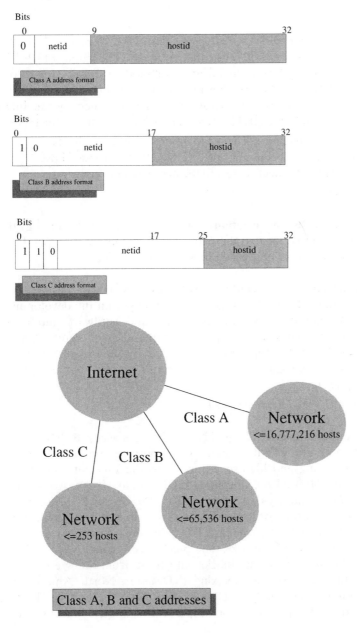

IP multicast   An IP addressing system, which is known as class D, and was developed at Xerox PARC. A multicast packet addresses a multicast group of nodes or hosts. The first multicast tunnel was implemented at Stanford University in 1988.
(See Mbone.)

IPv6 (Internet Protocol)   An advancement of the IP protocol that introduces 128 bit addressing and other improvements. The scaling of IPv4 32 bit addressing to 128 bit is intended to accommodate future growth of the Internet in terms of the growing number of network addresses. IPv6 is also called IPng (IP Next Generation), and is specified by the Internet Engineering Task Force (IETF). IPv6 supports addressing of the types:
- multicast, which connects a host to multiple addressed hosts
- unicast, which connects a host to a single other addressed host
- anycast, which connects a host to the nearest of multiple hosts.
(See IP address.)

IrDA (Infrared Data Association)   A wireless interface technology that is able to drive compatible peripheral devices. It is supported by Windows 98, and is integrated in numerous notebook systems designs.

ISAPI (Internet Server Application Program Interface)   An alternative technology to CGI. ISAPI consists of calls that permit the development of applications that offer performance gains and hardware and resource economies when compared with CGI scripts and programs. ISAP uses DLLs, and CGI-based applications can be renovated or converted to such DLLs. ISAPI filters can be used for encryption and decryption processes such as ciphering.
(See ASP, CGI and Cryptosystem.)

ISBN (Integrated Services Digital Network)   An access technology introduced by the CCITT, it is able to support reasonably sophisticated videoconferencing and high-speed access to the Internet and other networks. A BRI (Basic Rate Interface) ISDN line may have two 64 Kbps B-channels able to carry video, voice or data. ISDN uses PCM for encoding data in digital form, for transmission. Used in the Integrated Services Digital Network (ISDN) standard, PCM involves creating a data stream consisting of 8 bit PCM blocks. The blocks are created every 125 microseconds. By interleaving the blocks with those from other encoders, the result is time division multiplexing (TDM). In North America ISDN typically interleaves data from 24 64 Kbps sources or channels. This results in connections that provide 1.536 Mbps. Although the connection actually has a bandwidth of 1.544 Mbps, because each channel's frame has a marker bit 'F', adding 8 Kbytes. European ISDN typically interleaves 30 64 Kbps channels, giving 2048 Mbps. This and the 1.544 Mbps connection are known as primary rate multiplexes. Further interleaving of primary rate multiplexes sees:

- 6, 45, 274 Mbps in North America
- 8, 34, 139, and 560 Mbps in Europe.

While analogue modem speeds increased steadily throughout the eighties and early nineties, the arrival of the Web placed greater demands on available bandwidth. This encouraged telcos to provide ISDN services that were defined by the CCITT in 1971, and published in 1984 in the Red Book. ISDN was based on PCM (Pulse Code Modulation) that was conceived by A. H. Reeves, and experimented with in the Second World War, and was used in American telecommunications in the 1960s so as to increase network capacity. In 1986 a pre-ISDN service named Victoria was offered by Pacific Bell in Danville, California, offering RS232C ports that were configurable from 50 bps to 9.6 K bps. In the same year, official ISDN systems were introduced in Oak Brook, Illinois, and by 1988 some 40 similar pilot schemes were installed. ISDN digital networks eventually developed into B-ISDN where multiple lines could be used to provide data rates in increments of 64 Kb ps, and videoconferencing and high-speed Internet access were made possible. B-ISDN implementations could even be used to implement the lower data rates of 1.544 Mbps offered by modern T1 digital links that arrived some time later.

(See Access technology.)

ISO/TC 154   A technical committee, that addresses documents and data elements in administration, commerce and industry.

ISO 9736   A standard set of UN/EDIFACT syntax rules.

Issuer bank   A bank which provides credit to its customers usually through credit cards.

J

JAE (Java Application Environment)   A source code release of the JDK.

JAR   A Java archive file format used for concatenating files, and have the jar extension.
(See JAR File Format.)

JAR file format   A platform-independent file format that can be used to store applets and their components including images, sounds, resource files, and class files. JAR files may be used to download Java related data more efficiently using HTTP. It also offers support for compression and digital signatures.

Java   A general purpose, high-level language (HLL) which is:

- not platform or operating-system sensitive, yielding 'write-once-run-anywhere' code
- object-oriented
- multi-threaded
- class-based.

The resulting compiled bytecode can be run on Windows 3.x, Windows NT, Windows 95/98, Macintosh environments, Unix etc. OS independence is a key characteristic of Java[1], making it suitable for deployment of applets, where client OSs are of a heterogeneous nature. Web-based Java applets:

- are interpreted by Java-enabled browsers
- can access code libraries on the client machine
- may download class libraries from the server.

Development tools for Java include:

- the Java Development Kit JDK
- Microsoft J++ which is included in Microsoft Visual Studio
- Visual Age for Java
- Java Servlet Development Kit.

The Java language semantics, and high-level instructions are similar to C and C++. It is considered a static programming language[2], but is likely to be given a dynamic functionality through appropriate development environments and compilers. Compilation of Java source code yields in a bytecoded instruction set and binary format[3]. Java can also be used to develop client-side and server-side applications, perhaps using the CORBA-based Notification Services as its middleware or glue. Such Java code may be generated automatically from IDL files using an IDL2JAVA compiler.

References:
1. *The Java Language Specification* Sun Microsystems, 1996
2. *Dylan Reference Manual*, Apple Computer, 1995
3. *Java Virtual Machine Specification*, Addison-Wesley, 1996

Java applet   A program created using the Java programming language, and typically deployed over the Web. It resides on the server side, and is downloaded to a Java enabled-Web browser. It is then interpreted and run. The browser must feature the Java Virtual Machine which is a software-based processor.

Java array   A matrix of entities of the same type that may be simple or composite. The matrix or array may be multi-dimensional, and is declared using square brackets ([]).

```
int meters [ ];
char [ ] table;
long transform [ ] [ ];
```

The size of an array is not specified at its declaration.

JavaBeans   A standard component architecture offering Beans which can be used to build applets, sevlets and applications. The components are referred to as Beans, and complaint development tools provide access to the Beans using a toolbox. Visual programming plays an important role when architecting a Beans-based program; the developer simply selects Beans and modifies their appearance, behaviour and interactions with other Beans. JavaBeans-compatible development tools include:

- JavaSoft JavaBeans Development Kit (BDK)
- Lotus Development BeanMachine
- IBM VisualAge for Java
- SunSoft Java Workshop
- Borland JBuilder
- Asymetrix SuperCede
- Sybase PowerJ
- Symantec Visual Cafe.

JavaBeans Development Kit (BDK) A JavaSoft BDK aimed at Bean and tool developers, and not applications developers.

JavaBeans–ActiveX Bridge A Microsoft OCX control that permits the integration of JavaBeans as if they were ActiveX controls.
(See www.plash.javasoft.com/beans/bridge/)

Java Blend A database application development tool which is an environment for combining Java objects with enterprise databases. Applications can be developed by coding in Java, and resulting objects may be mapped to databases, and vice versa. It does not require knowledge of SQL. Java Blend was codeveloped by The Baan Company and Sun Microsystems.

Java Card A smart card implementation that uses Java technology. The Java Card specifications can also be applied to devices that have:
- 16 Kbyte ROM
- 8 Kbyte EEPROM
- 256 bytes RAM.

Java casting types A process of converting one data type into another. Casting often is necessary when a function returns a type different than the type you need to perform an operation. The `int` returned by the standard input stream (`System.in`) is cast to a `char` type using the statement:

```
char k = (char) System.in.read ();
```

Java comments and whitespace A textual comment, and whitespace consists of spaces, tabs and linefeeds.

```
/* multiple line comment */
// a single line comment
/** a multiple-line comment that may be used with
the javadoc tool to create documentation**/
```

Java data type A means of defining a storage method for information, such as the storage of variables in memory. The following statement declares a variable, a variable type, and identifier:

```
Type Identifier [, Identifier];
```

The statement:
- allocates memory to a variable type `Type`
- names the `Type` `'Identifier'`
- uses the bracketed identifier to indicate that multiple declarations of the same type may be made.

Java data types can be:

- simple, which include integer, floating-point, Boolean, and character
- composite, which are based on simple types, and include strings, arrays, classes and interfaces.

Java development tool   A tool/environment which allows programmers to create Java applets, Java programs, JavaBeans, and possibly Java Servlets.

Java Electronic Commerce Framework   A point-of-sale (POS) application framework.

Java floating-point data types   A data type which can represent fractional numbers that may be the:

- float type that is allocated a 32 bit single-precision number
- double type that is allocated a 64 bit double-precision number.

Such data types are implemented using the statements:

```
float altitude;
double angle, OpenRoad;
```

Java floating-point literals   A means of storing and processing fractional numbers that are expressed in decimal (i.e. 200.76) or in scientific notation (2.00.76e2). Floating-point literals default to the double type that is a 64 bit value. The 'f' or 'F' suffix harnesses the 32 bit value.

JavaHelp   A software product which allows the creation of on-line Help for Java applets, applications, OSs and devices. It can also be used to deploy on-line Help over the Web and intranets. JavaHelp is:

- written using the Java language
- implemented using JFC components
- platform independent
- browser independent
- supported by browsers that comply with the Java Runtime Environment.

Java identifier   A Java token that stores names that are applied to variables, methods, and classes.

Java integer data types   A means of representing signed integer numbers, and include:

- byte (8 bit)
- short 16 bit)

- `int` (32 bit)
- `long` (64 bit).

Integer variables are declared thus:

```
int x;
short ;scale
long lumin, light;
byte alpha, beta, gamma;
```

Java integer literals   A literal may be:

- decimal (base 10)
- hexadecimal (base 16) with the 'OX' prefix
- octal, with the '0' prefix.

By default, integer literals are stored in the `int` type that has a 32 bit value. They may be stored in the `double` type that has a 64 bit value, using the 'l' or 'L' suffix.

(See Java literal.)

Java keywords   A meaningful vocabulary of entities which perform specific functions, and include:

abstract	double	int	super
boolean	else	interface	switch
break	extend	long	synchronized
byte	false	native	this
byvalue	final	new	threadsafe
case	finally	null	throw
catch	float	package	transient
char	for	private	true
class	goto	protected	try
const	if	public	void
continue	implements	return	while
default	import	short	

Java lexical translation   A process by which Java source code[1] is converted into Java tokens. It is implemented by the lexical analyser facet of the compiler, which:

- translates Unicode escapes into Unicode characters, allowing the Java listing to be represented using ASCII characters
- generates a stream of input characters and line terminators
- generates Java input elements, or Java tokens that are terminal symbols.

1. *The Java Language Specification*, Sun Microsystems, 1996

Java literal   An element that maintains a constant value; it may be:

- numeric
- integer
- floating point
- Boolean
- characters
- strings.

Character literals refer to a single Unicode character. Multiple-character strings that are implemented as objects are also literals.

JavaMail   An API used to build Java-based mail and messaging applications.

Java Management API (JMAPI)   A library of objects and methods used for the development of network, and service management solutions targeted at heterogeneous networks.

Java Media and Communication APIs, including 2-D, 3-D, and Java Telephony   A Sun Microsystems' product family that allows developers to develop interactive multimedia applications for the Web.

Java Naming and Directory Interface (JNDI) A connectivity API which provides an interface with enterprise, heterogeneous naming and directory services. It is a JavaSoft API, and a Java Standard Extension.

Java.net   A package which has classes designed for networks. Java.net includes the URL class, which allows remote objects to be downloaded and can be used to read and write streams to and from the object.

JavaOS   A compact operating system dedicated to running Java programs/applets. The JavaOS family includes:

- JavaOS for Network Computers (NCs), which is described as a stand-alone Java Application Platform for NCs
- JavaOS for Appliances, which is intended for communications devices
- JavaOS for Consumers, which is aimed at consumer electronics devices.

JavaPC   A software solution for migrating PCs to Java platforms. JDK 1.1 compliant Java applications can be stored locally or on a network, and can be run on DOS and Windows 3.x platforms.

Java remote Method Invocation (RMI)   A technology used in Jini and designed by Ann Wollwrath of SunSoft. Java RMI permits object-to-object communications where the methods invoked may be on a remote application object.

JavaScript   An object-orientated scripting language optimised for the Web. Using JavaScript Web pages/HTML documents can be given:

- dynamic content such as animations
- integrated Java applets and ActiveX controls
- interactive content
- data entry forms.

Microsoft's implementation of JavaScript is JScript. The rationale behind JScript is echoed by VBScript: it is intended as a quick method of creating and tailoring applications. Unlike JScript, VBScript is not an OOP language. Like other objects, JavaScript objects have properties and methods, and include the:

- *window*, which is at the top of the HTML document's object hierarchy
- *frame*, which is a window
- *location*, which stores URL information
- *document*, which stores document characteristics such as its URL and title
- *form*, which stores form characteristics
- *test* and *textarea*, which store text information
- *checkbox*, which is standard Widows UI object
- *radio*, which refers to a single UI radio button
- *select*, which is an array of option objects
- *button*, which stores button information
- *password*, which is a text-entry box that disguises keyboard entries using asterisks
- *navigator*, which stores a visitor's version number of Netscape Navigator version number
- *string*, which provides methods for string manipulation
- *date*, which is dedicated to calendar date information
- *math*, which facilitates common constants and calculations
- *image*, which indicates image information on the current page
- *array*, which is dedicated to arrays.

JavaScript listings are integrated in HTMI code by enclosing them between the following tags:

```
<SCRIPT LANGUAGE="JavaScript">
<SCRIPT>
```

Development environments and applications that support JScript are numerous, and include the Microsoft ActiveX Control Pad that also supports CBScript. *(See CB Script.)*

JavaScript commands: Comments Single and multiple line comments can be included using the syntax:

```
// A single line comment
/* Multiple lines comment
require this syntax */
```

JavaScript operators

++	increment
_	decrement
*	multiplication
/	divide
%	modulus
+	addition
−	subtraction
<<	shift left
>>	shift right
>	greater than
<=	less than or equal to
>=	greater than or equal to
==	equal to
!=	not equal to
&&	logical AND
!	logical NOT
||	logical OR
^	bitwise
|	bitwise OR
&	bitwise AND

for The `for` statement has three optional expressions:

```
for ( initial.Expression; condition;
update.Expression) {
statement
statement
statement
}
```

- `initial.Expression` initialises the counter variable, which can be a new variable declared with `var`
- the `condition` expression is evaluated on each pass through the loop. If the condition is true, the loop statements are executed
- `update. Expression` is used to increment the counter variable.

while A statement used to implement a conditional loop, based on a true or false validation:

```
while (condition) {
statement
```

```
statement
statement
}
```

break   A break statement stops `for` or `while` loops, and diverts program execution to the line following the loop statements.

for . . . in   A for . . . in statement executes the statement block for each object property:

```
for (variable in object) {
statement
statement
}
```

function   A statement which allows you to create a named JavaScript function together with parameters. The `return` statement may be used to return a value. Nested, functions are not supported.

```
function name ([parameter] [ . . . , parameter]) {
statements . . .
}
```

if . . . else   A conditional statement that offers one of two conclusions.

```
if (condition) {
statement
statement
} [else {
statement
statement
}]
```

return   This is used to specify a returned value from a function.

var   The var statement is used to declare a variable that may be local or global.

```
var variableName [=value] [ . . . , variableName
[=value]]
```

while   Repeats a loop while an expression is true.

```
while (condition) {
statements . . .
}
```

with   Declares a default object as the focus of a set of statements.

```
with (object) {
statement
statement
}
```

(See CGI.)

java.rmi.RMISecurityManager
(See RMI Security.)

Java package   A set of Java classes which address specific functions, were for instance `java.io` addresses input and output functions, and `java.net` addresses Internet and network operations.

Java separator   A means of categorising Java source code, and directs the compiler appropriately, and includes: { } ; , :

JavaSoft   A company formed by Sun Microsystems in 1995. JavaSoft develops Java language products and technologies that include Jini.

JavaSpaces   A SunSoft technology that provides a means of writing, reading and transfering objects or entries between spaces. The JavaSpace interface defines methods to read or copy entries from a space, and to take or copy entries from a space, while removing them from spaces also. Locating entries in spaces is carried out using associative lookup, and a template is used to match entry contents. For example, you can use a template like:

```
CarCreditcard anyCreditcardTemplate = new
CarCreditcard ();
AnyCreditcardTemplate.name = null;
AnyCreditcardTemplate.cost = null;
```

The `null` fields operate like wildcards and any `Creditcard` entry will be matched regardless of its name or cost. `null` may also be used for the template so that all entries in a space are matched. The match may be narrowed merely by adding values and name strings like:

```
AnyCreditcardTemplate.name = "Shell";
```

The JavaSpaces interface has two read methods:

```
Entry read (Entry tmpl, Transaction txn, long
timeout)
```

and,

```
Entry readIfExists (Entry tmpl, Transaction txn,
long timeout)
```

both require three parameters: a template, transaction and a timeout value, which may be expressed in milliseconds. When a matching entry is found, a copy of it is returned, or it is merely read. Where multiple matches are found the space returns a single arbitrary entry. This clearly must be borne in mind when developing JavaSpaces services. The `read` method waits for the timeout if no matching entries are found in a space, or until a matching entry is found. If no matching entry is found, a `null` value is returned by the `read` method. The Long.MAX_VALUE may be used as a timeout value, causing the `read` operation to block until a matching entry is found. Alternatively using the JavaSpaces.NO-WAIT value for the timeout causes the `read` operation to return immediately. The `readIfExists` method is non-blocking, and returns immediately when no matching entry is found, irrespective of the timeout parameter value. The timeout parameter is relevant only when the `read` operation takes place under a transaction. So with a `null` transaction the timeout value is equivalent to NO_WAIT. Both `read` operations may throw the:

`InterruptedException` when the thread implementing the read operation is interrupted.

`Remote Exception` when a failure occurs on the network or in the remote space.

`TransactionException` when the supplied transaction is invalid.

`UnusableEntryException` when an entry retrieved cannot be deserialised.

The `take` method defined in the JavaSpaces interface is of the same form as the read operation:

```
Entry take (Entry tmpl, Transaction txn, long
timeout)
```

The `take` method removes entries from spaces provided no exception is thrown. The aforementioned exceptions for `read` and `readIfExists` may also be thrown by the `take` method. These include `Interrupted Exception`, `RemoteException`, `TransactionException`, and `UnusableEntryException`.

JavaSpaces write method   A JavaSpaces method that is used to write entries to spaces. The following code segment uses the `write` method to copy a `Creditcard` requirement to a space:

```
public void writeCreditcard (CarCreditcard
Creditcard) {
  Try {
    space.write (Creditcard, null, Lease.FOREVER);
  } catch (Exception e) {
    e.printStackTrace ();
  }
}
```

The `write` method is defined in the JavaSpaces interface is of the form:

```
Lease write (Entry e, Transaction txn, long lease)
  throws RemoteException, TransactionException;
```

155

An entry is manipulated using the `write` method that may use the arguments transaction and lease time. If given a `null` value the transaction is a singular operation and is detached from other transactions. The lease time argument simply specifies the entry's longevity in the new space. When the lease expires the space removes it, but if a `Lease.FOREVER` value is used the entry exists in the space indefinitely, or until it is removed by a transaction process or operation. The lease time may also be expressed in milliseconds like the three minute lease shown below:

```
Long time = 1000 * 60 * 3 ; // three minute lease
Lease lease = space.write (entry, null, time);
```

Leases may also be renewed using the renew method:

```
void renew (long time)
    ''
```

The `time` value is added to the lease time remaining. The renew method may raise the exceptions: `LeaseDeniedException`, `UnknownLease Exception` and `RemoteException`. The former is raised should the space be unable to renew the lease that may be caused by lack of storage resources. The `UnknownLeaseException` is thrown if the entry or object is unknown to the space, perhaps because its lease has already expired. In real world scenarios the use of `Lease.FOREVER` is considered an uneconomical use of resources. The is an intelligent solution to leasing is to use `Lease.FOREVER` may compress the development lifecycle, as it can reduce the probability of thrown exceptions. The write method also throws two types of exceptions including `RemoteException` and the `detail` field that holds the exception type. If the space is unable to grant a lease, a `RemoteException` is thrown. A `TransactionException` is thrown when the transaction is invalid or cannot be rolled forward or committed.

Java String Literals A string, or number of characters, within a pair of double quotation marks. String literals invoke an instance of the `String` class, which is assigned the character string.

Java Studio 1.0 A development environment that does not require Java coding on a line-by-line basis. It harnesses the JavaBeans object architecture, and is typically used to build Web applications. It is a product of Sun Microsystems.

Java swing A set of interfaces and components that permit the easy creation of GUI components. These include menus, dialogues and toolbars, and also the items JsplitPane and Jtree.

Java to IDL language mapping A mapping which equates the Java to the IDL equivalent.

Java tokens   A meaningful element of a Java program when compiled. The five categories of token include:

- identifiers
- keywords
- literals
- operators
- separators.

Tokens are compiled into Java bytecode, which can be interpreted by a Java Virtual Machine.

Java Unicode   A predominant character set with which Java source code is represented; it is:

- 16 bit, which gives up to 2^{16} or 65 536 possible characters
- used exclusively by Windows NT at the system level
- a worldwide standard.

In Java, three lexical translations[1] convert a raw unicode character stream into a sequence of Java tokens.

1. *The Java Language Specification*, Sun Microsystems, 1996

Java World   An on-line magazine dedicated to Java.
(See www.javaworld.com.)

Jaz drive   A removable storage device manufactured by Iomega. Jaz disks offer 1 Gbyte data storage capacity.

JBuilder   A Java based development software suite from Inprise.

JDBC (Java Database Connectivity)   A Java package, which allows Java programs to interact with compliant databases. It also includes a bridge to provide backward compatibility with ODBC databases.

JDK (Java Development Kit)   Sun Microsystems' development tool for creating Java applets and applications. It is freely available from JavaSoft (www.javasoft.com), and includes:

- appletviewer for viewing Java source code listings
- jar for compressing an packaging applications
- java for executing applications
- javadoc for documenting Java programs
- javac for compiling Java programs.

(See www.javasoft.com.)

Jetsend   A wireless connection technology for home appliances.

Jini   A SunSoft standard for distributing services over local and remote networks. Jini can be applied to implement self-configuring tier 0 devices sometimes called *smart devices* that include cell phones, DVD drives, palm PCs and organisers. The connection between a Jini device and a Jini service takes place using the TCP/IP transport protocol, and other Jini protocols that include Discovery, which is based on UDP. Jini networks comprise lookup services, which act as directors containing the network's registered services. A client may receive a proxy object from these services, which is downloaded to a JVM, and may also use UIs specific to services. Jini applications are varied and exist at every tier including tier 3 where transaction processing can be carried out, and may be applied to devices ranging from servers to simple household appliances as simple as a light switch with a single input and no JVM of its own. Docking stations are also available where Jini clients share a JVM. Mobile Jini applications can include smart devices able to connect to remote Jini services in the home or in the office.

(See JavaSpaces, Jini and jini.org)*

Jini API   Jini is made up of numerous Jini packages that combine to make the collective API, which implements the many required interfaces. These include the methods and exceptions that make light work of developing Jini applications and include the shown `TransactionManager` interface.

```
package net.jini.core.transaction.server;

import net.jini.core.transaction.*;
import net.jini.core.lease.Lease;
import net.jini.core.lease.LeaseDeniedException;
import java.rmi.Remote;
import java.rmi.RemoteException;

public interface TransactionManager
extends Remote, TransactionConstants {
   /** Class that holds return values from create
   methods. */
   public static class Created implements
   java.io.Sterializable {
     static final long serialVersionUID =
     -4233846033773471113L;
```

```
public final long id;
public final Lease lease;
public Created (long id, Lease lease) {
   this.id = id; this.lease = lease;
}
}
```

```
Created create (long lease) throws LeaseDenied
Exception, RemoteException;
```

```
void join (long id, TransactionParticipant part,
long crashCount)
   throws Unknown TransactionException,
CannotJoinException.
CrashCountException, RemoteException;
```

```
int getState (long id) throws
UnknownTransactionException, RemoteException;
```

```
void commit (long id)
   throws UnknownTransactionException,
CannotCommitException,
   RemoteException;
```

```
void commit (long id), long waitFor)
   throws UnknownTransactionException,
CannotCommitException.
   TimeoutExpiredException, RemoteException;
```

```
void abort (long id)
   throws UnknownTransactionException,
CannotAbortException,
   RemoteException;
```

```
void abort (long id, long waitFor)
   throws UnknownTransactionException,
CannotAbortException,
   TimeoutExpiredException, RemoteException;
```

Jini Community   A community at jini.org dedicated to the development of Jini, its framework, its applications, its services and marketplaces. *(See jini.org.)*

Jini docking bay A docking bay, which has a JVM that may be shared by multiple docked devices.

Jini Multicast Response Service A transparent connection which occurs between Jini devices and services, and communities. It relies upon simply communicating messages and protocols. Jini has protocols to:

- discover lookup services on LANs, which may be in your office, in your home, or even installed in a hotel room
- broadcast the presence of lookup services
- forge communications with a lookup service using WANs.

A new entity uses the multicast request protocol to find lookup services and then uses the multicast announcement protocol to receive multicast lookup announcements. This communication requires that the requesting entity has a multicast request client and a multicast response server that listens to the lookup services. Both may be run on a single JVM implementation. The lookup service has a listening multicast request server and a multicast response client that responds to requesting entities by providing them with a proxy that is used to converse with the lookup service. The multicast request service uses the transport layer of the network protocol so that lookup services can push their information to a requesting host. The actual protocol used is a version of UDP (User Datagram Protocol), and a multicast discovery packet has a maximum 512 byte payload. It may contain architecture neutral parameters and should be simple to decode. The packets form a contiguous stream like that from a `java.io.DataOutput Stream` to a `java.io.ByteArrayOutputStream` object.

Jini nested transactions A series of multiple transactions using Jini. At times a transaction requires the implementation of subtransactions for its successful completion. These nested transactions provide a logical hierarchy where a parent transaction is dependent on a nested transaction. Nested transactions are implemented using `TransactionManagers` which use the `NestableTransactionManager` interface:

```
package net.jini.core.transaction.server;

    import net.jini.core.transaction.*;
    import net.jini.core.lease.LeaseDeniedException;
    import java.rmi.RemoteException;

    /**
    * The interface used for managers of the two-phase
      commit protocol for
    * nestable transactions. All nestable transactions
      must have a
```

```
* transaction manager that runs this protocol.
*
* @see NestableServerTransaction
* @see TransactionParticipant
*/
public interface NestableTransactionManager extends
TransactionManager {
  /**
   * Begin a nested transaction, with the specified
   * transaction as parent.
   *
   * @param parentMgr the manager of the parent
   * transaction
   * @param parentID the id of the parent
   * transaction
   * @param lease the requested lease time for the
   * transaction
   */
  TransactionManager.Created create
  (NestableTransactionManager parentMgr,
         long parentID, long lease)
    throws UnknownTransactionException,
  CannotJoinException,
      LeaseDeniedException, RemoteException;


  /**
   * Promote the listed participants into the
   * specified transaction.
   * This method is for use by the manager of a
   * subtransaction when the
   * subtransaction commits. At this point, all
   * participants of the
   * subtransaction must become participants in the
   * parent transaction.
   * Prior to this point, the subtransaction's
   * manager was a participant
   * of the parent transaction, but after a
   * successful promotion it need
   * no longer be one (if it was not itself a
   * participant of the
   * subtransaction), and so it may specify itself
   * as a participant to
```

```
 * drop from the transaction. Otherwise,
   participants should not be
 * dropped out of transactions. For each promoted
   participant, the
 * participant's crash count is stored in the
   corresponding element of
 * the <code>crashCounts</code> array.
 *
 * @param id the id of the parent transaction
 * @param parts the participants being promoted to
   the parent
 * @param crashCounts the crash counts of the
   participants
 * @param drop the manager to drop out, if any
 *
 * @throws CrashCountException the crash count of
   some (at least one)
 * participant is different from the crash count
   the manager already
 * knows about for that participant
 *
 * @see TransactnManager#join
 */
void promote (long id, TransactionParticipant [ ]
parts,
    long [ ] crashCounts, TransactionParticipant
    drop)
    throws UnknownTransactionException,
CannotJoinException,
    CrashCountException, RemoteException;
}
```

When a nested transaction is created, the originating manager joins the parent transaction using the `join` method when the managers are different. The `create` method may raise the `UnknownTransactionException` if the parent transaction manager does not recognise the transaction because of an incorrect ID, or if it has become inactive, or if it has been discarded by the manager.

Jini smart device   A Jini-enabled device which usually has its own JVM and is able to consume Jini services.

Jini transaction creation   A process where a Jini transaction is created. To create a transaction it is necessary for the client to use a lookup service

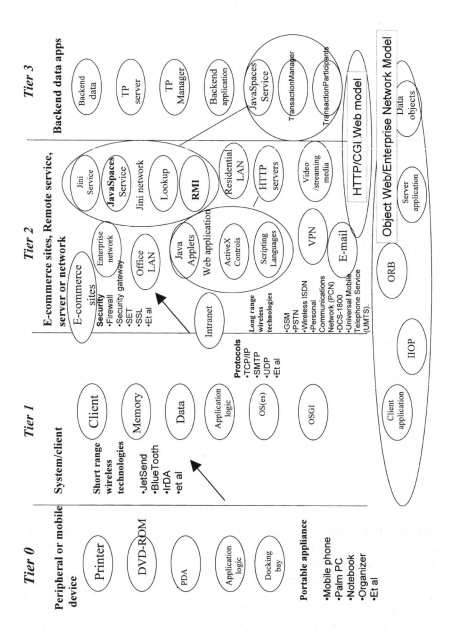

163

(or a similar directory services metaphor) in order to reference a TransactionManager object. A new transaction may be initiated using the create () method and by specifying a leaseFor period in milliseconds. The leaseFor duration is adequate for the transaction to complete, and the TransactionManager may forbid the lease request by throwing the LeaseDeniedException. Expiration of a lease before a transactionParticipant's vote with a commit or abort leads the TransactionManager to abort the transaction. Constants provide the currency of the described communications between Transaction participants and TransactionManagers and are defined in the TransactionConstants interface:

```
package net.jini.core.transaction/server;

/** Constants common to transaction managers and
participants. */
public interface TransactionConstants {
  /** Transaction is currently active */
  final int ACTIVE = 1;
  /** Transaction is determining if it may be
committed */
  final int VOTING = 2;
  /** Transaction has been prepared but not yet
committed */
  final int PREPARED = 3;
  /** Transaction has been prepared with nothing to
commit */
  final int NOTCHANGED = 4;
  /** Transaction has been committed */
  final int COMMITTED = 5;
  /** Transaction has been aborted */
  final int ABORTED = 6;
}
```

Jini transaction join   A process where a participant joins a transaction. To join a transaction a participant invokes the join method held by the TransactionManager using an object implementation of the TransactionParticipant interface. The TransactionManager uses the object to communicate with the TransactionParticipant. If the join method results in the RemoteException being thrown, the TransactionParticipant relays the same (or another exception) to its client. The join method has a crash count parameter that holds the TransactionParticipant's storage version which contains the transaction state. The crash count is changed following each loss or corruption of its storage. When a `TransactionManager` receives a `join` request it reads the crash count to determine if the `TransactionParticipant` is already joined. If the crash count is the same as that passed in the original `join`, the `join` method is not executed. If it is different, however, the `TransactionManager` causes the transaction to abort by throwing the `CrashCountException`.

Jini TransactionServer A two-phase commit using Jini. The two-phase commit protocol is implemented using the primary types:

1. `TransactionManger`, which creates and coordinates transactions.
2. `NestableTransactionManager`, which accommodates nested transactions or sub-transactions.
3. `TransactionParticipant`, which allows transactions to be joined by participants.

The two-phase commit protocol coordinates the changes made to system resources that result from transactions. It tests for their successful implementation, in which case they are committed. If not, and any one fails, they are each rolled back. In transaction processing (TP) this is left to a transaction coordinator whose function is integrated in the `Transaction Manager` using Jini. The `TransactionManager` is key to the two-phase commit protocol. This requires that all `TransactionParticipants` vote in order to indicate their state. The vote may be prepared (or ready to commit), not changed (or read only), or aborted (when it is necessary to abort the transaction). Having received information of the readiness to commit through a prepared vote, the *TransactionManager* signals `TransactionParticipants` to roll forward and commit the changes resulting from the transaction. `TransactionParticipants` that vote aborted are signalled to roll back by the `TransactionManager`.

JIT debugging A method of detecting bugs in a running program. It responds by running an appropriate debugging process.

Jobs, Steve A co-founder of Apple Computer, who later founded NeXT. His most significant achievements were those in the early years of Apple Computer. it was an era when a clutch of American companies, largely run and owned by college dropouts (including Bill Gates), revolutionised the computer industry by designing affordable microcomputers and accompanying software. Steve Jobs and Steve Wozniak revolutionised the world of computing by mass producing one of the world's most affordable PCs known simply as the Apple, and later the Apple II. It was designed by Steve Wozniak, whose dream was always to own a computer, once saying 'I don't care if I live in the smallest house, just so long as I have my very own computer.' This was a dream that he almost single handedly made realty for himself and for millions of people around the world.

(See Apple Computer.)

Join   A process of combining records from different tables/files in a relational database management system (RDBMS).

JPEG (Joint Photographics Experts Group)   An internationally agreed standard for still image compression and decompression that was devised by the JPEG, a specialist group set up by the ISO and CCITT. It is a symmetrical algorithm in that the processes required for compression mirror those of decompression. The processes include forward and reverse DCTs (Direct Cosine Transformations). It may be used to compress 8 bit, 16 bit and 24 bit graphics. Motion-JPG (M-JPEG) video uses individual frames compressed according to the JPEG algorithm, giving a full frame updates as opposed to the predominantly partial frame updates of standard MPEG video. The JPEG standard compression scheme for still photographic quality images began development in 1986. Compression and encoding techniques were evaluated during 1987 and 1988, until eventually the components of the symmetrical compression cycle were agreed, with DCT (Direct Cosine Transform) proving a central theme of the JPEG design.

(See DCT.)

JVM Java Virtual Machine   A software solution that yields an environment for running Java applets. Browsers such as Netscale Navigator and Microsoft Internet Explorer feature Java Virtual Machines. JVMs can be run on clients' desktop and notebook systems, or even consumer appliances so as they connect with Jini networks and consume compliant services. A rather cynical school of thought considers JAVA merely to be a slightly modified version of C++ but with the addition of a virtual processor, namely the JVM.

(See JavaPC.)

K

Kaband   A range of radio or electromagnetic frequencies 18–30 GHz.

Katakana   A character set used in a Japanese phonetic alphabet.

KB   *(See Kilobyte.)*

K band   A range of frequencies 10–12GHz.

Kbps (kilobits per second)   A unit of data transfer that equates to 1000 bits per second.

KBps (kilobytes per second)   A unit of data transfer that equates to 1000 bytes per second.

KBS (Knowledge-Based System)   An alternative name for an expert system, which includes a knowledge base of rules or heuristics, each comprising fact(s) and conclusion(s), i.e. IF disk drive light off THEN check ribbon cable. Such conclusions, and deductions may be weighted appropriately. The rule base is chained by an inference engine, which chains:

- backwards, comparing an inputted question with conclusions in the rule base, and may compare subsequently located facts with conclusions of other rules.
- forwards, comparing an inputted question with facts in the rule base, and may compare subsequently located conclusions with facts of other rules.

A KBS can offer informed decision-making skills, the effectiveness of which is a function of the accuracy and comprehensiveness of its rule or knowledge base. A knowledge engineer is responsible for generating rule base. Numerous KBS applications exist, including medicine, business, stock market, maintenance. Web-based KBS solutions exist.

Kermit   A file transfer protocol, which is asynchronous.

Kernel   A part of an operating system environment. The Windows kernel is responsible for a number of tasks, including memory management and dynamic linking.

Kernel driver   A driver which interacts with an internal or external device.

Kernel32.DLL   A DLL included in Windows 3.1 and Windows 95/98. *(See DLL.)*

Key   A means of making encrypted data unique.

Key field   A key field is included in a database in order to prevent the duplication of contained field values and to expedite information retrieval. Key fields are also used to link tables or files in relational databases. Where it is necessary to repeat values in a key field, additional fields are keyed. These are termed multi-field keys.

Key escrow agent   An entity that holds encryption keys under an escrow transaction, permitting parties such as government bodies to recover encrypted data.
(See Escrow.)

kHz (kilohertz)   A unit of frequency, which equates to 1000 cycles per second.

Kilobyte (or Kbyte or KB)   A unit of memory which has 1024 bytes. Occasionally disk drive manufacturers equate Kbyte to 1000 bytes in accordance with the metric interpretation of kilo. It is derived from a 10 bit address bus, or 10 bit pointer register, thus giving access to 2^{10} (1024) memory locations.

Kilostream   A digital service provided by BT, which requires the customer to have an Network Terminating Unit (NTU). It provides data rates of 2.4 Kbps, 4.8 Kbps, 9.6 Kbps, 48 Kbps, and 64 Kbps.

Kiosk application   A multimedia application intended to interface with the general public. The multimedia system may or may not be housed in a physical kiosk. Such applications might provide maps, tourist information, point-of-information, point-of sale etc.

Knowledge base   1. An information data base which is accessible via the Microsoft Web site. 2. A set of rules that determines the functionality of an expert system. The rules may be simple IF . . . THEN rules.

(See KBS.)

Knowledge engineer   A person responsible for programming an expert system.

(See KBS.)

L

L band   A section of the electromagnetic spectrum that ranges from 1.53 to 1.66 ghz and is applied in satellite and microwave communications.

LAN (Local Area Network)   A number of computers connected physically or wirelessly so that users can share directories, applications, services and resources such as printers and fax/modems. LANs are commonly used to connect all computers in a department, while Wide Area Networks (WANs) may be used to connect multiple sites. LAN data transfer rates over approximate speeds between 10 and 100Mbps though speeds up to 1000Mbps are possible. There are a number of internationally agreed standards by which computers forming a LAN are connected. Network topologies include the:

- star, where computers are connected using a centralised hub
- ring, where computers are connected in a chain; this is the chosen method for small networks that are perhaps peer-to-peer configurations which might be based on Windows 98/NT.

LAN standards include Ethernet, Token Ring and occasionally Fibber Channel (FC). The latter may be used to implement FC arbitrated loops.
(See 10 Base*, Active Web architecture, Client/server, Ethernet, Master/slave processing Server.)

Laser (Light Amplification by Stimulated Emission of Radiation)   A light source able to emit a coherent beam of light, which is of a fixed wavelength. The device is said to 'lase', when producing such a ray of light.
(See LED and Optic fibre.)

Launch   1. A process of starting a program or application. Synonyms: Load, Open and Run. 2. An angle at which a ray of light must be injected into an optic fibre to propagate the cable's entire length. The angles are within the fibre's *acceptance cone*, whose size is a function of the fibre's NA

171

or *numerical aperture*. The high the NA, the greater the light-gathering ability of the fibre.

(See Optic fibre.)

LCD (Liquid Crystal Display A form of display measuring a few milli-metres in depth. Available in monochrome and colour, LCDs are used in a wide variety of appliances including pocket televisions, notebook com-puters, PDAs, cellular phones, calculators, and portable CD-ROM readers/electronic books. Modern notebooks tend to use TFT and DSTN display technology. The former provides improved image definition.

(See LED and Notebook.)

Lease A time period assigned to an object, date element or service that dictates longevity. Services which register on a network can be assigned a lease, while objects in a JavaSpaces service can also be assigned leases placing time limits on their availability.

LED (Light-Emitting Diode) A semiconductor/optronic device, which emits visible light when excited electrically. It may provide a basis for:

- display technology, such as that used in notebooks and consumer elec-tronics devices such as pocket televisions
- laser light sources for fibre optic lightwave communications
- read heads for CD-ROM and DVD drives.

They are used in all types of consumer electronics and computers as power indicators and alphanumeric displays. Advantages over conventional fila-ment bulbs include: near-infinite life span, incredible durability, reliability, physical robustness, ease of manufacture in different colours, low power

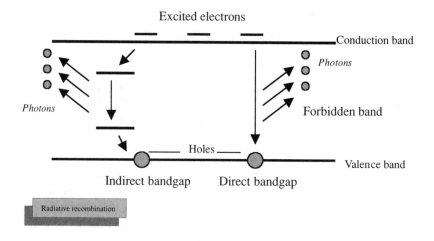

consumption and cheapness. Liquid Crystal Displays (LCDs) have displaced alphanumeric (LED) and graphical displays.

LEDs emit optical radiation, and the 800 nm (wavelength) emission is seen as red. Dividing the speed of light c (3×10^8 metres/second) by the wavelength (λ) of an (800nm) LED's emission, results in its frequency f:

$f = c/\lambda$

$f = (3 \times 10^8)/(8.00 \times 10^{-7})$

$f = 3.75 = 10^{14}$ Hz

The emission from an LED is commonly defined in terms of the external stimulation of electrons. Electrons exist in bands that surround a nucleus. the outer or valence band may share its electrons with other atoms that collectively form molecules. The valence band's elecrons are stimulated to higher energy state called the Conduction band. This condition occurs when electrons are:

- passed through a pn junction diode
- simulated by a high voltage
- simulated by light.

The difference that exists between the valence and the conduction bands is described as the forbidden gap. The type of semiconductor determines the behaviour of the bandgap, which may be:

- *indirect.* such as silicon, where eletrons may occupy intermediate levels as they pass from the conduction band tot he valence band
- *direct*, where electrons move directly through the forbidden gap, and provide the best results

Photon emission takes place as electrons are displaced from the conduction band, and united with holes in the valence band. The resulting emission of light from an LED might be referred to as *pn junction electroluminescence* or *recombination radiation*. The latter refers to the combination of electrons with holes. The resulting wavelength λ (in micrometres) is calculated thus:

$\lambda = hc/E$

where h is Planck's constant (6.63×10^{-34} joule seconds), c is the speed of light (3×10^{14} micrometres per second) and E is energy difference between the valence and conduction bands.

Legacy   A system, application or operating system (OS) that is of a past generation, usually based on mainframe technology. It may nonetheless be integrated into a modern IT implementation and coexist with modern client/server architectures.

(See Client/server.)

Level 1. A defined RAID architecture. *(See RAID.)* 2. High and low levels describe macro and micro features, respectively. In terms of programming languages, low-level languages relate most closely to machine code, such as assembly languages, or instance. High-level languages are those that are a considerable distance from the machine language (in terms of compilation processes), and include C++ and Visual basic. 3. A US-defined series of security grades. *(See Security.)*

LIFO (last in first out) A type of queue. the order in which items are regurgitated opposes that in which they are deposited; the last item placed in the LIFO queue is the first to be retrieved. It may be used to store the return addresses, when a subroutine is called. In this guise it is called a stack.
(See FIFO and Queue.)

Li ion (Lithium ion) A battery cell technology used widely in notebooks.

Linux An open-source operating system.

LIM memory (Lotus Intel Microsoft) An alternative name for EMS (Expanded Memory Specification), this is a method of addressing memory in a PC architecture. Introduced by Lotus, Intel and Microsoft (LIM) in 1984, it was used in Windows 1.x to cache DOS applications. The specification has evolved and numerous different versions are available. In the early days many PCs were fitted with EMS-compliant memory cards. However, growing extended memory (XMS) on motherboards and their EMS compliance drove EMS memory cards into obsolescence. Expanded memory is accessed by reading 16 Kbyte pages from EMS into the memory area between 640 Kbyte and 1Mbyte RAM. A device driver such as EMM386 responds to EMS requests.

Line speed A data transmission rate over media which may be physical or wireless. The unit measurement is typically in Kbps or Mbps.

Linear medium A medium that does not permit user interaction in order to control its sequence. Conventional broadcast television is a linear medium. A non-linear medium such as the Web provides the user with the ability to control its sequence.
(See Multimedia and Web.)*

Lingo An OOP-based multimedia authoring language, which was developed by MacroMedia, it is a most intuitive language even to non-programmers. It can be used in conjunction with Macromedia Director and Macromedia Authorware Professional. Lingo's functionality, syntax and structure are comparable to those of OpenScript, which is a proprietary language included with certain versions of Asymetrix ToolBook. It has become the industry's chosen language for authoring multimedia titles. Using Lingo, Director movies may be interwoven with interactivity by coding handlers that respond to events. Messages that result from such events may be defined in the program code.

Lingo events   Director is driven by four key event categories, which are associated with:

- Frame
- Keyboard
- Mouse
- Movie.

Lingo program form

```
on eventOfSomeSort
go to frame 15
end
```

This simple script operates thus: if the specified event occurs, the play head is moved to frame 15.

Lingo messages   Events invoke the messages:

```
mouseDown
mouseUp
— are sent when the mouse button is either pressed or
released
keyDown
keyUp
— are sent when is either pressed or released
enterFrame
exitFrame
— are sent when the playback head passes over frames
startMovie
stopMovie
— are sent when the movie either starts or stops
idle
— is sent during dormant states
timeOut
— is sent after a specified period following a previous
action
```

Additional messages may be defined.

Lingo if . . . then form

```
on keyDown
  if the key = ESCAPE then
    alert "Cue previous video clip"
    beep
  else
    alert "Escape?"
  end if
end keyDown
```

Further reading:

Roberts, Jason, *Director Demystified*, Berkeley, CA, CA, Peachpit Press, 1995.

Thompson, John and Gittlieb, Sam *MacroMedia Director Lingo Workshop*, Indianapolis, IN, Hayden, 1995.

Callery, Michael, *Learning Lingo, Programming with Macromedia Director*, Addison Wesley, 1995.

(See Multimedia authoring tool, Object*, OpenScript, www.asymetrix,com and www.macromedia.com.)

Link   1. A process by which the object (.OBJ) files are linked with libraries, which include functions, procedures and classes. *(See Compiler and DLL.)* 2. A means of connecting related information in a hypertext model for information storage and retrieval. Hence, user-interaction may be given context. They provide the user with a means of touring non-linear paths through information. Such links of association are taken to limits that are imposed by the design's levels of granularity. Nodes, representing text or images, are linked to provide a potentially infinite number of meaningful paths. For example, a single node representing a linear structure, such as an article, might be linked to numerous other articles and images. Links can naturally exist at a number of levels, either to link complete documents (macro features) or to reference words or phrases (microfeatures) within documents, or complete documents or Web sites that are identified by their URLs. 3. A means by which tables/files may be connected in a relational database management system (RBMS). In the case of a multi-table form within a relational database, such links can refer to how master tables and detail tables are associated as follows:

- One-to-one: each master record is linked to only one detail record at any given time.
- One-to-many: each master record is linked to a group of detail records.
- Many-to-one: a number of master records may be linked to a single detail record.

- Many-to-many: each master record is one of a group, which can be matched to one of a group of detail records.

Such RDBMSs make possible multiple table changes and updates using a single form as a data entry interface. *(See Database, Data warehouse and Relational database.)* 4. A communications path between devices, which may be processors as is the case in MPP designs. *(See MPP.)*

List box   A windows component that provides a means of selecting files. Where the number of files exceeds a certain figure, a vertical scroll bar is provided in order to assist in the process of their selection.

Literary Machines   A book written by Theodore Nelson, which put forward his hypertext concept, its methodologies, its data storage models, and its applications. Theodore Nelson is also remembered for his Xanadu project, which to some is the conceptual birth of the Web. To others the conceptual birth of the Web and of the Internet is accredited to Vannevar Bush through what he described as Memex. Both Xanadu and Memex were perceived as unified information storage architectures, which could be accessed through specific technologies. Through his writings, including 'As We May Think', Vannevar Bush predicted the miniaturisation of information storage media. *(See Bush, and Xanadu.)*

Load balancing   1. A method of distributing the workload across processes and system resources in an effort to optimise performance. it is usually applied dynamically in OO distributed systems. *(See Distributed computing.)* 2. A method of distributing the workload in an MPP architecture, so as processors are as close to the heightened states of operation as is possible. It is carried out dynamically, and may be referred to as dynamic load balancing. *(See MPP.)*

Local bus   A method of connecting video cards, hard disk controllers and other devices more directly to the processor's data bus, thus overcoming the data transfer bottleneck of ISA. Theoretically, local bus technology should permit the accommodation of expansion cards running generally at clock speeds equal to that of the processor's external data bus. Local bus standards have emerged including VL-bus and Intel's PCI (Peripheral Component Interconnect). PCI generally performs better than VL-bus.

Local class   A class which is local to a given block of Java code.

Local glue   A collection of entities that unite client components so that they may operate collaboratively. OLE, OpenDoc, ActiveX and JavaBeans components require local glues so that their running operations may be coordinated. These common OO component architectures use different local glues, where:

- OLE uses ODL (Object Definition Language).
- ActiveX uses COM.
- OpenDoc uses CORBA IDL (Interface Definition Language).
- JavaBeans uses a subset of the Java programming language.

(See ActiveX, Glue, JavaBeans, OLE, and OpenDoc.)

Login and Log off   A model which sees the interaction of components and programs where messages are typically used to request services and data. Software components may act as:

- servers, providing client components with data
- clients, which request data from servers
- server and clients.

Typically it is a distributed OO software architecture platformed on a physical client/server system.

(See Client/server.)

Logical client/server model   A process of connecting to and disconnecting from a computer, network, remote server, Internet service provider or Internet service. A login name is required, as might be a password.

(See Firewall and Security.)

Lomem   The lowest user memory address in system.

Look-and-feel   A term which broadly describes the user interface or presentation element of an application.

(See Application software.)

Lookup service   A directory which stores links or objects relating to available or registered network services.

Loop   1. A repetition of code in a program. The loop is normally conditional, and rarely unconditional. 2. A series of video frames which is repeated.

(See Micon.)

Loose coupling   *(See Coupling.)*

Loss   1. A level of attenuation a signal is subjected to while passing through media that may be physical or wireless. Optic fibre signal losses are caused by impurities in the silica core, and by fibre couplings. 2. A measure of the number of lost telephone calls or connections due to congestion.

Lossless compression   A compression technique which does not rely on the omission of pixel information from a video or image file. Authentic lossless compression should result in video or image quality that is equal to that provided by the uncompressed files. However, the attainable compression ratios are lower than those of lossy compression algorithms.
(See DCT, JPEG and MPEG.)

Lotus Notes   A Groupware implementation remembered as the first commercially successful variant. An evolving solution, it provides network services such as e-mail and documents publishing, and provides easy migration of resulting Notes applications to the Web.
(See Groupware.)

Low-level language   A programming language that provides access to the low-level elements of a computer such as memory locations and processor registers. Assembly language is considered to be a low-level language. Assembly languages are indigenous to the processor type. The language consists of mnemonics, which replace, and translate into, hexadecimal processor instructions.

M

Macintosh   *(See Apple Macintosh.)*

Macro   A short program or series of instructions. A macro is usually provided for repeated use in a program or an application (e.g. MS Word). Macros are useful for automating processes, or for performing tasks that would otherwise take a great deal of time to implement. Typically macros are written when the user interface is restrictive for a given task, or for particular usage habits. They are also written when there is no predefined macro that will perform a desired task. Sometimes certain predefined macros can be improved upon or edited to perform different tasks. Sophisticated word processors such as Microsoft Word and Word Pro have indigenous macro languages. Standard macro languages include Visual Basic for applications.

(See VBScript and Visual Basic.)

Macro level   Links which exist at the macro level relate comparatively large documents or 'chunks'. They are said to exist at a high level, forming part of the chunk-based model of hypertext and hypermedia.

Macromedia SoundEdit   A wave file recorder and editor.

Mailing list   An electronic conference based on e-mail.

Mainframe   A powerful computer that typically offers centralised processing, serving a number of connected dumb terminals. In terms of its positive characteristics, a modern mainframe may:

- process data at speeds beyond those attainable on desktop systems, and those based on conventional 32 bit and 64 bit processors that might be CISC or RISC.
- provide long-term archiving of data

181

- be a massively parallel processing (MPP) architecture, where processes are run concurrently, offering efficient scalable processing
- offer industrial strength operation through robust operating systems and applications
- provide easy diagnosis of faults as they are isolated to the network or to the mainframe itself, though the mainframe with all its electronics and mass storage remains a complex fault diagnosis domain
- provide effective migration paths to client/server architectures
- prove a more durable IT solution in terms of longevity, because mainframe technology advances more slowly than microcomputer technology.

The disadvantages of mainframe computers revolve around the following factors:

- high initial cost
- high cost of ownership brought about comparatively high maintenance and servicing bills
- fault tolerance is at a low threshold, because a mainframe fault may render an entire IT solution inoperable. However, the fault tolerance of the connected mass storage (which may be shared) might be high
- the dumb terminals are typically green-screen, but there is scope for renovation (*See Application renovation*)
- mainframe languages like COBOL tend to be old-fashioned, though this is a changing situation.

MAN (Metropolitan Area Network)   A UK-based network.

MAPI (Messaging Application Program Interface)   A standard that permits e-mail messages to be sent from any application. Originally developed by Microsoft, it is a DLL containing C functions, which allows developers to exploit Windows messages. Calls to the DLL may allow applications to be given e-mail functions.

Marquee   A message scrolled across Web pages, which may be a promotion, advertisement, announcement etc.
(See ActiveX.)*

Mass storage device   A device used to store data. Can be assumed to be either magnetic, optical or magneto-optical.
(See CD-ROM, DVD, Hard disk and RAID.)

Master/slave processing   An architecture where a master computer is connected to slave (intelligent) computers, which are connected to dumb ter-

minals. Processing is distributed from the master computer, which can be assumed to be a mainframe, to the slave systems.
(See Client/server.)

Mbone (Multicast backbone)   A virtual infrastructure to deliver multicast packets over the Internet. It is composed of tunnels and provides limited bandwidth, but enough for audio/video data. A restriction mechanism integrated in MBONE routers or mrouters drops packets over tunnels where a predefined threshold rate is exceeded. Mrouters forward multicast packets to specified destinations. The MBone topology maps are available at www.cs.berkeley.edu:
(See IP multicast, and www.cs.berkeley.edu.)

McAfee   A large international software publisher of tools and anti-virus solutions.

MCIS (Microsoft Commercial Internet System)
An evolving suite of servers used to architect Web solutions. The servers are Windows NT compliant, and include:
- Address Book
- Chat
- Content Replicator
- Internet locator
- MCIS Mail
- MCIS News
- Membership
- Merchant Server
- Personalisation.

(See Address Book, Chat, MCIS Mail, MCIS Nes, Membership and Merchant Server)

MCIS Mail   A Windows NT-based server which can be used to implement mailboxes across multiple Web sites. DPA (Distributed Password Authentication) and SSL (Secure Sockets Layer) are supported. E-mail protocol support includes:
- POP3 (Post Office Protocol)
- SMTP (Simple Mail Transfer Protocol)
- MIME (Multipurpose Internet Mail Extensions).

(See DPA, MIME, POP3, SMTP and SSL protocol.)

MCIS News   A Windows NT-based server that is part of the MCIS, and supports electronic conferencing and newsgroups. It supports the NNTP (Network News Transport Protocol) together with its extensions.
(See MCIS.)

Media Player   A Windows program able to play a variety of different media files. With the appropriate driver selected and installed using the Control Panel, it can be used to play various different media types including:

- CD-DA
- MIDI files.
- Wave (.WAV) files
- Video files.

When launched it shows controls common with typical audio/visual appliances, including Play, Pause, Stop and Eject. Finer control over playing various media files and tracks is provided by a horizontal scroll bar.
(See Video* and Wave audio.)

Megabyte (Mbyte, MB)   A megabyte (MByte or MB) equates to 1024 Kbyte. Sometimes it is wrongly referred to as 1000 Kbyte, as is the case when some manufacturers specify hard disk data storage capacities. Derived from 20 address lines resulting in 2^{20} (1 048 576) memory addresses.

Member class   A member of an enclosing class which is defined using the static modifier.

Membership   A Windows NT-based server which is part of the MCIS and allows visitors to become members of your site.
(See MCIS.)

Memex   An information and storage system concept which was put forward in the 1940s by the visionary Vannevar Bush, Science Advisor to President Roosevelt and administrator of the wartime Manhattan Project. He believed that all published information should be made available through access points, and clearly set out the advantages of association through links. Calling the system Memex, and describing it as a sort of private file and library, he thought that some kind of workstation would be used with user-interaction accommodated through mechanical levers. If there were errors in his vision, it was a total underestimation of the sheer quantity of information that would be published in future, and an overestimation of the technology of the day, i.e. microfilm, facsimile and telegraph. It was Bush's misfortune to live in the era of valves. The solid state

transistor had yet to be invented, and it was some thirty years before the first reasonably sophisticated microprocessor was made commercially available. As such, Memex remained in the minds of a select few.
(See Hypertext, Multimedia, Web and Xanadu.)

Merchant   An entity which accepts payment for goods or services using physical or electronic payment transaction technologies.

Merchant Server   A Windows NT-based server that is part of the MCIS, and permits the construction of virtual shopping sites. *(See E-commerce and MCIS.)* The server consists of a:

- Controller, which is used to define language, currency, date and other preconfigurable parameters.
- Router, which is an ISAPI (Internet Service Application Programming Interface) DLL. This routes requests from the client to relevant parts of the Store server, and routes responses to those requests back to the client browser.
- Store Server, which is the system's backbone, and functions to implement tasks such as order requests and to interact with the backend database.

The Merchant Server may be used to implement sites that allow customers to:

- peruse product databases
- purchase items using a shopping cart metaphor
- receive e-mail confirmation of orders placed.

Merchant Server permits the vendor to:

- query customer details, and purchase habits
- conduct promotions
- conduct marketing campaigns
- create membership accounts using IDs and passwords
- offer membership discounts
- integrate ActiveX, OLE and COM components into the server
- use ODBC-compliant databases
- secure credit card transactions using the SET (Secure Electronics Transfer) protocol together with Verifone's vPOS application.

(See Server.)

Merchant services   A bank department that processes information for merchants.

Message   A request sent from one object or component to another, commonly used in OO systems. The message will be of a standard or proprietary format, with address information and appropriate data. The messages might require an acknowledge message before the originating component may continue processing. OO client/server architectures use messages and underlying protocols as their collective glues.

(See Glue.)

Message authentication   A process or usually sub-process that verifies that a message is received from the appropriate or legal sender.

Message wrapper   A top-level data structure that conveys information to message recipients.

(See Wrapper.)

<META>   An HTML tag to enclose descriptive meta data that may be used by search engines as an alternative to the 200 characters that follow the <BODY> tag.

```
<HEAD>
     <TITLE>Francis Botto home page</TITLE>
     <META name="description" content="IT Research" >
     </HEAD>
```

Francis Botto

The <META> tag may also be used to add keywords of up to 1000 characters to Web page, and may be retrieved through appropriate search phrases, i.e.:

```
<META name="keywords" content="Multimedia, MPEG,
DVD">
```

(See Search engine, <BODY>, <TITLE> and HTML.)

Metadata   A term used to describe data that indicates the information types and subjects. The data may be stored in an information storage and retrieval system. In the context of the Web, metadata such as indexes and URLs are gathered and stored by search engine implementations. This provides clients with the ability to search and retrieve documents from the Web.

(See Search engine.)

Method   A code fragment which is able to perform an operation of a certain type; like writing or reading data or making a connection with a remote server application, or simply sending a message. Methods may be defined in a set of APIs and they may define an object's behaviour in terms of how it responds to an expected event such as a mouse click, and to other stimuli. Other events might be the reception of messages from other objects and how the underlying methods might interpret them and initiate an appropriate response. The response might be an acknowledge message, or a return value such as the contents of a variable.

(See Java, OOP, OpenScript and Visual Basic.)

MHz (megahertz)   A measurement that equates to one million cycles or pulses per second. It is commonly used to describe the clock speed of computers, thus providing indication of speed of operation. A 50 MHz machine will therefore yield 50 million clock cycles per second, and a single clock cycle will have a duration of 1/50 000 000 of a second.

Micon (Motion icon)   An animated icon represented by a number of frames run in a continuous loop. Invented by Hans Peter Brondmo, these manifest more clearly the purpose, feature, application or program to which options lead. Micons manifest more clearly the information, features or applications to which screen options are tagged. It is reasonable to assume that they will consolidate with the current (commercial) user interface approach, coexisting for some time with the generally accepted buttons and icons.

MicroJava   A processor from Sun Microsystems which is optimised for the Java programming language. it is used in network devices, telecommunications hardware and consumer games.

(See Java* and Sun Microelectronics.)

Micropayments   A minor transaction purchase over the Web.

Microsoft   A large software producer and vendor founded jointly by Bill Gates and Paul Allen. Microsoft is a leading computer software company targeting mainly the PC platform. Its best known products are Windows, Microsoft Office, the MS-DOS operating system. It also produces multimedia titles, and has recently extended its operations to the Internet through the Microsoft Network (MSN), and numerous related ventures.

Microsoft ActiveX SDK   An SDK dedicated to the creation of ActiveX controls, compatible with Visual C++ 4.2 (or higher).

(See ActiveX*.)

Microsoft Commercial Internet System   *(See MCIS.)*

Microsoft Design-Time Control SDK   An SDK that is used to create Design-Time ActiveX controls, which, as their name suggests, is active only during design. The resulting controls may be used with FrontPage, InterDev, Visual C++, Visual basic etc.

Microsoft DirectX SDK   A toolset that is used to develop multimedia elements, which includes:

- Direct3D for three-dimensional graphics
- DirectDraw for 2-D graphics
- DirectInput for connectivity to input devices such as joysticks
- DirectSound for exploiting sound card/software capabilities
- DirectPlay for connecting to remote applications.

Microsoft Forms 2.0 ActiveX control   A suite of ActiveX controls included in Visual Basic Control Edition.

Microsoft IIS (Microsoft Internet Information Server)   *(See MCIS.)*

Microsoft Index Server   A search engine which may be used to find information on a Web site. It is included with Microsoft IIS, as is the Crystal Reports reporting engine. It is also a Web server used with Microsoft Windows NT operating system and is bundled with Microsoft Windows NT Server.
(See Crystal Reports and IIS and Web server.)

Microsoft Internet Client SDK   A comprehensive set of tools, components and utilities for ICPs, Internet developers and Web authors.

Microsoft Internet News   A technology which allows Web browser users to subscribe the newsgroups, submit messages and read messages. Microsoft Internet News is invoked from Internet Explorer by selecting Read News on the Go menu.

Microsoft MDK (Multimedia Developers Kit)   A collection of tools which can be used to develop sophisticated multimedia titles.

Microsoft NetShow   A streaming technology server which may be integrated into a Web site/application. Its inclusion results in the ability to serve client browsers with streaming audio, video and multimedia. Web site and Web application developers may integrate it into IIS-based Web application solutions.
(See ASF, IIS, Multimedia and Streaming.)*

Microsoft NetShow Theater Server   A streaming MPEG video media server which extends Windows NT Server NetShow Services to deliver higher quality video, MPEG1 and MPEG2 video streams from 500 Kbps to 8 Mpbs, including:

- scalability of up to thousands of video streams
- a distributed, fault-tolerant PC architecture for mission-critical applications.

(See Streaming media and MPEG*.)

Microsoft Office An integrated software package, which features the following applications in some or all versions of the package:

- Word word processor
- Excel spreadsheet
- Access database
- Outlook contact management program
- PowerPoint presentation program
- Publisher desktop publishing program (in later editions only)

(See Application software, Microsoft*, and Windows.)

Microsoft Proxy Server A server implementation which may be used to deliver Internet access across an enterprise. The Internet Service Manager is used to manage the Proxy Server, as it can for Chat and Mail servers. The Microsoft Proxy Server:

- is compatible with Intel and Risc platforms
- uses caching algorithms to optimise access to LAN data
- includes an Auto-dial feature which connects the user with the ISP if the user's requested data does not reside in the cache
- assign users with access rights to specified Web sites.

(See Server.)

Microsoft SDK for Java A superset of the JDK, it includes Microsoft class libraries, JIT compiler and the Microsoft Virtual Machine for Java.

(See Java*.)

Microsoft SQL Server A relational database management system, (RDBMS) that provides mutli- and concurrent user access to enterprise data. The Microsoft SQL Server's utilities include:

- SQL Enterprise Manager, which provides management features
- SQL Service Manager, which provides start and stop functions
- Interactive SQL for Windows, which permits sessions with multiple SQL servers
- SQL Security Manager which provides access to security features

- SQL Setup which can be used to upgrade MS SQL Server, as well as to change default settings
- SQL Client Configuration Utility, which is used to manage SQL Server client software configurations
- SQL Performance Monitor, which offers performance readings
- SQL Server Web Assistant, which permits the generation of Web pages that use SQL Server data
- SQL Trace, which is used to track SQL Server user habits.

(See Server.)

Microsoft Transaction Server   A transaction manager. A Microsoft solution for integrating transaction processing in Web applications. Its component architecture includes:

- Transaction Server Explorer, which is used for administration and management purposes
- Transaction Server Executive, which is a DLL providing functions used by the application's server components
- ActiveX Server Components, which is used to deploy ActiveX server components
- Server Process, which hosts the application's components
- ODBC Resource Dispenser, which manages database connectivity
- Shared Property Manager, which gives access to a Web application's properties
- Microsoft Distributed Transaction Coodinator, which coordinates transactions, and is integrated in Microsoft SQL Server 6.5.

Other transaction managers include CICs and Encina.

(See ACID and Server.)

Microsoft Video for Windows (VfW)   A video playback, capture and editing program suite. It includes the VidCap video capture program, VidEdit video editing program, BitEdit 8 bit graphics editor, and PalEdit 8 bit colour palette editor. Compression algorithms such as MPEG, Microsoft RLE (Run Length Encoding) and Microsoft Video 1 can help reduce video file sizes by varying amounts. the size and quality of the video files can be controlled using compressors through the adjustment of compression settings, about which more shall be said later. The resultant video may be added to applications through OLE (Object Linking and Embedding). It supports the AVI (Audio Video Interleaved) format and features a number of compressors including Microsoft 1, Microsoft RLE and Intel Indeo.

(See Video*.)

Microsoft Visual Basic *(See Visual Basic.)*

Microsoft Web Wizard SDK A tool that may be used to create Wizards that may be used to build Web sites using tools like FrontPage and Visual InterDev. Tools created using Design-Time Control SDK may be used with the Web Wizard.

Microsoft Windows An industry standard operating system and graphical user interface (GUI) for the PC. It uses the windows metaphor as a means to contain documents and applications. Up until late 1995 when Windows 95 appeared, its foundation was considered to be the Program manager, a main window that contained program group windows. the group windows contain selectable icons of related applications. Windows 95 offered a replacement for Program Manager by way of Task bar. By default it under-scores all applications, providing buttons to select open applications and it anchors the all-important start button which invokes the start menu. This shows options that lead to programs as well as to submenus which replace the group windows of Program Manager. Once invoked the menu system can be navigated by dragging the mouse rather than by clicking menu items and programs are opened through a single mouse click. Application menu systems echo its operation.
(See Windows.)

Microsoft Windows CE (Compact Edition) A version of the Windows OS designed for palmtops, organisers and other small-scale system solution including those targeting the consumer market. It also supports UpnP.

Microwave radio Short wavelength radio waves that have a frequency above 1000MHz or 1 GHz.

Middleware 1. A software implementation or glue which exists between the client and the server. It makes the network protocols and other server workings transparent to the client. Middleware implementations include those based on the OMG's CORBA-based Notification Service that supports push and pull style communications of an asynchronous nature. There is no real-time synchronistation between client (consumer) and server (supplier) applications, rather the client may invoke operations even when a supplier application or complete server is occupied. Both consumers and suppliers invoke operations in the API, which includes modules or files written in the CORBA Interface Definition Language loosely based on C++. Within the files are defined interfaces, operations (or methods), exceptions and certain error codes. 2. Database middleware connects client applications with back-end applications, and consists of:

- an application programming interface (API)
- network and database translators.

(See Glue.)

MIDI (Musical Instrument Digital Interface)   An industry-standard file format and specification for producing and playing electronic music using computers and compatible devices such as MIDI keyboards and MIDI guitar interfaces. It covers hardware, cables, connectors and data protocols (MIDI messages) and file formats. The single most significant advantage of MIDI is the compactness of resultant so-called MIDI song files. These consume a fraction of the data capacity required by digitised waveform audio such as .WAV files. A one-hour stereo MIDI file can consume around half a Mbyte. Even using compression techniques an equivalent .WAV file would consume literally hundreds of Mbytes.

MIME (Multipurpose Internet Mail Extensions)   A standard specification which permits e-mail messages to include multimedia elements. It supports:

- ASCII alternatives, such as foreign language character sets
- images
- multiple objects
- audio
- video
- PostScript.

Included in served files is a MIME code, which has a type and subtype denoting the media included. Types of media such as HTML and GIF may obviously be displayed by any browser. Others such as MPEG video require helper programs. MIME was developed by Nathaniel Bernstein of Bellcore and by Ned Freed of Innosoft.

(See E-mail.)

Mirroring   A function of hard disk controller that writes data to more than one disk drive simultaneously.

Mirror site   An internet site that duplicates functionality of another site. Mirror sites help provide an improved service for users by lowering usage demands on individual sites.

M-JPEG (Motion-Joint Photographics Experts Group)   A type of video that uses individual frames compressed according to the JPEG algorithm. It gives full frame updates as opposed to the predominantly partial frame updates of MPEG-1 video. M-JPEG video therefore provides random access points and lends itself to non-linear editing. In this respect it is more flexible on playback because applications can simply show any frozen frame of an M-JPEG sequence or play any selected frames of a sequence either backwards or forwards. Another advantage of M-JPEG is that it can be compressed into other formats, including MPEg-1/2. A principal disadvantage of M-JPEG, however, is its comparatively low overall compression ratio. *(See MPEG-1 and MPEG-2.)*

MMX Technology   A set of extensions (or additional instructions) that gives a processor improved multimedia performance. The Intel Pentium and Pentium II processors have MMX Technology that consists of 57 instructions. The addition of MMX results in dramatic performance gains in video and 3-D graphics. MPEG refused to adopt the whole of Intel's now obsolete DVI (Digital Video Interactive) technology as a video standard, allegedly causing Intel to abandon its initial plans for an Intel processor with built-in DVI functionality. Intel once announced that it would integrate the functionality of its i750 DVI chipset into a general-purpose processor design. However, the year of 1995 saw Intel unveil its MMX Technology, which is not an acronym but a trademark. MMX delivers performance gains to multimedia-, graphics- and video-related applications that range from 3-D animation programs to videoconferencing. The array of multimedia-related standards, such as those of the MPEG continuum and those that have yet to emerge, fits within the open framework that is MMX Technology. This gives ISVs the freedom to adopt current, emerging and even proprietary compression standards. MMX Technology delivers improved matrix manipulation through some 57 new instructions and gives higher levels of concurrency through Single Instruction Multiple Data (SIMD). Fred Pollack, an Intel Fellow (1997), once stated, 'Preliminary tests have shown performance benefits between 50 and 400 per cent, depending upon the application.'
(See DCT, MPEG* and Pentium.)

Mobile network   Key mobile networks include GSM (Global System for Mobile Communications), PCN (Personal Communications Network) or DCS-1800, and the many UMTS (Universal Mobile Telephone Service). These have displaced the earlier networks like AMPS, and currently account for the vast majority of wireless data and voice traffic. There are also mobile satellite networks like Teledesic, Globalstar and Odyssey. The cost of wireless technology is set to plummet in the early years of the new millennium. For telcos the implications are as serious as those when the copper networks of the 1990s began to be replaced by the then revolutionary optic fibre links. The level and rate of displacement of physical networks and media carries with it important questions for analysts and for many others attempting to forecast the growth of these new deregulated network infrastructures which coexist with those of the telcos, but at the same time which compete with them. As an example, voice telecommunications have bypassed the comparatively regulated international telcos since 1995 when the first Internet phones were introduced. This clearly illustrated that IP networks could provide services other than Web applications. By 1998 growing number of voice calls migrated from the switched networks that were once the preserve of international telcos like AT & T, Cable & Wireless, BT (UK) and Telstra (Australia), to the largely unregulated packet switched (PS) networks using what became known as IP or Internet telephony. With appropriate IP telephony gateways (which are now standard), virtually anyone can set themselves up as a carrier and corporate data networks have done the same with their own IP telephony gateways.

Modal   A term used to describe interaction where the user moves between different modes of program operation. The multimedia authoring too, Asymetrix ToolBook is modal in that the user switches between Read and Design modes.

(See OpenScript and ToolBook.)

Modem (Modulator/demodulator)   A hardware device used for modulating and demodulating data normally received and transmitted over voice-grade communications systems. It may be:

- an internal modem that consists of an expansion card that plugs into the expansion bus
- An external modem connects with the serial port of a computer. It typically measures about 15cm by 10 cm by 2.5 cm
- an external PCMCIA (Personal Computer Memory Card International Association) modem that is little bigger than a credit card.

56.6 Kbps modems are asymmetrical, offering wider downstream bandwidths; thus downloading times are shorter than those of uploading. The ITU has considered two industry standards:

- X2
- K56flex.

The resulting V.90 standard was specified provisionally and finally released in 1998.

(See Shannon's theorem.)

Moderator   A person who checks all contributions to newsgroups before posting them.

MOLAP   An OLAP implementation that supports Multidimensional Database Management Systems (MDBMS), which may be assumed to use proprietary data storage techniques.
(See Data warehouse, DBMS, OLA.)

Monitor   A display device used with computers, multimedia and digital video playback systems. Desktop systems may be assumed to include CRT (Cathode Ray Tube) displays, but increasingly flat-screen TFT displays are being used. Notebooks and other portable systems may be assumed to integrate LCD (Liquid Crystal Displays), TFT or DSTN display technology. Principal technical factors that dictate a monitor's specification are its:

- screen size
- supported resolutions
- non-interlaced and interlaced screen refresh rates (in the case of CRT-based designs)
- supported number of colours that is irrelevant with CRT-based designs.

Moore, Gordon   A founder of the Intel Corporation.

Moore's Law   A law stating that the number of devices that may be integrated onto a single silicon will double annually. The founder of Intel Corporation, Gordon Moore authored his law in t he 1960s.

Morphing   An animation techniques where one image is evolved into another. Its full name is polymorphic tweening. Numerous commercial morphing programs exist. Using such programs, the first step in the creation of a morphing animation might involve loading two bitmaps. The animation program can then be used to produce an animation which merges one of the bitmaps into the other. Modern morphing programs for Windows are able to create animations in the .AVI format, so providing full compatibility with all fully specified presentation programs and multimedia authoring tools. Morphing animation effects provide a means of enhancing the appeal of many multimedia presentations and applications.

MOTO (Mail Order/Telephone Order)   A transaction that emanates from a cad-not-present scenario, and may take place using voice communications or most often using an e-commerce Web site.

Mouse   A hand-held input device. By dragging it on a flat surface it provides a means of moving a screen pointer/cursor in both x and y directions. It is typically connected to the serial port, but may also be wireless. It has two or three push buttons that are used to make selections either by pressing a button once (or single-clicking) or by pressing a button twice in succession (or double-clicking). The mouse is also used for dragging (or moving) objets to move them from one point to another, or for resizing windows by dragging their borders. Dragging is carried out by holding down the left mouse button above an object or window border, and then moving the mouse appropriately. Modern notebook systems use mechanism-free touchpads instead of the traditional mouse.

MP3   A compressed stream of digital audio created according to level 3 of the MPEG-1 audio/video specification, which dates back to 1990. It is a popular format for distributing audio using the World Wide Web and numerous MP3 Web sites exist from which such audio may be downloaded free of charge. An MP3 player application such as WinAmp or even a consumer appliance may be used to play resulting files and they may be recorded or created using an appropriate MP3 recorder. MP3 file quality is determined by the:

- source recording quality
- source format (which may be analogue cassette, CD, DAT etc.)
- source playback device
- sample rate (which be 11.025 KHz, 22 KHz or 44.1 KHz)
- sample size (which may be 4 bit, 8 bit or 16 bit).

(See MPEG*.)

MPEG frames   An MPEG video sequence consists of partial frames in the form of Predicted (P) frames and Bi-directional (B) frames, and full frames or Intra (I) frames. I frames are compressed in a similar way to JPEG (Joint Photographic Experts Group) images and do not rely on image data from other frames. They exist intermittently, perhaps between 9 and 30 frames, and provide non-linear entry points. Increasing the frequency of I frames provides a greater number of valid entry points, but the compression ratio of the overall file diminishes proportionally. Realistically, the compression ratios achieved using MPEG may be assumed to be around 50:1. Higher compression ratios lead to an unacceptable loss of quality and it is wise to forget about 200:1 ratio which MPEG is supposedly capable of producing. Normally this is achieved through a pretreatment process which dramatically reduces the number of frame pixels. I frames and P and B frames are termed Groups of Pictures (GOPs), and the occurrence of each frame might be predefined through the careful adjustment of MPEG parameters prior to encoding.

However, this fine level of control over compression parameters may not be provided by low-cost MPEG encoding programs.

MPEG-1 (Moving Picture Experts Group Algorithm) An internationally agreed digital video compression standard. It is used widely for local playback, and for streaming multimedia over the Internet, and other IP and multimedia networks. *(See MPEG-2.)* The early days of digital video were plagued by the problem of how digital video data should be compressed, thus illuminating the need for international standards for the digital storage and retrieval of video data. Sponsored by the then ISO International Standards Organisation) and CCITT (Committée Consultitif International Télégraphique et Téléphonique), the Motion Picture Experts Group (MPEG) was given the task of developing a standard coding technique for moving pictures and associated audio. The group was separated into six specialist sub-groups including Video Group, Audio Group, Systems Group, VLSI Group, Subjective Tests Group and DSM (Digital Storage Media) Group. The first phase of MPEG work (MPEG-1) covered DSMs with up to 1.5 Mbps transfer rates, for storage and retrieval, advanced Videotex and Teletext, and telecommunications. The second phase (MPEG-2) of work addressed DSMs with up to 10 Mbps transfer rates for digital television broadcasting and telecommunications networks. This phase would cling to the existing CCIR 601 digital video resolution, with audio transfer rates up to 128 Kbps. MPEG-1 was finally agreed, developed and announced in December 1991. MPEG participants included leaders in: computer manufacture (Apple Computer, DEC, IBM, Sun and Commodore); consumer electronics; audio-visual equipment manufacture; professional equipment manufacture; telecom equipment manufacture; broadcasting; telecommunications and VLSI manufacture. University and research establishments also played an important role. It provided a basis for the development of Video CD which was specified publicly by Philips in late 1993. This is an interchangeable format that may be played using both PCs fitted with an appropriate MPEG video cards and compatible CD-ROM drives, as well as Philips CD-I players fitted with Digital Video cartridges. Its development is constant, to accommodate the increasing data transfer rates of both DSMs and other video distribution transports. MPEG-1 compression is optimised for DSMs with data transfer rates of up to 1.5Mbps. MPEG-2 accommodates DSMs and video distribution transports capable of supporting higher data transfer rates of up 10Mbps. MPEG-4 video compression is designed to transmit video over standard telephone lines. An MPEG video stream generally consists of three frame types:

- intra
- predicted
- bi-directional.

Central to MPEG encoding is the use of reference or intra (I) frames that are complete frames that exist intermittently in an MPEG video sequence. The video information sandwiched between intraframes consists of that which does not exist in the intraframes. Information that is found to exist in the intraframes is discarded or 'lossed'. Intraframes can act as key frames when editing or playing MPEG video as they consist of a complete frame. Generally, editing compressed MPEG video is difficult owing to the paucity of authentic access points. However, editable MPEG files to exist, one of which is backed by Microsoft. Additionally an MPEG video stream composed entirely of I frames lends itself to non-linear editing. The quality of MPEG video depends on a number of factors ranging from the source video recording quality to the use of important MPEG parameters that affect the overall compression ratio achieved. Contrary to popular belief the logical operations that provide a basis for obtaining high quality MPEG video are by no means the preserve of expensive video production bureaux. Equipped with a reasonably specified PC and a basic understanding of MPEG video, there is nothing to stop you producing good quality White Book-compatible video on your desktop. Probably the most obvious elements that influence MPEG video quality include the analogue or digital source recording, the video source recording format, and the video source device specification. It can be assumed that the higher resolution S-VHS format will provide slightly better results than VHS, but there will not be a dramatic improvement in resolution because the MPEG SIF is standardised at 352 × 288 pixels for PAL. If you are digitising the sound track of the source video recording also, then you will probably obtain the best results with camcorders and VCRs that offer hi-fi quality stereo sound. When capturing a video file so that it may eventually be compressed, it is important to choose an appropriate capture frame rate, capture frame size and image depth. The capture frame rate should be set for 25 fps for PAL and 30 fps for NTSC. Frame rates that differ from these will cause the MPEG video sequence to run at the wrong speed, and it will not be White Book-compliant. The capture frame size should correspond with the MPEG-1 SIF which is 352 × 288 pixels for PAL and 352 × 240 pixels for NTSC. Authentic MPEG requires a truecolour image depth of 24 bits per pixel giving a total of over 16.7 million colours which are generated by combining 256 shades of red, green and blue. The quality of captured audio that is used as an input audio stream obviously depends upon the sample size, recording frequency and whether mono or stereo is chosen. You can assume that your wave audio recorder or video capture program will provide sampling rates of 11 KHz, 22 KHz and 44.1 KHz, and samples sizes of 8 bit and 16 bit. While higher sampling rates and larger sample sizes yield improved audio quality, the resultant audio stream can consume an unacceptably large portion of the available MPEG-1 bandwidth. With regard to careful adjustment of the MPEG compression parameters there is not much you can do if the MPEG encoding software provides no control over them. If it does, then it can be assumed that a greater number of I frames can improve the quality slightly, though this will introduce an overhead in terms of lowering the compression ratio.

(See MPEG-2.)

MPEG-2 (Moving Pictures Experts Group) An improved version of MPEG-1 video compression supported by DVD technology. It was developed for media and networks able to deliver 10 Mbps data transfer rates. MPEG-1 was developed for narrow-bandwidth media, such as the original single-speed CD drive variants, which offered average data transfer rates of approximately 150 Kbps or 1.2 Mbps. MPEG-2 video may contain considerably more audio and video information than MPEG-1. The most noticeable improvement is the higher playback screen resolutions that are possible, making possible D1 or CCIR 601 quality. DCT is key to MPEG-2, as it is to MPEG-1 and JPEG (or even M-JPEG). As is the case with MPEG-1, MPEG-2 requires decoding solutions, which may be hardware-based such as set-top boxes (STBs), or equivalent hardware implementations integrated in computers. Applications of MPEG-2 video include video-on-demand, multimedia, videoconferencing, etc. It may also be stored and delivered using DVD variants.

(See CCIR 601.)

Further reading: *Information Technology – Generic Coding of Moving Pictures and Associated Audio.* ISO/IEC 13818.

MPP (Massively Parallel Processing) A computer using processors, which may operate independently and concurrently, as well as interacting with one another through interprocess communications. The strict definition of MPP is a system that offers scalability where resulting processor gains increase in multiples that equate to the processing power of a single unit processor. For example, the collective processing power of an MPP system with n processors should increase by x MIPs per added processor(s). The processors may have their own memory and I/O capabilities, and constitute complete computers, or use shared memory. The processors also exhibit channels of interconnection between other processors. These connections constitute the network, and its bandwidth naturally influences the collective processor power of the system. The network is not to be confused with external, industry standard networks such as IP and Ethernet. An MPP network is internal, with the rationale of optimising system performance by permitting the processors to communicate as quickly as possible. Typical network topologies include ring, two-dimensional mesh, three-dimensional mesh, and hypercube. The resulting MPP interconnection network may be specified in terms of its:

- link bandwidth, or the rate at which data may be sent via a direct link, which is a function of clock speed, and data bus width
- switching latency, which might be defined as the period between a processor data request and the reception of that request. This is a function of clock speed, the network topology and the physical location of the serving processor in the network; the farther away it is, the most extended the switching latency.

The processing power of an MPP may be measured in:

- millions of floating point operations per second (MFLOPs)
- billions of FLOPS (Giga FLOPs or GFLOPs)
- trillions of FLOPS (Tera FLOPs or TFLOPs) – in future
- millions of instructions per second (MIPS)
- SPECmarks.

The optimim processing yield depends on distributing processes evenly across the processor array, matrix or network. Program algorithms may perform this function of dynamic load balancing, which is carried out in real time. A common denominator in current networks, is that not all processors are connected directly. MPP architectures are divided between:

- Multiple Instruction Multiple Data (MIMD)
- Single Instruction Multiple Data (SIMD).

MIMD architectures feature memory that may be:

- distributed
- or shared.

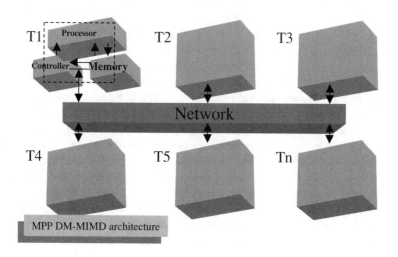

MPP DM-MIMD architecture

The SIMD architecture has a single controller driving multiple slave processors, each with independent storage. The distributed memory DM MIMD architecture has a multiplicity of such processors, and controllers, too. An MPP architecture variant may be explained in terms of its electronic storage, controller(s) and processor(s). Leading MPP manufacturers include Cray, Thinking Machines, Intel and nCube. Concurrent programming languages include Occam, which has its origins in Inmos (UK) where it was developed as part of the Transputer parallel processor. Java is the first mainstream programming language which supports the parallel programming model. Languages that are optimised for parallel processing systems offer authentic concurrency. One of the earliest transputer-based supercomputers was developed by Meiko though the Computing Surface. This was used in the development of DVI, and modern transputer-based implementations are used as video-on-demand servers. Among the advantages of such parallel processing systems is scalability, where for example, growing numbers of subscribers to a Vod service may be accommodated through additional processors, and even complete servers.
(See NUMA and SMP.)

MReply   An e-mail autoresponder, with added features including the ability to send multiple messages to recipients on a mailing list.

MSDN (Microsoft Developer Network)   A Web site targeting developers using Microsoft tools and technologies. Hyperlinks to the site are also included on hybrid CD-ROMs included with the Microsoft Visual Studio.
(See www.msdn.com.)

MSN (Microsoft Network)   A superset of the Web, providing additional services that are comparable to those of CompuServe. Its four main category headings are:

- communicate
- Essentials
- OnStage
- Find.

MTBF (Mean time between failures)   An average period time that indicates the frequency at which a device, component, subsystem or complete system will fail.
(See MTTR and Reliability.)

MTTR (Mean time to Restore)   An average period required to return a failed system to its fully operational state.
(See MTBF and Reliability.)

MTS (Microsoft Transaction Server)   A package which combines a TP monitor and an ORB. These are used to deploy scalable ActiveX component-based e-commerce Internet applications that include:

- transactions
- scalability services
- connection management
- point and click administration.

MTS 2.0 integrates with:

- Microsoft Internet Information Server 4.0 (IIS)
- Oracle and DB2 databases to give transactional connectivity
- Microsoft Message Queue Server 1.0 (MSMQ)
- Microsoft SNA Server 4.0 and the COM Transaction Integrator to give transactional mainframe connectivity.

Multi-field key   *(See Key field.)*

Multimedia   A broad term which may be applied to a system or process which embodies and combines various different media. Modern (digital) multimedia may comprise computer animations, text, still images, digital audio, synthesised sound, digital video and interactivity. Combining still and moving images, sound, audio, text and interactivity, multimedia has initially culminated in a re-evaluation media. Unlike linear, non-interactive media such as broadcast television, it provides users with a choice of numerous meaningful paths. The underlying technology has spawned off-shoots, of which the most notable will be video-telecommunications and videoconferencing. Distribution media disc-based multimedia include Compact Disc – Read Only Memory (CD-ROM). Other less known, distribution media include Compact Disc Interactive (CD-I), and CD-ROM XA (Extended Architecture) discs. The 12cm diameter CD-ROM and CD-I discs typically support up to about 660 Mbyte data storage capacity. A single-sided, single-layer DVD-ROM disc supports 4.7 Gbyte, and supports MPEG-2 video playback. Increasingly, however, multimedia networks are being used, and the most significant of these is the ubiquitous Internet.
(See Hypertext and Web.)

Multimedia authoring tool   A software tool intended for the development of multimedia. Many such tools require no programming skills.
(See ToolBook.)

Multimedia development team   A team given the task of designing and developing a multimedia application. It may consist of experts in all disciplines required to generate the multimedia title, including:

- a producer/director, to enforce an appropriate degree of creative control and oversee amalgamation of media types
- a project manager, to ensure budget and schedule are observed and adhered to
- a high-level language programmers, to design the retrieval system or to write other routines
- a multimedia author, to implement interactive design
- content provider/advisor, who possesses expertise in the material/ information to be communicated
- an associate producer
- a project planner
- an interface designer
- an animation director
- a writer
- an art director
- a lead programmer
- a Quality Assurance (QA) manager
- a sound designer
- an audio visual (A-V) designer.
- 3-D modeler
- a video editor
- a graphic designers/computer graphics artists, to produce original artwork
- sound engineers for recording etc.
- studio technician(s)
- various production staff
- Web site/Internet developer(s).

How many of the aforementioned experts should be included depends upon the complexity of the material and upon what percentage, if any, of the production process is contracted out.

Multimedia presentation   A multimedia-based presentation that might combine audio, MIDI, video, text, animations and graphics. It might be presented on a desktop or even notebook computer using their attached displays, or it might be presented using an LCD projector. Popular multimedia presentation programs include Microsoft PowerPoint, which is included with Microsoft Office. Multimedia authoring tools such as ToolBook, IconAuthor and Authorware may also be used, but these are not dedicated to the production of presentations.

Multimedia producer   An individual given the task of captaining the production of multimedia application/titles. Typically he/she will:

- liaise with investors, if he/she is not the sole investor in the project

203

- often have control over the hiring of personnel ranging from directors to programmers and multimedia production staff, who might include camera operators and even sound engineers
- be responsible for optimising the application of a given budget
- be responsible for originating marketable project ideas
- understand the technical issues that control the quality of a multimedia application
- direct personnel effectively, perhaps toward the use of contracted services and sources of multimedia or Web content
- receive praise or criticism for the complete project.

Multimedia production A process of gathering media files for inclusion in a multimedia application. Multimedia production embodies the implementation of all tasks necessary to attain (in appropriate format) audio and visual materials required. The following components are typical of the production process. The end result should be a collection of usable digital files that can be included in an application. It may involve the following processes:

- capturing video using an appropriate video capture program and capture card
- editing digital video using a video editing program such as Adobe Premier or Microsoft VidEdit supplied with Microsoft Video for Windows
- editing 8 bit video/graphics colour using a palette editor
- compressing video according to preselected parameters that are appropriate to the bandwidth of the target platform
- recording digital wave audio using a sound card/sound feature together with wave audio recording software
- editing wave audio files
- compressing wave audio files
- obtaining still images by scanning, using a still video camera or using Photo CD
- compressing graphics files and/or converting them into the appropriate file formats
- digitising text using a scanner
- marking up text files using a language such as HTML (HyperTextMarkup Language)
- creating Web pages
- creating Java applets.

(See ActiveX*, Java*, JAVAScript, Multimedia, Multimedia authoring tool, OOP, VBScript and Visual Basic.)

Multimedia streaming A real-time delivery and playback of multimedia that may be local or remote. Typically, it takes place over the Web or

Internet, and requires a server and client. Web applications include real-time monitoring or surveillance of remote locations, WebTV and video playback.
(See ASF, Multimedia, Streaming* and Video*.)

Multiple inheritance A concept where subclasses inherit methods and data from more than one superclasses. It defines a class of objects, which inherit attributes and behaviour from multiple superclasses.
(See C++ and OOP.)

Multiplexing 1, A process by which an MPEG video stream is mixed with an MPEG audio stream to form an MPEG system stream. (*See MPEG and Video capture file.*) 2. A process by which multiple signals may be communicated along a single transmission path that may be serial or parallel. The Integrated Services Digital Network (ISDN) standard uses multiplexing, which involves creating a data stream consisting of 8 bit PCM blocks. The blocks are created every 125 microseconds. By interleaving the blocks with those from other encoders, the result is time division multiplexing (TDM). In North America ISDN typically interleaves data from 24 64 Kbps sources or channels. This results in connections that provide 1.536 Mbps, although the connection has a bandwidth of 1.544 Mbps, because each channel's frame has a marker bit 'F', adding 8 Kbps. Europe sees ISDN that typically interleave 30 64 Kbps channels, giving 2.048 Mbps. This and the 1.544 Mbps connection are known as primary rate multiplexes. Further interleaving of primary rate multiplexes sees:

- 6, 45, 274 Mbps in North America
- 8, 34, 139, and 560 Mbps in Europe.

PCM was conceived in 1937 by Alec Reeves, but was not applied widely for many years.

Multisync monitor A monitor that may synchronise itself with various incoming signals. There are many technical implementations of the 'multisync monitor', the simplest of which will automatically synchronise with perhaps two or three vertical frequencies. The term multisync was coined by NEC that it registered. Professional versions are able to automatically synchronise with a range of horizontal and vertical frequencies. This is called the scanning range, and the greater it is, the greater the number of acceptable signal sources. Yet higher specification monitors economise on scan range, thus concentrating on the narrow band of professional graphic controllers beginning with VGA. Such monitors may be considered non-proprietary.

Multithreading A process by which multiple processes within the same application are executed concurrently, or what is perceived to be concurrently.

My Computer An icon/feature on the Windows Desktop, which provides access to practically the whole feature array of Windows 98/2000. It may be considered as the highest level window, in a hierarchical context. Double-clicking the My Computer icon results in the My Computer window that may be used to:

- open important folders such as the Control Panel
- generally access features
- browse, and work with files on mass storage devices that are fixed or removable.

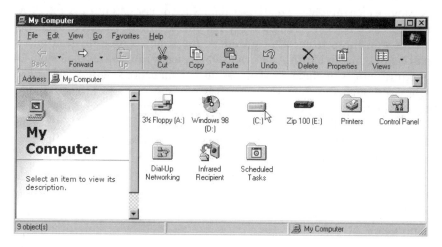

(See Windows.)

N

Nanosecond   A billionth of a second.

Naturally speaking   A popular dictation application.

NC (Network Computer)   A computer designed for connection to the Internet or to an IP network. The subsequent rationalisation of hardware results in low system costs, and reduced costs of ownership. Base case NCs are not fully specified standalone, multimedia devices. They do however offer streaming multimedia functionality, which plug-ins and ActiveX controls can provide to the client.

NDIS (Network Driver Interface Specification)   A standard specification for network interface cards (NICs). It provides functions, collectively referred to as a wrapper, which may be used by TCP/IP protocol drivers. It was developed by Microsoft and 3-COM. Its implementations for Windows may be assumed to be proprietary.
(See Network interface card.)

Nelson, Theodore   The inventor of the term hypertext, and a dedicated hypertext evangelist. He also began project Xanadu, which paralleled the functionality of the Web.
(See Hypertext and Xanadu.)

Nested   1. *Nested transaction*: a technique that sees the integration of subtransactions within transactions. The subtransactions are said to be nested. *(See Transaction* and Server.)* 2. *Nested loop*: a loop in a computer program that is encapsulated within another.
(See Java*.)

Nested top-level class   A static member of an enclosing top-level class.

Net   An alternative shorthand name for the Internet or The Net.
(See Internet and Web.)

Netbanx   A credit card clearance solution.

NetMeeting   A Microsoft technology which permits a multiplicity of communication and information exchange types over the Internet and over compatible IP networks such as intranets. The communications types supported include:

- Internet telephony
- Whitboards
- Application sharing
- File transfer
- Chat
- Multiple participant conferences.

(See Videoconferencing.)

NetMeeting SDK (Software Development Kit)   A software suite that can be used to integrate conferencing features into applications.
(See API.)

NetPC   A PC specification designed for network systems.
(See NC.)

Netscape   A company founded by Marc Andreeson, who developed its initial flagship product, the Netscape Navigator Web browser. The company continues to produce Internet software for users and for developers, including the Netscape Communicator.
(See Netscape Navigator.)

Netscape Navigator   A Web browser produced by Netscape. Its functionality is improved through the addition of plug-ins. Plug-ins for streaming audio and video are available. Like many other browsers, Navigator can be used to send e-mail messages, but it is not an e-mail application. A bookmark window assists users to list and revisit Web sites that are of interest. Images that are shown in the client area can be saved to disk by right-clicking on them.
(See Browser and Web.)

Netware   A network operating system (NOS).

Network   1. A physical or wireless entity that unites computer systems. *(See Client/server, Internet, LAN and Web.)* 2. A physical entity which interconnects processors in an MPP. *(See MPP.)* 3. A interconnecting scheme for neural networks.

Network computing A broad term denoting the use of systems that are connected to physical networks.
(See Internet, LAN and NC.)

Network interface card (NIC) An device used to connect a system to a network. It may be one (or even more) of a number of standard and proprietary variants, including:

- Ethernet
- Token Ring
- ISDN interface
- Fibre channel interface (arbitrated loop)
- Modem (such as an analogue or cable variant).

(See Ethernet.)

NNTP (Network News Transfer Protocol) A protocol for transferring Usenet news between servers, clients and a central server.

Non-interlaced A mode of CRT-based monitor/display operation in which the screen image is generated by scanning all lines in a single scan field. The rate at which all lines are scanned is termed the refresh rate or the vertical scan rate. The frequency that lines are scanned is termed the horizontal frequency.

Non-linear medium A medium whose sequence may be controlled by the user or viewer; interactive television and the Web are non-linear media

Non-preemptive multitasking A type of multitasking in which the operating system does not interrupt applications. It is less seamless than preemptive multitasking in that a reasonable degree of concurrency is not achieved. Windows 3.1 (and earlier) and Windows for Workgroups 3.1x offer non-preemptive multitasking.

Norton A large international software publishing company that produces system diagnostic tools, anti-virus software and other software variants.

Notebook A portable computer with a footprint about the size of an A4 page. A sub-notebook is slightly smaller.

Notification Services An extension to the OMG Event Service that defines interfaces and operations for transmitting events between client and server applications.
(See CORBA Notification Service.)

Novell   A corporation which markets and sells Internetworking products. Its flagship product is Netware.

(See Novell Netware.)

Novell Netware   A network operating system that is optimised for serving information to a large number of users. It caches data read from servers in RAM.

NS message (Notification Services)   *(See CORBA Notification Service.)*

NT (New Technology)   A 32 bit version of Windows, which features an extra layer to prevent general protection faults and unrecoverable application errors.

***n*-tier client/server architecture**   A client/server architecture which sees multiple divisions of application logic and data. The division are distributed across four or more systems, which represent the number of tiers (*n*).

(See Application software and Client/server.)

NUMA (Non-Uniform Memory Architecture)   A variation of the SMP system architecture. NUMA attempts to solve the bottleneck of using a single shared bus to interconnect processors. Instead a number of internal buses are introduced, thus promoting processor scalability. NUMA systems have modules called quads, which include processors, memory and I/O devices that share an internal bus. the modules are called quads, which

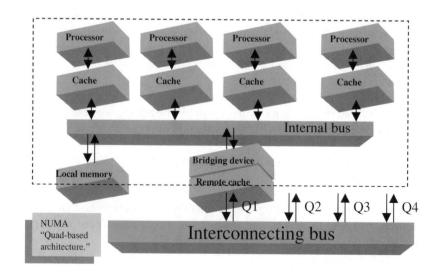

interconnect via a main bus. The NUMA architecture permits processors to access

- local and external caches
- local and external memory.

Its non-uniform characteristic hinges on the varying access time between local and remote memory access. Though NUMA is architecturally superior to SMP, it is not classifiable as an MPP system.

(See MPP and SMP.)

O

Oak An original name for the Java programming language, which was developed largely under the Green project that commenced in December 1990 at Sun Microsystems.
(See Java.)*

OBI (Open Buying on the Internet) A protocol aimed at the standardisation of e-commerce on the Internet.

Object A software entity which may have its own logic, data and member functions that determine its behaviour and response to simulii, such as events, and events it initiates itself. When objects are built they are said to be instantiated. Consider a currency object where we have an object named MyCurrency, and we would get its *value* using the expression:

```
value = MyCurrency.GetValue ();
```

- MyCurrency is the object's name or identifier.
- The period or full stop indicates the part of the object that is addressed.
- GetValue () is a member function that returns a value or an *out parameter*, (and is sometimes referred to as a 'getter'). These member functions may be *set* or *changed* and an *in parameter* is applied using the form:

```
MyCurrency.SetValue(Value);
```

Object factory An entity in an OO programming language that instantiates objects by collecting data required to make instances of an object's class, and invoking class constructors.
(See Object.)*

Object implementation A coded solution which dictates an object's behaviour and response to events. The code represents the object's methods.
See OOP.)

Object interface   An object's outer layer, which intercepts messages and directs them appropriately. The layer is sometimes referred to as a shell. It is the first entity which an inbound message meets. The message may then be processed internally by the object's methods.
(See Object* and OO*.)

Object-oriented   *(See C++, Java* and OOP.)*

Object-oriented language   *(See C++, Java* and OOP.)*

Object-oriented programming   *See C++, Java* and OOP.)*

Object-oriented programming language   *(See C++, Java* and OOP.)*

Object schema   A structure that defines the interactions and relationship of objects in an OO system.
(See OO*.)

Object scraping   A method of mapping data from a server to objects. The objects are used to perform transactions or other types of processing. It may be applied in an application renovation solution.
(See Application renovation and Screen scraper.)

Object-based   *(See C++, Java* and OOP.)*

OCR (Optical Character Recognition)   A program that converts scanned text into text files.

OCQ   A control or object which was a forerunner to ActiveA. OCX controls may be integrated into compatible applications, yielding functionality gains that may take the form of complete applications such as grammar checkers. OCX controls may be written using Visual C++.
(See ActiveX* and C++.)

ODBC (Open Database Connectivity)   An internationally agreed standard, covering database connectivity. Most modern databases offer ODBC compliance.
(See DBMS.)

ODBC 3.0 SDK   A set of tools, libraries and headers which may be used to integrate ODBC 3.0 connectivity access in Web sites.
(See Data warehouse and ODBC.)

OLAP (On-Line Analytical Processing)   A data analysis technique used predominantly in the client/server computing environment. It is a decision-making support technique which may be applied to interrogate data from disparate sources. Resulting data may also be analysed. OLAP implementations may be assumed to embody multidimensional data analysis techniques, and to integrate:

- an OLAP GUI for user communication
- OLAP analytical processing logic
- OLAP data processing logic.

OLAP empowers users to generate query data in order to answer complex questions based on what-if scenarios, or on current and historical data. It is an advancement of the primitive querying techniques harnessed in RDBMS designs. These include Borland (now Inprise) QBE, and even to query languages such as the industry standard SQL.

(See Data warehouse, MOLAP and ROLAP.)

OLE (Object Linking and Embedding)   An object architecture. It is a method by which one application may be linked with or embedded into another. An OLE server application is the underlying source of an OLE client application. Objects may be video, wave audio, speech synthesis, MIDI files, graphics or text. The objects can be shown in the client OLE document or application as an icon, and can be launched by double-clicking that icon. OLE may be used to embed Windows Media Player into client applications to add voice or video annotations to documents. Using OLE1-compliant applications the process of embedding an object is more intensive than that associated with OLE2 applications. Object embedding is made easier using OLE2-compliant applications, because objects can simply be dragged from one application to another. An increasing number of Window applications are OLE2-compliant.

(See ActiveX.)*

OLE client (Object Linking and Embedding client)   An application which has an embedded object or application from an OLE server application.

(See Object and Visual Basic.)*

OLE DB SDK   A Microsoft database access specification which bases itself on OLE and COM object architectures. It complies with SQL and non-SQL databases.

(See Database, ODBC and ODBC 3.0 SDK.)

OLE server (Object Linking and Embedding server) An application which provides an object for an OLE client application, providing a means of running that object from within the client application.
(See Object* and Visual Basic.)

OMG Notification Service (NS) An extension tot he OMG Event Service which defines interfaces and operations for transmitting events between client and server applications. In OMG terminology such connected entities are termed consumers and suppliers, and in some NS implementations the terms are interchangeable with consumers/receivers and publishers. The OMG NS is a *defacto* industry standard messaging architecture. It is a mainstay for many client/server implementations that adhere to the push and pull models as a means of driving information-on-demand. It enhances the OMG Event Service by allowing:

- clients to specify received events by filtering proxies in a channel
- event transmission in the form of structures data types, adding to the Anys and Typed-events of the OMG Event Service
- defined operations (or methods) to provide parameters to suppliers, thus informing them of event types required by consumers on a channel, and providing information about usage habits *(See CORBA*.)*
- event types offered by suppliers to an event channel to be discovered by consumers of that channel so that consumers may subscribe to new event types as they become available
- quality of service (QoS) properties to be set for individual channels, proxies or structured events (relevant CORBA operations include `set_qos` and `get_qos.`)
- optional event type repositories that facilitate filter constraints by end users, and make available information about the structured events flowing through the channel.

The NS is based on a series of CORBA IDL (Interface Definition Language) modules which define operations and interfaces that may be used by consumers and suppliers to connect to a client/server environment. They include:

- CosNotification *(See CosNotification)*
- CosNotifyFilter
- CosNotifyComm
- CosNotifyChannelAdmin.

(See www.omg.com.)

One-click sales A facility that permits on-line purchases to be made without the re-entry of address and credit card details. Instead they are retrieved from data held in a cookie on the client side.

On-line advertising   Advertising which takes place on the World Wide Web. It takes the form of advertising banners that may be placed on many major sites for a fee.

On-ling banking services   A banking service which is platformed on the World Wide Web or other networks.

On-line brokerage services   A brokerage service which is platformed on the World Wide Web or other networks.

On-line state   A state in which a computer or peripheral can perform its intended purpose. For example, a printer may print when it is on-line and it is possible to communicate with a remote computer when it is on-line.

OO (Object Oriented)   A prefix used in object-oriented systems, software and development tools.
(See ActiveX, C++, Java, JavaBeans, Object and OOP.)

OODBMS (Object-Oriented Database Management System)   A data base used to store and to retrieve complete objects including the their code and their data. Stored objects can be categorised and stored in compound structures or objects. OODBMSs are characterised by their ability to:

- store complex objects
- be renovated or updated without radical renovation of data table structures associated with RDBMS implementations
- be extensible, providing a means of defining new data types
- support OO methodologies and concepts, including encapsulation, where objects' inner workings are hidden, and inheritance, where objects may be granted and methods and data of other objects. Multiple inheritance may also be supported where subclasses inherit methods and data from more than one superclass.

(See Data warehouse, DBMS, OO and OOP.)*

OODL (Object-Orientated Dynamic Language)   A programming language which is both object-oriented and dynamic, of which Dylan is a commercial example.

OOL (Object-Oriented Language)   A programming language which adheres to the object-oriented programming model.
(See C++, Java and OOP.)

OOP (Object-oriented programming)   A modular programming approach that depends upon reusable objects. OOP programming tools include

Inprise Delphi, Optima++ and PowerSoft PowerBuilder. OOP languages include C++, Java and Visual Basic. In the real world we unconsciously place objects in classes. We know, for example, that cars, holiday chalets and computers are from different classes, but each time we see a car we don't ask ourselves: which class does a car belong to? Or why is it different from a holiday chalet? We know that it is a member of the class vehicle because we have learned how it behaves, and that behaviour, with all its methods, is in our mind. We do not have to learn or consider an objects' behaviour each time we come in contact with it. For example, you know that you cannot drive the holiday chalet because of its behaviour, and the class to which it belongs. You know these things without having to, repeatedly, decide that a holiday chalet cannot be driven because it has no wheels, no axle, no engine and so on. Object-oriented programs are much the same. Classes of objects are carefully defined. Hierarchies form another important part of classes where, once again, like in the real world, classes are subdivided into further classes. This helps distinguish between, say, a sports car and a jeep. The jeep would be a member of the class OffRoadVehicles which is a member of the class, Cars, which in turn is a member of the class, Vehicles. This additional information tells us that a sports car cannot be driven up a steep muddy slope etc. Everything in the real world is a member of a class, of which there are an infinite number. Some Windows databases come with a number of in-built methods to choose from. These cover standard activities such as opening tables and forms, and even opening the Help window. This type of database building is achieved through a so-called 'pick and build' interface. The OOP model embraces:

- data hiding
- encapsulation
- reuse
- polymorphism.

OOP languages include:

- Java
- C++
- Smalltalk
- Visual Basic

(See C++, Data hiding, Encapsulation, Java, Polymorphism and Smalltalk.)*

OOUI (Object-oriented user interface *(See OO user interface.)*

OO user interface A user interface which uses the object model as its underlying interface components. They are typically graphical user interfaces (GUIs or 'gooey'). The Apple Macintosh is remembered as one of the first systems to feature a commercially successful OO UI, followed by NextStep which was founded by Apple Computer's co-founder, Steve Jobs. This was followed by the Microsoft Windows and IBM OS/2 OSs, which featured OO user interfaces.

(See ActiveX, C+o+, Java*, Object*, OO*, Windows and UI Builder.)

Open buying on the Internet   A protocol aimed at the standardisation of e-commerce on the Internet.

OpenDoc   A standard object or component architecture initially aimed at the creation of compound documents. It is not as widespread as OLE or Microsoft ActiveX component technology.

(See ActiveX*, Compound document, OLE, and JavaBeans.)

Open loop   A relationship that sees cardholders and merchants maintained by different banks.

OpenScript   A programming language included in many versions of Asymetrix ToolBook. It fits into the same programming language category as Lingo, but is dedicated to the ToolBook environment and is not used as widely. ToolBook operates in two basic modes: Author level and Reader level. The Author level mode provides access to ToolBook's drawing and programming tools. It lets you create books, create and modify page objects and program in OpenScript. The Reader level mode provides all necessary features to run ToolBook applications, but does not provide access to the development tools. It lets users:

- navigate through pages, and add pages
- type, edit and format text in fields
- print
- run OpenScript programs.

To prevent users from changing ToolBook applications you can use the runtime version of ToolBook. While authoring an application you can switch between Author level and Reader level instantly in order to test applications under development. You toggle between Reader and Author levels either by selecting Reader or Author from the Edit menu, or by pressing F3.

Scripts   A typical OpenScript is shown below. It plays a MIDI file and shows a page of a video file in a stage. Take for example the script for page 1 which is shown below:

```
to handle enterPage
mmOpen clip "intro"
mmShow clip "intro" in stage "intro"
mmPlay clip "music"
end
```

Like all the scripts associated with page objects this event handler is activated by simply opening, or moving to, the page number. The second line simply opens the video clip stored as intro in the Clip Manager. With the intro clip open the third line shows the first page, or a current page, of the intro video file. Finally, the fourth line plays a Midi file clip stored as music in the Clip Manager. All the page scripts operate in the same way, except they have extra statements to close Midi file clips. The button script below simply closes a MIDI file clip that is played by the page script, and plays the video file in the stage. This requires just two lines of code using the mmClose and mmPlay commands:

```
to handle buttonClick
mmClose clip "music"
mmPlay clip "intro" in stage "intro"
end
```

The script below illustrates a Pause button. It requires an additional if . . . then structure to determine whether or not the video clip is playing. This has to be included because an attempt to pause a clip that is not playing causes an application to crash.

```
to handle buttonClick
if mmStatus of clip "intro" = "playing" then
mmPause clip "intro"
end if
end
```

The status of any clip may be obtained using the mmStatus command.
(See Authorware Professional, Lingo and ToolBook.)

Open-to-buy   An item of information on a credit card that is the difference between the line-of-credit and the balance owed by the cardholder.

Operating system (OS)   A generic term used to describe the software elements that manage system resources and so provide an interface between the user and the system, as well as between software and the system. The shell, user interface or front-end is sensitive to a number of user commands. Popular operating systems include Windows 98/NT, OS/2 Warp, MS-DOS, DR-DOS, OS/2 and Unix.
(See Windows.)

Operation   A term which is interchangeable with method, as used in languages such as C+O+ and Java.
(See C+O+, CORBA-based Notification Service and Java.)

OPIE (One Time Passwords in Everything)   *(See OTP.)*

Optic fibre   A silica-based fibre that can propagate a light signal while inducing minimal losses. Light propagation is driven by total internal reflection. This is made possible using a core fibre and surrounding cladding of different refractive indexes. The light source must emit light into the cable at the critical angle in order to achieve total internal reflection. Applications include:

- lightwave communications
- flex sensing in gloves and bodysuits, which are used in VR

Numerous different types of optic fibre exist, including graded and step index. A step index is one in which the core silica is of one refractive index and its coating silica is of another index. A graded fibre consists of a core fibre that is coated with a number of grades of silica of differing refractive index. The advantages of optic fibre include:

- light and easy to install.
- immunity to electrical and reasonable levels of electromagnetic interference.
- exceptionally wide bandwidth when compared to electrical conductors.
- cost-effectiveness.

The operation relies upon total internal reflection, given by reflecting injected rays in the cladding. The core and the cladding, therefore, have a different refractive index.

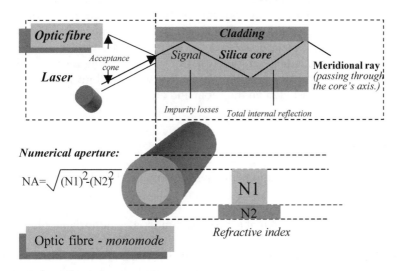

The angle at which rays are injected into a fibre is critical, in order to achieve total internal reflection, and to propagate the ray appropriately. The numerical aperture (NA) of a fibre is a measure of the size of its acceptance cone, or the range of angles at which rays must be injected. Propagated rays may be:

- meridional, which repeatedly intersect the core's axis
- skew, which spiral through the core without ever intersecting the axis. Their launch angle tends to be greater than that of meridional rays.

The light source must be an LED or laser device, which lases at an appropriate wavelength. A multimode step-index fibre may have a core diameter of between 125 and 500 micrometres, and an NA of the order of 0.15 to 0.4. They are able to propagate a substantial amount of emitted light from an LED. Injected light is dispersed into many thousands of paths called modes (hence the term *multi-mode* fibre.) A monomode step-index fibre as a smaller core, and an equally low NA (which is typically 0.1).

(See LED.)

Optical medium   A generic term used to describe a medium which is read using an optical read head. CD variants are optical media, and include Audio CD, Philips CD-I discs, CD-ROM, CD-V, CD-ROM XA, photo CD, Video CD and DVD. Other optical media include LaserVision and Sony Mini disc.

(See CD-ROM and DVD.)

ORB (Object Request Broker   A software entity, which acts like a conduit or bus, enabling objects and applications to communicate and cooperate over local, and over remote paths in client/server architectures. The communicating software components may be written in different languages and may invoke methods or operations that are defined using an IDL, which may also define exception handling. In a client/server architecture the ORB may be physically installed on the client and on the remote system.

(See IDL.)

Orbix Web   An ORB.

Oracle   A database development environment, produced by a company of the same name.

Oracle Media Objects   An object-based multimedia authoring tool.

Orange Book   A set of security standards developed by the United States Department of Defense, and formally named the Trusted Computer Standards Evaluation Criteria.

(See Security.)

OS/2 (Operating System/2)   A PC operating system. Launched in mid-1987 to coincide with the release of the IBM PS/2 family of computers, it is a multitasking operating system able to run applications simultaneously, and is downwardly compatible with DOS. OS/2 is used in conjunction with Presentation Manager, a GUI. Relaunched in 1992 by IBM under the name OS/2 2.0 it is now a relatively successful 32 bit operating system. It is also able to run Microsoft Windows applications in either real of standard modes. The release of OS/2 2.1 in mid-1993 saw the inclusion of multimedia extensions, which compare with those of Windows.

OSGi (Open Standard Gateway interface)   A standard for residential networks.

OSI (Open System Interconnection)   A seven-layer industry standard reference model which is applied extensively to client/server architectures and was introduced in 1983 by the ISO (International Standards Organisation). It provides a standard infrastructure for the applications, glues and communications required of modern client/server implementations. The seven layers include:

- *Application*, which encompasses client- and server-side programs, such as e-mail clients and browsers at the front-end.
- *Presentation*, which is the formatting layer, delivering such operations as protocol conversion and compression. A typical application sees clients' SQL requests converted to a format that complies with the SQL server.
- *Session*, which permits a conversation between programs, objects or processes.
- *Transport*, which provides error detection and correction operations for communicated data, and adds a transport layer ID.
- *Network*, which operates to break down transmitted data into packets (with sequence numbers), and to reassemble them into a readable message on reception. It may be assumed to route packets to an appropriate node.
- *Data-link*, which receives packets from the network layer and adds control information to their headers and trailing regions. The resulting frames are passed to the physical layer when appropriate access is detected.
- *Physical*, which converts frames into binary data so that it may be transmitted, and returns this data to frames upon reception at its intended destination.

(See Application*, Client/server* and Glue.)

OSPF (Open Shortest path First)   A protocol used in routers.

OTM (Object Transaction Monitor)   A middleware variant which exists in an EJB-based server application. It is a TP monitor in the design context of an ORB and is best thought of as an object bus.

OTP (One-Time Password) A password protection security policy to prevent illegal access. In many instances it does not prevent hackers from monitoring the network and gaining access to information. OTP variants include:

- Wietse Venema's LogDaemon
- Bellcore's S/KEY Version 1.0
- BellCore's Commercial S/KEY Version 2.0
- United States Research Laboratory's (NRL) One-Time Passwords in Everything (OPIE).

(See Encryption.)

P

Package   A set of Java classes that address specific functions, where for instance `java.io` addresses input and output functions, and `java-net` addresses Internet and network operations.

Packet   *(See Packet-switched network.)*

Packet filtering   A method used to promote network security, where packets are filtered according to predefined criteria. Packet filtering is possible using screening routers and security gateways.
(See Screening router and Security gateway.)

Packet-switched network   A data transmission and reception technique where data streams are divided into packets coded with origination and destination information. The packets may be interleaved with different data transmissions. For instance, the packets that may be providing a two-way audio communication link in IP telephony, might be interleaved with other streams such as videoconferencing data. Packets may follow dissimilar routes over a network, and are directed over what are perceived as the quickest and least congested routes. If available routes or logical channels are congested, then packets are buffered before transmission. The buffer is a FIFO (first in first out) storage, where the first packet placed in the buffer is the first to be retrieved and transmitted when the appropriate virtual channel is available. The X-25 protocol standard dictates that a packet may contain between tree and 4100 octets or bytes. *(See X.25.)* Up to 4095 logical channels might be accommodated on a single physical link (1997). The logical channel followed by a packet is determined by its header information. There is also error correction, where the receiver might request that a particular packet is re-transmitted. The original packet switching standard for public data networks is CCITT X.25. This is a multi-tiered recommendation embodying everything from physical connectors to data formatting and code conversion. Packet switching is rather like the logistics

225

involved in shipping a motor car part by part. The disassembled parts are sent and then assembled at the factory of destination. Equally, if a part is damaged, the factory will request that it is sent again. The packets may have one of two identities:

- multicast packets (or items of transmitted information) can be delivered to more than one destination
- unicast packets have one destination only.

Packet-switched networks (that use IP) are currently displacing switched networks in the telecommunications industry, and drive the growing use of IP telephony or Internet telephony. The comparative advantages of IP telephony include reduced costs and reduced cost of ownership, for telcos and corporations running IP-compatible networks such as intranets. The reduced costs are largely brought about by the fact that IP and Internet traffic is unregulated. Corporations and government departments may experience savings in the cost of voice traffic that might reach as much as 80 per cent. Flexibility is also an advantage. IP telephony makes better use of bandwidth. For example, Australian telecommunications giant, Telstra, introduced the virtual second line in the late 1990s. This allows subscribers to its ISP (Telstra Big Pond) to receive incoming calls while connected to the Internet.

(See Internet telephony.)

PaintShop Pro   A popular graphics capture and editing program. It has numerous special effects.

Palette   An item of colour information accompanying 8 bit digital video sequences and images.

Palette editor   A program used to edit the palette of 8 bit graphics or video. Palette editors such as Microsoft PalEdit are used to alter the colour characteristics of 8 bit video sequences. They are also useful for building palettes that work with a number of different 8 bit video files. The importance of this relates to switching between two or more different 8 bit sequences on screen that contain different palettes, which can result in a flicker. The degree to which the flicker occurs depends upon the difference that separates the palettes, as well as upon the general video and graphics speed of the playback system. Building a common palette is easiest if you run multiple instances of the palette editor, provided the program has this capability, or where it is able to open multiple palettes.

Palette switching   An instant when a colour palette is switched from one to another. Palette switching occurs most often when 8 bit video is cut from one sequence to another which has a different colour palette, or when one 8 bit still image is cut to another which has a different palette. Palette switching can result in a brief screen flicker. The screen flicker may be eliminated using a common palette for all bitmaps (images) and video clips. A common palette can easily be achieved using a palette optimiser or by using an editing program such as PalEdit.

Palm Pilot   A PDA that is the modern equivalent of an organiser, it may provide much of the functionality gained from personal computers and mobile telecommunications devices.

Palmtop   A small-scale portable PC that runs a streamlined operating system such as Windows CE.

PAN (Payment Account Number)   A number on the front of payment cards.

PARC (Palo Alto Research Centre)   A research establishment founded in 1970 by Xerox. It is the birthplace of many multimedia-associated technologies and concepts including laser printing, local area networks, the graphical user interface (GUI) and object orientated programming (OOP). The GUI system integrated into the Apple Macintosh launched in 1984 was a direct result of Apple's Steve Jobs visiting PARC. During his visit he saw a GUI platformed on PARC's Alto system.
(See Windows.)

Parser   A function of a compiler, interpreter or translator that attaches semantics to tokens, which are generated by the lexical analyser.
(See Java*.)

Pascal   A high-level, general purpose programming language that is used in Inprise Delphi. The original implementation was developed in the mid-1960s by Prof. Niklaus Wirth of Eidgenössische Technische Hochschüle, Zurich. A structured language, it was one of the main advancements in computer programming languages to follow Algol 60. The most popular and successful implementation of Pascal was Turbo Pascal from Borland (now called Inprise).
(See BASIC, C++, Java and Visual Basic.)

Passsword   A series of alphanumeric characters used to protect a system against unauthorised access. By using TCP/IP, the password file, /etc/ password are used to prevent unauthorised access. Servers like Apache, NCSA and Netscape integrate facilities for authenticating users who do no require programming. The principal files are the *access file* (.htaccess) and the *password file* (.htpasswd) that is stored in a secure directory on the server and listed below:

```perl
#!/usr/bin/perl

$passfile = "/disk/mysite.com/ood/.htpasswd";

require "ctime.pl";
$method=$ENV{"REQUEST_METHOD"};
$type=$ENV{"CONTENT_TYPE"};

%input_values=&break_input;
$username= normalize_query
($input_values{"username"} );
$password=&normalize_query
($input_values{"password"} );

open (PWFILE,"+< $passfile") || &croak("Can't open
$passfile: $!");
$salt=reverse time;
seek (PWFILE,0,2);
print PWFILE $username,":",crypt
($password,$salt),"\n";
close (PWFILE);
&croak ("All done");
exit;

sub break_input {
local ($i);
read(STDIN,$input,$ENV{'CONTENT_LENGTH'});
@form_names = split ('&',$input);
foreach $i (@form_names) {
  ($html_name,$html_value) = split ('=',$i);
  $input_values{$html_name} = $html_value;
  }
return %input_values;
}

sub croak {
local ($msg)=@_;
&print_header("System Error");
print $msg;
&print_footer;
}
```

```
sub print_header {
local ($title) = @_;
print "Content-type: text/html\n\n";
print "<HTML>\n<HEAD>\n<TITLE>$title</TITLE>\n";
print "</HEAD>\n<BODY>\n<H1>$title</H1>\n";
}

sub print_footer {
print "</BODY>\n</HTML>\n";
}

sub normalize_query {
local ($value) - @_;
$value =~ tr/+/ /;
$value =~ s/% ( [a-fA-F0-9] [a-fA-F0-9])/
pack("C",hex($1) )/eg;
return $value;
}
```

The access file (.htaccess) holds the following:

- `AuthUserFile/disk02/.htpasswd` which points to the file containing user names and passwords.
- `AuthGroupFile/dev/null` which points to groups of names, although this is unusual in a Web context.
- `AuthName Name goes_here` which specifies the realm.
- `AuthTypeBasic` which specifies the user authentication system.
- `<Limit GET>` which specifies the server method that may also be POST or PUT.
- `Require valid-user` which ensures only valid users access the implementation.

Using HTML the `passwd.cgi` program is integrated as follows:

```
<BODY>
<H1>Input Password</H1>
<FORM ACTION=http://,botto.com/bgi-bin/passwd.cgi"
METHOD=post>
User name: <INPUT TYPE="text" NAME="username"><P>
Password; <INPUT TYPE="text" NAME="password"><P>
<INPUT TYPE="Submit">
</FORM>
</BODY>
```

(See Security.)

path_info   A CGI variable that holds the URL's suffix or that data which follows the script's name.

Path/trail   1. A path through a series of links in hypertext, hypermedia or multimedia material. 2. A statement which points through the hierarchy of directories to a file or folder, and may take the form: C:\jini1_1/source/examples\. They are often included in autoexec.bat files so the user need not type the path of a file or program in order to run it.

Pattern language   A vocabulary of entities which defines the problems and the forces that drive them, as well as the actions that may be taken to obtain acceptable solutions. The language can exist in many domains and sciences and can even be the basis of a new science or technology or simply provide the decision-making frameworks and rules and changes to a business community or organisation. Christopher Alexander, the founding father of pattern languages, invented three key concepts:
1. *'Quality Without a Name'*: an essence held by living things giving qualities such as freedom, wholeness, completeness, comfort, harmony, habitability and durability.
2. *'The Gate'*: an entity which provides access to the quality.
3. *'Timeless Way'*: a flow of patterns through the gate that ultimately evolves and shapes a design or entity.

Payload   A user data capacity of a packet, block, cell or frame that forms part of a protocol.

Payment gateway   A gateway which translates SET messages to and from standard bank financial data formats.

Pay-to-view   An e-commerce site which is created to sell content rather than tangible goods. Pay-to-view may vary from a virtual publication to a TV broadcasting facility or on-line juke box. Implementing such sites requires password access to selected areas and forms for gathering credit card or bankcard details.

PC card   *(See PCMCIA.)*

PCI (Peripheral Component Interconnect)   A local bus implementation which permits the addition of expansion cards to a system. Such cards typically include graphics controllers, internal modems and sound cards. Local bus technology provides high performance communications between such devices and the system processor and memory. It does this by providing a data path width and operating clock speed that is more closely matched to the internal and external data bus of the processor. While PCI has become the industry's chosen local bus standard, Vesa Local Bus (VLB) is also used. Non-local bus variants include:

- IBM's 8 bit XT bus
- IBM's 16 bit ISA (Industry Standard Architecture) or AT (Advanced Technology) bus
- IBM's MCA (Micro-channel Architecture)
- EISA (Enhanced Industry Standard Architecture).

PCM (Pulse Code Modulation) A method of encoding data in digital form for transmission over a network or for storage on DSM. Used in the Integrated Services Digital Network (ISDN) standard, multiplexing involves creating a data stream consisting of 8 bit PCM blocks. The blocks are created every 125 microseconds. By interleaving the blocks with those from other encoders, the result is time division multiplexing (TDM). In North America ISDN typically interleaves data from 24 64Kbps sources or channels. This results in connections that provide 1.536 Mbps. In fact the connection has a bandwidth of 1.544 Mbps, because each channel's frame has a marker bit 'F', adding 8 Kbps. Europe sees ISDN that typically interleave 30 64 Kbps channels, giving 2.048 Mbps. This and the 1.544 Mbps connection are known as primary rate multiplexes. Further interleaving of primary rate multiplexes sees:

- 6, 45, 274 Mbps in North America
- 8, 34, 139, and 560 Mbps in Europe.

PCM was conceived in 1937 by Alec Reeves, but was not applied widely for many years.

Sampling Using ISDN, an 3.4 kHz analogue signal is sampled at 8 kHz. The sampling rate is more than twice the bandwidth of the analogue signal, in accordance with Nyquist's sampling theorem, and prevents aliasing. A sampling frequency in a multiple of 4 kHz was used because the existing networks used 4 kHz carriers, and would cause audible interference in the form of whistles.

Coding The amplitude of each sample is measured, and encoded using standard 8 bit values that give ± 2048 possible values.

Compression The 12 bit samples are reduced to eight bits using logarithmic compression that may be:

- 'mu-law' in North America
- A-law in Europe.

Compression standards permit the system to be embedded anywhere in an analogue network.

(See ISDN, ATM and T1.)

Further reading: *CCITT Recommendation G.711. Pulse Code Modulation (PCM) of voice frequencies.*

PCMCIA (Personal Computer Memory Card International Association)
A slot which connects with almost credit card-size peripheral devices that may be modems, NICs, interfaces to CD-ROM drives, hard disks etc. The original PCMCIA was designed for memory cartridges only, but in September 1991 the PCMCIA Type II (PCMCIA 2.0) specification was launched facilitating hard disks and modem/facsimile devices.

PCX   A bitmap file format developed by ZSoft featuring RLE compression.

PDA (Personal Digital Assistant)   A portable device which serves a number functions including that of an e-mail client, Web browser and organiser.

Peer-to-peer network   A network that permits each network user to access the directories and the peripheral devices associated with any connected computer. When computers are linked together so that they can share the resources of one or more computers, a network is formed. You can build a peer-to-peer network using Windows 95/98, simply by adding Ethernet cards to connected systems. Another type of local area networks (LAN) is the server-based variant, which permits users to access and share information stored on a powerful computer commonly termed a server.

PEM Privacy Enhanced Mail   An encryption standard for e-mail, created by the IETF.

Pentium   A fifth-generation Intel processor, and successor to the 486DX family of processors. Currently the Pentium with MMX Technology is the *de facto* Intel fifth-generation processor. MMX Technology is the registered trade name for Intel's additional instructions that lend themselves to multimedia. They drive performance gains through such applications as speech recognition, video, and 3-D graphics. The clock speed of the Intel Pentium processor has increased steadily, and currently are 200 MHz, 233 MHz, and 266 MHz versions. The more modern Intel Pentium II processor offers yet higher performance.
(See MMX Technology and Pentium II.)

Pentium II   An Intel processor that integrates MMX Technology as standard.
(See MMX and Pentium.)

Pentium Pro   A sixth-generation Intel PC processor which integrates SMP design features. It is used for servers and for workstation-class PCs.
(See Pentium and SMP.)

232

Perl (Practical Extraction and Report Language)   A programming language for processing text. It was developed by Larry Wall who once joked that Perl stood for 'Pathologically Eclectic Rubbish Lister'. He describes Perl as: '. . . an interpreted language optimized for scanning arbitrary text files, extracting information from those text files, and printing reports based on that information. It's also a good language for many system management tasks. The language is intended to be practical (easy to use, efficient, complete) rather than beautiful (tiny, elegant, minimal). It combines (in the author's opinion, anyway) some of the best features of C, sed, awk, and sh, so people familiar with those languages should have little difficulty with it. (Language historians will also note some vestiges of csh, Pascal, and even BASIC-PLUS.) Expression syntax corresponds quite closely to C expression syntax . . .'

Perl variables   Scalar variables are assigned single data values, which may be integer, floating-point or string:

```
$tasform-25;
$response="You did not enter the correct patient
symptoms.";
```

Numeric variables are incremented using the syntax:

```
$transform- transform+1;
```

or

```
$transform++;
```

Numeric variables are decremented using the syntax;

```
$transform—;
```

Subroutines are named using the sytax:

```
&subroutine;
```

perl arrays   An array of scalars is defined using the syntax:

```
@trans(2,4,5);
text:The number '4' in the defined three-element array is
addressed thus:
$tate=@trans(1);
```

Arrays may be combined using the syntax:

```
@combine=(@trans, @forward);
```

The definition of array variables is accompanied by the generation of scalar variables (of the same name) that have the @ # prefix. These store the array size, or more precisely the sequence number of their final element. The array size need not be defined, and it is legal to insert elements into an array at whatever point, thus:

```
@transform = (10,25,35,55);
$transform[25] = 7;
```

An associative array of scalars may be assigned to a variable (with the % prefix) thus:

```
%transform = ("x",100, "y",20, "z",20);
```

This equates transform to the element strings x, y, and z, whose values are 100, 20 and 20.

subroutines   Subroutines begin with the word sub and its code or block is contained within opening and closing braces, this:

```
sub transformt_every {
    $tate=@trans(1);
}
```

(See CGI.)

Persistence   A preservation of states which may be reestablished following a network or system failure.

Personal Web Server   *(See PWS.)*

PGP (Pretty Good Privacy)   An asymmetric cryptosystem that is in the public domain, and was invented Phil Zimmerman. It is used along with RSA by SET (Secure Electronic Transactions) for security and authentication services.

(See Adymmetric*, Brute Force*, Ciphertext, Cryptosystem, Dictionary attack, Encryption, Plaintext, Public key encryption, RSA*, SET* and Transposition.)

PHP   An *active server page* technology for Unix Web servers.

Piano   A wireless and spontaneous networking technology for small networks. Piano provides discovery and lookup services within a 5 m range. Piano supports peer-to-peer networking and uses the Internet Protocol (IP). Piano may provide Internet access using Jini pods or gateways that unite Piano networks and Jini-enabled IP networks.

(See Jini.)

PicoJava   A chipset from Sun Microelectronics, which is optimised for the Java programming language. It is used in cellular phones, and computer peripherals.

(See Java* and Sun Microelectronics.)

PIN (Personal Identification Number)   A number assigned to an ATM cardholder.

Ping   A name for ICMP (Internet Control Message Protocol) Reply/Echo. It is also used to describe programs that use ICMP. ICMP is used to test the reliability and connection speed to a remote host. The reply to such a test is called a pong.

Pipe   A network communication channel, which provides a means of transferring packets between local or wide destinations. Pipes have addressable names and may be used to send and receive data (which is typically assembled into packets) to and from a central computer over a WAN.

P & L (Profit and Loss)   A report that documents the difference between an enterprise's profits and losses, and is usually published annually as part of a company report that is typically used by business analysts and investors and even by potential employees as they gauge the performance and current state of the enterprise.
(See balance sheet.)

Plaintext   An input into an encryption algorithm or cipher, which becomes ciphertext. Wen ciphertext is processed by a decryption algorithm it is returned to plaintext.
(See Asymmetric*, Brute Force*, Cryptosystem, Dictionary attack, Encryption, Public key encryption, RSA, SET* and Transposition.)

PLC (Public Limited Company)   An enterprise which has been floated on the stock exchange. It has shares which may be bought and sold on the share market using on-line brokerage or traditional brokerage services. Various types of shares exist, and agreed dividends are paid annually by the company to shareholders who have certain democratic rights and may vote at meetings of the shareholders. They may decide on such matters such as whether or not a merger or a buyout should take place.

Plug-in   A software component which is in the same market space and functionality domain as ActiveX controls and applets, and typically adds capabilities to browsers. Netscape is remembered as having introduced plug-ins for the Navigator browser. They are not downloaded as part of an HTML page, and are not architecture neutral as is the case with applets. Instead the user installs them and many exist on the Internet as freeware and shareware. Browsers may harness plug-ins using the EMBED tag which includes the SRC attribute that points to the file used.

PnP (Plug and Play)   A hardware specification that ensures easier installation using Windows 95/NT. PnP hardware devices can be detected and installed by Windows 95/NT.

POI (Pont-Of-Information)   A means of exhibiting products electronically through the Internet or other medium such as CD-ROM or DVD-ROM. Traditionally, consumer education has consisted of publishing product brochures, advertising, allowing the potential customer to peruse in a shop or showroom, and product demonstrations. These generally accepted ways in which the consumer chooses an appropriate product may be aided or replaced using multimedia in a point-of-information (POI) guise. POI terminals present the customer with the ability to browse through product ranges, or experience just those items that fit a user-defined profile. POI can be a powerful marketing and advertising tool, providing the means to display products. The benefits are clear: it gives an opportunity to promote products in a medium that cannot be rivalled by (current) television advertising. It also allows small and medium-sized companies to promote products on terms that only large companies and corporations could previously afford. Furthermore, if products may be demonstrated adequately through multimedia, the need to exhibit them physically becomes unnecessary and so floor space may be saved. Research also indicates that users of POI terminals spend more money than those shoppers using conventional means. Finally, the possibility of fewer sales staff is raised. With the growing number of multimedia systems in the home and with the falling price of disk replication, POI may be distributed free like junk mail. In the computer industry, there is also the possibility of distributing short advertisements/demonstrations containing video sequences on floppy disk. Museums of various kinds throughout the world have installed POI terminals. These give visitors the opportunity to follow user-defined guided tours. Such an approach also allows visitors to experience interesting items which might otherwise be catalogued and hidden away from public view. Many other areas such as careers advice, geographic information systems, surrogate travel (brochures) are also possible through POI.

Polymorphism   An object-oriented concept where an entity has many forms. For example, a function call can be used to apply an object in different ways. The object might be button, whose various forms include different methods which determine its response to mouse clicks. Polymorphism allows messages to stimulate context-sensitive processing. For instance, the message might be interpreted by one of a number of methods in a single object.

(See C++, Java* and OOP.)

POP3 (Post Office Protocol)   A protocol for sending and receiving e-mail. Compliant e-mail applications are called POP3 agents.

Port 1. A channel through which a computer communicates/drives a peripheral device. Standard PCs include Centronics parallel ports, and serial ports (which are often referred to as COM ports). Typically parallel ports are used to connect with such peripherals as printers, mass storage devices and scanners. Serial ports are often used to connect with external modems. Other ports include Five wire and USB (Universal Serial Bus). 2. A method of translating a program from one platform to another, or from one language into another. 3. A port number used by a server.

Portable Object Adapter A CORBA 3.0 technology which gives portability across different ORBs for server-side components.

Portal site A site that provides multiple links or search engine functions which give access to Web sites, their metadata and their Web pages. It may be arranged to search categorised information such as shopping, MP3 files, video files and graphics. It is sometimes interchanged with the less popular term *gateway*. Examples of portal sites include Yahoo, Excite, Netscape, Lycos, CNET, Microsoft Network, and America Online's AOL.com. Niche portals are subject oriented and might address weather forecasts, gardening and many other topics. Some portals may be customised to suit the user's search habits. *Portal space* refers to the market for portal sites of a certain category.

POS (Point-Of-Sale) 1. An automated credit card or bank card transaction. 2. A method of selling products or services from e-commerce Web sites, or even multimedia booths.

post method *(See CGI*.)*

PostScript A standard formatting language used to store and print documents. Many commercial printers and reprographics bureaux are able to accept files in the PostScript format, from which they are able to print or produce films. The language itself is the property of Adobe. PostScript printers are more expensive than others, mainly because Adobe require licence fees.

Post-transactional page A page that confirms an order, it is often accompanied by a further confirmation using e-mail.

PowerBook A range of notebooks manufactured by Apple Computer. Such notebooks may operate as DOS, Windows and Windows NT using emulation software.

PowerPC   A processor architecture designed for Microsoft and Apple OS compatibility. The technology is integrated in Apple desktop and notebook systems.

PowerPoint   A presentation program that is marketed and sold by Microsoft. It may also be used as a drawing package, and is include in the Microsoft Office integrated package.

PowerPoint Animation Player   A Microsoft animation player, which can be added to Web pages.
(See ActiveX control.)

PPP (Point-to-Point Protocol)   A standard protocol used with Internet access technologies. It is a way of assigning an IP address to a customer of an ISP.
(See SLIP.)

Precedence   In C++, arithmetic operators have a precedence value. These indicate the order in which such operators are implemented, which is significant with expressions such as:

```
dev = xx + yy * zz + yy;
```

Control over such arithmetic operations is obtained by using parentheses, i.e:

```
 dev = (xx + yy) * zz;
```

Parentheses may be nested.
(See C++.)

Preemptive multitasking   A type of multitasking in which the operating system interrupts applications running concurrently. It is more seamless than non-preemptive multitasking in that a higher degree of concurrency is achieved. Windows 95 and OS/2 Warp embody preemptive multitasking.

Pretty Good Privacy   *(See PGP.)*

Private key encryption   An encryption model that requires the sender and the receiver of encrypted matter to use a secret password key. The size of the key (in bits, such as 56 bit) is a function of the encryption techniques harnessed.
(See Encryption.)

Process flow   A diagram which shows the processes included in a system architecture. It shows how the processes, and their leaf processes, interrelate and interact with entities that might be data or program modules.

Processing fees A fee charged by acquirers and merchants for using inter-change networks or for using merchant account services.

Processing power A measure of a system's processing performance. It can be measured in:

- millions of floating point operations per second (MFLOPs)
- gigaFLOPs or billions of FLOPs (GFLOPs)
- tera FLOPS or trillions of FLOPs (TFLOPs)
- the rate at which instructions are executed in millions of instructions per second (MIPs)
- SPECmarks
- whetstones
- dhrystones.

Processor A device that embodies the functionality of a CPU (Central Processing Unit). The familiar Intel PC processor continuum broadly equates to: 4004, 8088, 80286, 80386DX, 80836SX, 80486DX, 80486SX, 80486DX2, Pentium, Pentium II, Pentium Pro. The generic PC processor continuum is a little more complex with companies such as AMD (Advanced Micro Devices) and Cyrix producing reverse-engineered, and often enhanced, Intel compatible processors.

Programmer An individual that creates programs and works in a software development environment. Typically programmers have specialist skills and concentrate on certain programming languages. The most popular languages are of the general-purpose OOP variety that include C++ and Java. Visual basic is also popular but there is a school of thought that believes it is not an authentic OOP language. However, a contesting school believes that it is an OOP language. Such high-level languages may be used to create standalone applications, ActiveX controls, clients, applets and many other software types. Scripting languages are also popular and include the object-based JavaScript and JScript that may be used to create dynamic content for Web applications. An equivalent scripting language is VBScript, though this is not considered to be object-based at present. The most popular scripting language is HTML (HyperText Markup Language) that is used to format and create Web pages and on-line applications. An improved version of HTML is called XML.
(See Software development.)

Programming language A language used to create an operating program, component or even script. Typically programmers have specialist skills and concentrate on certain programming languages. the most popular languages are of the general-purpose OOP variety that include C+o+ and Java. Visual Basic is also popular but there is a school of thought that believes it is not an authentic OOP language. However, a contesting school believes that it is an OOP language. Such high-level languages may be used to create standalone applications, ActiveX controls, clients, applets and many other software types. Scripting languages are also popular and include the object-based JavaScript and JScript that may be used to create dynamic content for Web applications. An equivalent scripting language is VBScript, though this is not considered to be object-based at present. The most popular scripting language is HTML (HyperText Markup Language) that is used to format and create Web pages and on-line applications. An improved version of HTML is called XML.

(See C++*, Java*, OOP, OO* and Software development.)

Programming tool   An item of software used to develop software.

Project planning   A process of planning a project so that its component parts are completed on time. The compilation of a design, development and production schedule is essential for the efficient use of studio time or for providing a completion date. As with costing, estimation may play a role, the accuracy of which will increase with greater experience. A reasonable starting point for accurate scheduling is a design network, within which the frequency of targets or milestones depends upon fineness of granularity. A low-level approach will yield a more accurate basis upon which to build a precise schedule, where each stage can be allocated a precise period of time. the real function of a design network, however, is to illuminate a critical path, highlighting those stages whose target dates will, if exceeded, set back the entire project. Equally, less important stages manifest themselves. For example, it might be found that certain production processes running in parallel with application development can overshoot target dates without setting back the completion date.

Properties   A set of attributes associated with an entity which may be a simple font or window, or a complex container that has an embedded application.

Proprietary   A prefix denoting non-standard hardware or software.

Protocol   A format used to transmit and to receive data. Examples of industry standard protocols include IP, Ethernet, SMTP and HTTP. Each protocol is optimised for the information it is intended to carry and for the network over which it is to used. A protocol often consists of:

- an information field for data
- the destination address
- error detection and correction codes
- originating address

All of this information is held together in a single unit that might be a *packet, cell* or *frame*. In IP networks, such as the Internet and intranets, they are called packets, but it is just a new term; really they are all the same thing. The packets are assembled at the point of transmission and sent over various different paths to their destination. Once received they are checked for errors and then appropriately assembled. Network protocols are analogous to the Royal Mail: the packets are comparable to envelopes, and they have destination and originating addresses etc.

Proxy object An object that may be passed to a client to provide access to remote objects via an interface. Jini has consumer services in this area, where a proxy object is passed to a JVM.

Proxy server A intermediate server on the communications path between server applications and data entities, and the client systems and software.

Pseudo-conversational communication A communication regime between two software components or objects that exists only for the duration of interaction.

Psion A manufacturer of portable devices that include organisers.

PSTN (Public Switched Telephone Network) A voice-grade, public telephone network.
(See Packet-switched network.)

Public domain CGI script A script that is freely available from a Web site and requires no payment.
(See www.eff.org.)

Public key *(See Cryptography.)*

Public key encryption An encryption technique that requires both private and public keys. A public key is used to encrypt sent data.
(See Encryption.)

Publishing medium A medium that may be used to publish information. The Internet, CD-ROM and DVD-ROM are publishing media.

241

Pure transaction   A transaction which occurs under control and all shared access to resources is coordinated.

(See Transaction*.)

Push technology   A technology with which a user is served requested Web-sourced information. It is sometimes referred to as the push model.

PWS (Personal Web Server)   A downsized implementation of IIS bundled with Microsoft FrontPage. It can be used to:

- test Web applications
- build intranets.

Python   An OOP language.

Q

QBE (Query By Example) A proprietary database querying method introduced by Borland through the Paradox RDBMS. It involves completing forms and using arithmetic operators, to interrogate tables. It offers users the basic functionality of SQL, but is not a language.
(See SQL.)

Quality of Service (QoS) A set of attributes that determine the reliability and performance of a given service that may be a real-time event channel in an OMG NS middleware implementation, or a complete network service. Factors that typically influence QoS of numerous and include software attributes that may be given values such as the maximum number of channels supported, or the time out values, or leases that objects hold. Collective system elements that include network coupling, read/write latency, protocols, protocol translation, NICs, networks, servers, clients also determine QoS values.
(See Reliability.)

Query A question that may be implemented in code such as SQL or by completing a query table, that is presented to a database which returns an appropriate result.

QUERY_STRING A CGI variable that holds the 'query' part of an HTTP GET request, which is the URL's suffix portion following '?'.

Queue A contiguous series of memory locations utilised as a temporary storage area. It is a FIFO (First In First Out) system in that the order in which items are dispensed is the same as that in which they were deposited.

QuickTime A video compression standard. It appeared in advance of the Microsoft Video for Windows (AVI) video standard. QuickTime files may be converted into Video for Windows (VfW) format using a utility supplied with VfW.

(See AVI.)

QuoteChar ( )   In the JDK 1.0 this can be used to specify a character which delimits strings.

Qxl.com   An on-line auction site.

R

RAD tool (Rapid Application Development tool)   A development tool that expedites application development. Its identity hinges on a number of identifying features, which may include:

- authentic object-oriented programming (OOP)
- visual programming methodologies
- industry-standard component architectures such as ActiveX or JavaBeans
- useful program libraries
- features that are appropriate to the collaborative team development environment. These may include security features that can be used to provide team members with access rights to objects so that they may be developed.

(See ActiveX*, C++, Java* and Visual Basic.)

Radio button   A series of buttons in which only one may be selected at a time. For example, using HTML you may add radio buttons using the following form that merely displays four radio buttons labelled £30, £40, £50 and £60:

```
<FORM> NAME="Customer"
ACTION="http://botto.com/cgibin/form/cgi
METHOD=get>

<INPUT TYPE="radio" NAME="rad" VALUE="1">
£30
<INPUT TYPE="radio" NAME="rad" VALUE="2">
£40
<INPUT TYPE="radio" NAME="rad" VALUE="3">
£50
<INPUT TYPE="radio" NAME="rad" VALUE="4">
£60
</FORM>
```

RAID (redundant Array of Independent Disks)　A mass storage device that has many individual disks. Identifying features of RAID may include:

- high levels of fault tolerance
- scalability through the addition of hard disks
- hot-swappable disks, meaning that they may be removed and replaced without the need to power down the RAID
- redundant power supplies for improved fault tolerance
- shared mass storage, serving disparate computers/networks
- heterogeneous characteristics, where they may be integrated into environments comprising multiple OSs
- high-speed interfaces such as Fibre Channel and Ultra SCSI.

The original RAID specification originated from UC Berkeley in 1987, and was named Redundant Array of 'Inexpensive' Disks. The aims of the Berkeley group were threefold:

- to improve fault tolerance of mass storage
- to reduce mass storage costs
- to improve mass storage performance.

Realising the inescapable fact that no single mass storage system could be optimised in all three of the aforementioned areas, the group defined what were to become a number of industry-standard solutions. Achieving its objectives to varying degrees, the Berkeley group defines a series of RAID levels employing several tried and tested data storage techniques. One of these was mirroring where data is written to, and read from, pairs of disks concurrently in order to deliver fault tolerance. Modern RAID systems may be specified in terms of:

- maximum data storage capacity which is typically in the Gbyte range for a single RAID unit and is in the Tbyte range for multiple connected units
- average access time measured in millseconds (ms)
- average and burst data transfer rates
- cache size
- interface type
- multiplicity of host types that may be connected
- OS compatibility.

RAID performance has obvious effects, and high-performance echoes performance gains that are felt locally and remotely. The five levels of RAID defined by the Berkeley group include the following:

- Level 0, which stripes data across multiple disks, but provides no error correction or redundancy.
- Level 1, which uses duplexing or mirroring, where data is written concurrently to pairs of independent disks, promoting a high degree of fault tolerance.

- Level 2, which stores and reads data by dividing it into bits and storing them on different drives, otherwise known as *striping*. It also stores ECC codes on dedicated disks.
- Level 3, which divides data into blocks, storing them on different independent disks. One additional disk contains parity data.
- Level 4, which stripes data blocks across multiple disks. One additional disk contains parity data.
- Level 5, which stripes data blocks across multiple disks, while parity data is stored multiple disks.

Other RAID configurations include Level 6 and Level 7, neither of which were devised by the Berkeley group. Level 7 offers improved fault tolerance, and is patented by Storage Computer Corporation.

(See Hard disk.)

RAM (Random Access Memory)   A volatile form of electronic memory. It is described as random access because the access time is constant. DRAM is used for system memory and is used mainly in the form of SIMM (Serial In-line Memory Module) electronic assemblies and occasionally SIPP (Serial In-line Pinned Package) assemblies. The principal advantage of DRAM is its low cost, while its disadvantage is its comparatively slow speed. Typically slow RAM will be of the order of a 100 ns (nano seconds. Fast RAM will be of the order of 60 ns or even 50 ns). Enhanced Data Out (EDO) RAM offers higher performance, while Static Dynamic RAM (SDRAM) might offer access times of 10 or 12 ns. Static RAM (SRA is generally faster than DRAM because it does not require constant cyclic refreshment. Its disadvantage is that of high cost. It is used widely for external processor caches.

RAS (Remote Access Services)   A RAS feature/program permits you to dial-in to remote networks and to ISPs. Windows NT features RAS compliance.

RDBMS (Relational Database Management System)   *(See DBMS.)*

RealAudio   A streaming audio technology for deploying real-time audio over the Web.

(See Streaming.)*

RealNetworks   A software publisher which manufactures media players that include RealPlayer, RealPlayer G2 and RealPlayer Plus.

(See RealPlayer.)

RealPlayer   A media player which is able to deliver streaming audio and video, as well as play local media files. It provides options to connect to streaming media sites including those associated with radio and broadcasting.
(See Streaming media.)

Real time   1. A program or system that responds to user interaction, instantly. 2. A program or system which captures and/or compresses data at the rate it actually occurs. For example a live satellite broadcast link is in real time.

Real-time compression   A technique where an uncompressed video stream is compressed while it is played at full speed.

Real-time video capture   A video capture technique where a source video recording is digitised and stored as it is played at full speed.
(See Video capture file.)

Record   A row in a database table, or a collection of fields that contain field values.

Recursion   A property of a programming language that enables procedures to be called by their own code. Such compliant languages are termed recursive.
(See C++.)

Red Book Audio   An industry term used to describe the official Compact Disc-Digital Audio (CD-DA) specification that defines the audio CD.

RedHat   A popular version of the Linux operating system.
(See OS.)

Redirected URL   A page or URL which converts one URL into another.
(See URL.)

Referrer log   A log that tracks the user's visited pages.

Referring site   A site that offers links to other sites.

Refresh rate   A measurement of the rate at which all lines on a CRT-based monitor are scanned. It is quoted in Hz.
(See Monitor.)

Relational database An information storage and retrieval application. Using a relational database, information is stored in records that are divided into fields of different types including text, numeric, data, graphic, and even BLOB (Binary Large OBject). The records are stored in tables or files. Records from one file can be linked to records stored in a separate file or table. Codd's standard text about relational databases published in the 1960s specified different types of relational links. Types of link include one-to-one, one-to-many, and many-to-many. There are many commercial examples of the relational database that base their design on the original writings of Codd. Relational databases are formally referred to as RDBMSs (Relational Database Management Systems) whereas flat-file databases are termed simply DBMSs (Database Management Systems). Commercial examples of software products that permit the development of RDBMSs include Borland Paradox for Windows, dBase, Microsoft Access, Ingres, and Compsoft Equinox. All fully specified RDBMS development tools include an indigenous programming language. For instance, Paradox for Windows has ObjectPAL (Paradox Application Language) which is a visual programming language. Important relational database features include:

- ODBC1 or 2 (Open Database Connectivity) compliance
- maximum table or file size
- speed of operation
- BLOB (Binary Large OBject) support permits the storage of field values that include executables and digital video files.

(See Data warehouse, DBMS and OODBMS.)

Reliability A measure of the period of down-time which a system will endure. It may be expressed as a percentage value, indicating the portion of time that the system will be fully or even partially operational. Such a measure of availability (A) may be applied to devices, components, sub-systems, systems, networks etc. Availability may be calculated using the:

- MTTF (Mean time to restore), which is the average time period required to return a failed system to its fully operational state
- MTBF (Mean time between failures), which is the average time period that indicates the frequency at which a device, component, subsystem or complete subsystem will fail.

```
Availability (A) = MTBF/(MTBF + MTTR)
```

Collective Availability   (Ac) of a complete system is equated to the product of the Availability for each individual component. For example:

```
Availability (Ac) = Clients (Au) * Server (As) *
Network (An) * ......* Router (Ar)
```

Remote   An application or data entity that is not local, and is not on the user's machine in a permanent form.
(See 3-tier.)

REMOTE_ADDRESS   A CGI variable that holds the clients' or proxy's IP address from where the request is being made.

REMOTE_HOST   A CGI variable that holds the hostname of the client or proxy making the request, or its IP address only when NO_DNS_ HOSTNAMES is defined in the config.h file.

Remote Method Invocation (RMI) over Internet Inter-Orb Protocol   *(See RMI over IIOP.)*

Removable medium   A medium that may be removed from the computer. Examples include floppy disks, CD-ROM disc, DVD disc and Iomega Zip disks.
(See CD-ROM and DVD.)

Requester path   A uni-directional path from the client to the server that supports GET requests and may deliver to the server such information as the client's:
- domain
- e-mail
- user agent denoting the browser type
- variables such as a list of file types with which the browser is compatible

The requester path naturally coexists with the uni-directional path from the server to the client which may deliver:
- Web pages
- streaming media.

(See CGI and CGI environment variables.)

Resolution   A measurement of the concentration of dots or pixels in a digital image. In display technology, resolution is specified in terms of screen dimensions expressed in pixels and the dot-pitch is expressed as the distance between displaying pixels. Typical display resolutions of commercially available monitor include 640 × 480 pixels, 800 × 600 pixels, 1024 × 768 pixels, 1280 × 1024 pixels, and 1600 × 1200 pixels. In terms of printer technology, resolution is expressed in terms of the number of dots per inch (dpi). Generally, low-cost laser printers produce output composed of 300 dpi. More expensive variants offer 600 dpi and 1200 dpi resolutions.
(See Monitor.)

Restore   A method by which a maximised or minimised application or document window is returned to its previous size and position.

Reverse engineer   A process which begins by a studying the inputs and outputs of a system or devices and progresses to designing an implementation that echoes the same input and output characteristics.

Reverse engineer ER diagram   A process of beginning with a database and then arriving at an ER diagram representation.

Rhapsody   An operating system built around OpenStep technology that was developed by NeXT Software.

Risk exposure (RE)   A product of risk probability (RP) and risk cost (RC):

```
RE=RP * RC
```

- RP is the probability of attempted attacks on a system leading to a security breach
- RC is the estimated cost of a particular (or average) security breach.

(See Firewall and Security.)

RLC (Run Length Coding)   A lossless compression process. It may be used in conjunction with DCT and forms part of the JPEG algorithm.

RMI over IIOP   An implementation of RMI which may be used to develop CORBA-compliant distributed applications, using the Java programming language. It was developed jointly by Sun and by IBM. It does not require an IDL of its own, and allows the transmission of serialisable Java objects between communicating applications. It also uses IIOP as a communications protocol which can glue applications running on the Java platform to C+O+, SmallTalk and to any CORBA-compliant program.
(See IDL, Java* and RMI*.)

RMI security   A security perimeter for RMI-reliant applications. Downloading entities and classes dynamically reveal the obvious need for security which typically approximates all those things that security gateways are designed to address, such as the filtering of unwanted ActiveX controls, Cookies, Applets and plug-ins. In order to prevent the downloading of potentially hostile code the standard `SecurityManager` is installed, which prevents the downloading of entities of all their program elements', including classes and stubs. It is effective in many applications, though some may require additional flexibility or the ability to configure the security policies as you would using a security gateway. RMI has another security manager called `java.rmi.RMISecurityManager` which may be used to implant a security policy that gives certain permissions depending on the code's origins. The security manager also operates on local code and may render certain functions inoperable as they try to connect with remote URLs, so a policy file must remedy this block. More information about RMI security is available on the Web, and particularly at jini.org and at the Sun site.

Robot   *(See Search engine and Crawler.)*

ROLAP (Relational On-line Analytical Processing)   A data analysis environment using RDBMS data structures and query language implementations and techniques.
(See OLAP and Data warehouse.)

Route   1. *Noun*: a path taken by a packet or message which leads from a sending device to a receiving device. The path might involve the interaction with software components which may form part of an OO distributed system. 2. *Verb*: an action taken in order to send or forward a packet or message to a receiving device, or even software component.
(See Screening router.)

Router   A device which receives and routes messages between network systems or between complete networks. The messages may be packets, cells or frames, depending on the protocol used.
(See Frame relay, Packet switched network, Protocol and Screening router.)

Routing   An action which sees a packet, cell or frame allocated a path.
(See Frame relay, Packet switched network Router, Protocol and Screening router.)

RS232   A standard from the Electronic Industries Association (EIA) for the serial transmission of data over relatively short distances, but greater than those internal to most computer systems. Standard representation of digital data, using TTL for example, is limited in terms of transmission distance. To overcome this, signal strength is broadly increased. RS232 represents an industry standard for achieving this, to increase transmission distance and give interchangeability of computer peripherals.

RSA   A public key or asymmetric cryptosystem, or algorithm developed by MIT professors Ronald L. Rivest, Adi Shamir, and Leonard M.

Adleman in 1977. It is used by numerous e-commerce site developers and e-commerce product vendors. Its aim is to make difficult the derivation of the private key from the public key using a one-way function. For example, if the public key is a known function of x, $f(x)$, it may be made theoretically difficult to determine the unknown x that is the private key. The same cannot be said of the reverse, where x is known and $f(x)$ is unknown, particularly in the case of factorising. This was illustrated in 1977 when RSA-129, a 129 digit integer, was published by Martin Gardner in Scientific American. He laid down the gauntlet, challenging readers to factorise it, for which they would receive a small cash prize. Not until March 1994 was it factorised by Atkins *et al.*, using the resources of some 1600 computers and the quadratic sieve factoring method that has been superseded by the more economical general number field sieve. A one-way function is appropriately effective when attempting to factorise the product of two large primes, which is implemented as follows:

1. Two prime numbers are selected: p and q
2. Calculate their product n, or the public modulus
3. Another chosen number $e < n$
4. e is relatively prime with $(p - 1)(q - 1)$ e and $(p - 1)(q - 1)$, therefore, have only 1 as their common factor
5. Calculate $d = e^\wedge -1 \bmod [(p - 1)(q - 1)]$
6. e is the public exponent
7. d is the private exponent
8. The public key is the pair, (n,e)
9. The private key is the pair, (n,d)

The chosen prime numbers p and q maybe kept with the private key, or destroyed. Using PGP, p and q are retained in encrypted form and help expedite operations through the Chinese Remainder Theorem. The reverse process is difficult, thus obtaining the private key (n,d) from the public key (n,e) is deemed secure. Factorising n would result in p and q, leading to the private key (n,d). The encryption process involves:

- dividing the target message into blocks smaller than n
- modular exponentiation: $c = m^\wedge e \bmod n$
- decryption or the inverse is driven by: m x5 $c^\wedge d \bmod n$.

(See Brute Force* and Cryptography.

RTP (Real-time Transport Protocol) A protocol which supports real-time audio/video communications.

(See ASF.)

S

SAA (Systems Application Architecture A strategy initiated by IBM for enterprise computing, which defines the three layers:

- Common User Access
- Common Programming Interface
- Common Communications Support.

Sample A digital value derived from an analogue source,
(See ADC and ISDN.)

Sales ledger A listing of sales which can include the date of sale, the product description, the product code, the net cost, and the total cost including a breakdown of sales and shipping charges, and other miscellaneous charges, including storage.

Sampling rate (or frequency) A frequency at which an incoming analogue signal is digitised. The sampling rate of an ADC influences the effectiveness of conversion.

SAP R/3 A client server development environment, which is the successor to SAP R/2. The transition was a response to the shift from the two-tier client/server model to the three-tier client/server model. The product is used globally and came to prominence through its application in German industry, notably the automotive sector.
(See Client/server.)

Satellite system A medium or communications technique which uses orbiting satellites fitted with microwave antennas. These provide line-of-sight communications with microwave antennas at earth stations. Applications are used extensively in telecommunications and in television broadcasting. Geostationary satellites orbit above the equator, revolving in unison with the earth, hence they are stationary relative to the earth's rotation. The concept was originated by science-fiction writer, Arthur C. Clark.

Scanner   A device used to digitise printed material such as photographs. With optical character recognition (OCR) software, a scanner can be used to convert text into machine-readable form. Types of scanner include:

- Hand-held scanners typically offer a scanning width of around 10 cm. Operation involves passing the scanner over images to be digitised.
- Flat-bed scanners are the most popular. Paper handling is comparable to that of a photocopier. Flat-bed variants can allow complete A4 or A3 pages to be scanned, and are ideal for digitising manuscripts, together with illustrations. If digitisation of a significant amount of material forms part of development, then a flat-bed scanner is essential. Conversion of text into a computer readable format requires optical character recognition (OCR) software.
- Sheet-fed scanners are easier to use than hand-held scanners. Paper handling approximates that of fax machine, where motorised rollers simply pass sheets over the scanning array. A principal disadvantage is that bound publication pages have to be removed before they may be scanned.
- Drum scanners are very highly specified and tend to be used by commercial printers and bureaux. They offer very high resolutions that provide true photographic-quality images.
- Slide scanners enable the production of images using 35mm slides alone.

Scanners may be greyscale or colour. The simplest greyscale variants will produce 8 bit images so generating images with 256 (2^8) shades of grey. More sophisticated colour versions may generate colour images using 24 bits per pixel so producing 16.7 million (2^{24}) colours. Image depths of 30 bits, 32 bits or 36 bits may also be supported. Most scanners come complete with scanning software, picture editing programs and OCR (Optical Character Recognition) software. Such software may be essential in the production stage of multimedia, and also in electronic publishing when transcribing older texts into digital form. Drivers supplied with a scanner do much for compatibility with various software packages. For example, a standard Twain driver will allow the scanner to be used with Twain-compliant programs like HiJack Pro. Equaly HP Scanjet drivers allow the device to understand HP protocols.

SCM   *(See Supply Chain Management.)*

Screen refresh rate   *(See Refresh rate.)*

Screen scraper A client/server software component or function that removes or 'scrapes' display information from requested data and formats so that it can be displayed by the client system. It may also do the same for outgoing traffic from the terminal or client system.
(See Client/server.)

Screened subnets A subnet which restricts TCP/IP traffic from entering a secured network. The screening function may be implemented by screening routers.
(See Firewall, Screening router and Security gateway.)

Screening router A router variant able to screen packets which match a predefined criteria, including the:

- source address
- destination address
- protocol type.

(See Firewall, Packet filtering and Security.)

Script A series of instructions that can be interpreted by a program, sometimes referred to as macros. Scripts can sometimes be generated through menu selections or by writing code.
(See Perl and VBScript.)

Script-based authoring tool A multimedia authoring system/environment which requires coded program sequences or scripts. They are generally difficult to use for non-programmers.

SCRIPT_NAME A CGI variable which holds the name and path of the CGI script being executed.

Scroll bar A user interface component that is used to scroll an image of item of text that is too large to be shown in the display area. Horizontal and vertical scroll bars are available.

SCSI (Small Computer System Interface) A universal and internationally agreed interface standard backed by ANSI (American National Standards Institute), intended to provide interchangeability between peripherals and computer systems from different manufacturers. Apple Computer has long since realised the importance of SCSI, fitting Machintosh machines with appropriate controllers. The SCSI continuum approximates:

- SCSI-1
- SCSI-2

- Wide SCSI
- Fast Wide SCSI
- Ultra SCSI.

(See Firewire.)

SDK (Software Development Kit)   A library of functions that may be used to implement specific solutions. Microsoft SDKs are numerous and include those associated with:

- ActiveX
- Java
- NetMeeting
- Design-Time Control
- Active Template Library
- OLE DB.

SDRAM (Static Dynamic RAM)   A type of random access memory (RAM) that offers a comparatively short access time. Such access time is measured in nanoseconds (nS), or billionths of a second.

Search engine   1. A site used to retrieve documents from the World Wide Web, which operates using gathered and evolving indexes stored locally. The indexes are not common to all search engines, though they share a standard format which dictates the following:

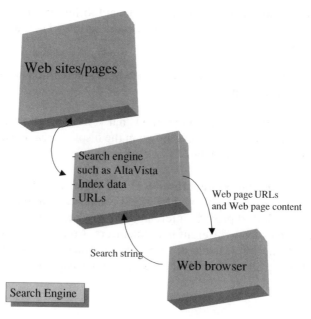

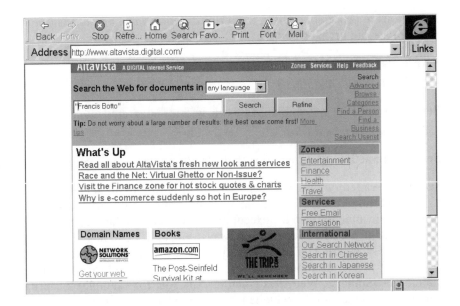

- the heading must be enclosed by HTML <TITLE> tags
- the description must consist of the 200 characters that follow the <BODY> tag, or the matter enclosed by <META> tags.

The interface permits the entry of search words and phrases which may include logical operators. Popular search engines include:

- Alta Vista
- Yahoo
- HotBot

A search engine is also a feature which permits a Web site to be searched. *(See HTML, <META> and <TITLE>.)*

Search string   A single word, phrase, sentence (or a number of words, phrases, sentences) for which a document or number of documents are searched. A search engine or retrieval system retrieves documents (or document details) based on the search string. Search engines and retrieval systems support wild cards and logical operators. For instance if it were necessary to find documents containing the name Van Gogh along with the city Amsterdam, using logical operators you would use the phrase Van Gough AND Amsterdam.
(See Search engine.)

Second-generation language   A programming language where instructions are represented by concise mnemonics. Such 'assembly languages' are indigenous to processors. Often the terms *assembly language* and *machine code* are used interchangeably.

Secure mail   An e-mail that is suitable encrypted.
(See Cryptosystem and RSA.)

Secure systems   A system that has cryptosystems integrated into its design.
(See Cryptosystem and RSA.)

Secure transaction   A transaction that is made secure using cryptography.

Security   A method of restricting access to applications, data and systems to their intended users. The term may include automated virus checks on incoming documents and on executable code such as Java applets and ActiveX controls using security gateways. Firewall technology is key to Web security, as are data encryption and password protection. Security is paramount to organisations deploying corporate data, and for companies running e-commerce Web sites (such as Amazon, for example). Security standards include those developed by the United States Department of Defense, and named the Trusted Computer Standards Evaluation Criteria, otherwise known as the Orange Book. This was introduced in 1985, and was originally aimed at mainframe and mini computers for many years. It is also applicable to databases and to networks, through the Trusted Database Interpretations, and the Trusted Network Interpretation. The Orange Book is a multi-tier set of guidelines, including:

- Level D1. which is the lowest level of security, rendering the system untrusted.
- Level C1, which is a discretionary security protection system, requiring a login name and password, and in which access rights are allocated.
- Level C2, which includes Level D1 and Level C1 security and integrates additional security features. For instance, this level requires the system's relevant events be audited.
- Level B1, or Labelled Security Protection, which provides tiered security. Compliance sees object permissions that may not be changed by file owners.
- Level B2, or Structured Protection, which requires the labelling of all objects.
- Level B3, or Security Domains level, which requires terminal connections via a trusted path.
- Level A, or Verified Design level, which is the highest Orange book security level.

(See Encryption, Firewall, Packet filtering, Risk exposure, Screening router, Security gateway, SET and Web.)*

Security boundary Also known as security perimeters, such boundaries encapsulate systems, software, objects etc. They may be implemented in software, hardware using firewalls, in passwords, by encryption, or by the assignment of dongles to users. Boundaries exist at a number of different levels including:

- Physical, which covers tangible resources such as systems
- Application, which cover access rights to applications
- Data, which covers access and editing rights to data
- System, which dictates who may log on to a network or system.

(See Firewall.)

Security gateway A security layer which fortifies a network against hostile virus attacks by screening incoming executables and data. The executables might be Java applets, ActiveX controls or plug-ins. Each of these represents a potential threat, not just in terms of viruses, but in terms of what they may do to client-side documents, files and even system files such as those concerned with the initialisation of Windows variants. For instance, an ActiveX control might take control of a client's Word documents, performing operations on them, such as converting them to HTML, and then possibly abstracting them, for display or even processing on a remote Web site. For many security managers, this is unacceptable behaviour. Additionally, the unregulated Internet means that virtually anyone can deploy applications, which may potentially damage clients. It is desirable, therefore, to attempt to check and possibly screen such inbound traffic. Such a comparative centralisation of the anti-virus security layer, makes redundant the need for standalone variants on clients, though these may still be employed particularly if removable media are being used for file transfer. Such a security gateway may:

- provide multiple OS support, such as Windows, DOS or Netware, though many are confined to Windows NT
- support ActiveX, Java. cookies, plug-ins, JavaScript, VBScript and various executables
- check all Java classes on downloaded applets
- provide intelligent filtering features.

(See Firewall and Security.)

Security protocols A protocol that integrates a cryptosystem.
(See S-HTTP.)

Security proxy A Web proxy that integrates security features used to authenticate connections to servers.
(See Firewall, Security and Web.)

Semantic Visual Café   A visual programming development tool. *(See Visual Basic.)*

Semaphore   A communications method, involving physical signalling, which was invented by the French in 1792. Even today the semaphore principle is applied in programming, where flags may be used to relay certain states and events. In computer terms, semaphore may be applied to coordinate processes.

Sequential prose   A continuous stream of linear text. *(See Hypertext and Nelson Theodore.)*

Serial port   An input/output port through which data is transmitted and received sequentially. RS232 is a standard serial port used to transmit serial digital information over modest distances to connect communication devices and other serial peripherals to computers. The PC COM (COMmunications) ports are serial ports. *(See Firewire and USB.)*

Server   1. A transaction server is allocated the task of transaction processing (TP), and it often invokes the application logic necessary to perform database interactions and manipulations. The process(es) invoked directly or indirectly by the client are collectively referred to as the transaction. Transaction servers may include UI logic, driving the client UI, relegating the client device as little more than a dumb terminal. Typically mainframe-based transaction systems might adhere to this model. Alternatively, the UI logic, or presentation may be distributed to the client. The server consists of a TP monitor, which performs transaction management and resource management. Transaction management ensures the so-called ACID properties of transactions. These include *Atomicity, Consistency, Isolation* and *Durability*. ACID property compliance is achieved through the two-phase commit protocol. *(See ACID and Two-phase commit.)* Resource management is intended to optimise the use of resources, which include memory, mass storage and processing. it may also be involved with load balancing between resources and between the software processes which may be threads. *(See MPP.)* 2. An entity that serves clients. The services provided might include the implementation of processes and the distribution of data, and may be categorised as follows:

- Fax, where the server provide fax reception and transmission facilities for connected client systems.
- Database, in the client/server configuration in which SQL requests from the clients perform the necessary data requests.

262

- Communications, which enable client systems to make remote connections to external networks and servers.
- Print, where the server is dedicated to printing locally or remotely.
- File, where a centralised server, perhaps connected to RAID storage devices, is utilised by clients to provide high-volume data storage, and high performance disk access and data transfer rates.
- Transaction, where the server updates data which may form part of simple client/server two-dimensional database, or warehouse data that may be multidimensional (in data cubes) or even hypercubes. *(See Data warehouse.)* 3. Web server is the hardware platform that supports one or more Web sites. Traditionally Web servers have been based on the Unix or Windows NT OSs. 4. A Web server can also be considered as the software implementation that serves HTML pages. *(See Web.)* 5. An intranet server may considered in the same terms of a Web server, but with a security perimeter to prevent public access. 6. A peer-to-peer server is a system on a network in which the resources of any connected system may be shared. While any system on a peer-to-peer network might be a server, typically the most highly specified system performs as a server. 7. A file server provides centralised resources for network users. 8. A database server provides centralised data storage. 9. An object or application that serves an application or object with embedded or linked data. The server might be OLE 2.0 compliant, or may conform to another component architecture. *(See ActiveX*, Object* and OLE.)* 10. A CD-ROM server dynamically distributes requested information from CD-ROM drives to LAN users. If the maximum number of drives per server is exceeded, additional servers are added. The incorporation of additional servers, prior to reaching the network maximum of drives per server, leads to better service for users. There are several commercially available CD_ROM network packages, many of which are software orientated. 11. A video server is a hardware solution which provides the basis for a video on demand (VoD) service. It may be implemented using MPP. Advantages of such parallel processing systems include scalability, where, for example, growing numbers of subscribers to a VoD service may be accommodated through additional processors and even complete servers. *(See MPP.)* 12. A video, audio or multimedia server that serves client systems with streaming media.

(See ASF, E-commerce, and Streaming*.)

Server application   A term used to describe a server-side application that may drive, or provide services for client applications and systems. The latter tier is the front-end, with which the user interacts. Between the back- and front-end applications is middleware or glues that exist at a number of

levels. These may bind together and coordinate application logic, data and presentation distributed across the back- and front-ends.
(See Application*, Client/server, Front-end and Glues.)

Server crash   A state where a Web server is rendered inoperable by a hacker who has in some way overloaded the services it provides. Examples include subjecting the server to excessive e-mail traffic, or using a program which continually attempts to access content files.
(See Asymmetrical*, Brute Force*, cryptosystem, Dictionary attack, Hacking and public key encryption.)

SERVER_NAME   A protocol which contains the name of the host on which the server is running.

Serve object   An object that runs on a server or at some location at tier 3.
(See 3-tier.)

SERVER_PORT   A CGI variable which holds the port on which server is running.

SERVER_PROTOCOL   A CGI variable which contains the protocol version.

SERVER_SOFTWARE   A protocol which holds the name and perhaps version of the server software.

Service   An entity which may be used or provide functions of some kind which may be relevant to users, devices, applications or to other services that are typically on a network. Jini services are an example, which may provide access to communications applications, printers, remote residential networks etc.

Servlet   A Java program which exists on the server-side and publishes services which may be dynamic Web content to clients, and coexists with an HTTP server. Servlets are compiled, support-threading, and may be added to Web sites using programs like JRun or a Java module for the Apache server. An e-commerce site may use a servlet which is perhaps based on the `HttpServlet` abstract class which provides support for handling requests from the client-side, and to respond to them accordingly. Servlets may be loaded either:

- when specified using a URL
- when the Web server starts.

The Web server calls the servlets' `init` method to begin, and the servlet calls `service, doGet,` or `doPost` method requests to serve requests. When unloaded the servlet may invoke the destroy method to release itself from committed resources and to save state changes to a persistent state, and these may be retrieved using the `init` method. When called, the `init` method is passed a `ServletConfig` object that holds configuration information about the particular Web server implementation including the initArgs parameter which is held in the servlet properties file, and is obtained by calling the `config.getInitParameter ("parameter")` method. Servlets may also interact with, and make use of EJBs (Enterprise JavaBeans). A HTTP servlet may handle requests and responses using its `service` method, and accepts:

- the `HTttpServletRequest` object that holds the client's sent headers and streams
- the `HttpServletResponse` object that holds the servlet's output stream response.

SET (Secure Electronic Transaction)   A standard means of securing payment transaction made to on-line merchants. By integrating cryptosystem techniques, it is perceived as a credit card security system and was initiated by Visa and Microsoft. SET implementations are an amalgam of cryptosystems, protocols, secure protocols and techniques.
(See Cryptography* and SET*.)

SET application   An application which uses the SET internationally agreed technologies and methodologies.

SET ASN.1 (Abstract Syntax Notation One)   A standard that defines the encoding, transmission and encoding of data and objects which are architecture neutral.

SET baggage   A method of appending ciphered data to a SET message.

SET CDMF (Commercial Data Masking Facility   A ciphering technique based on DES which is used to transfer messages between the Acquirer Payment Gateway and the Cardholder in SET implementations.

SET Certificate Authority   A trusted party that manages the distribution of SET digital certificates, where layers of the Tree of Trust has the representation of a digital certificate.

SET certificate chain   A group of digital certificates used to validate a certificate in a chain.

SET certificate practice statement   A group of rules that determine the suitability of certificates to particular applications and communities.

SET certificate renewal   An event that sees the renewal of a certificate for continued transacting purposes.

SET Consortium   An international organisation which was formed when Mastercard and Visa announced SET, whose initial objective was to create an agreeable standard, and to consider STT and SEPP.

SET digital certificate   A means of linking an entity's identity with a public key, and carried out by a trusted party.

SET digital signature   A digital signature may be applied to an encrypted message. A message digest is ciphered using the sender's private key and then appended to the message, resulting in a digital signature.

SET E-wallet   An element of a cardholder which creates the protocol and assists in the obtaining and management of cardholder digital signatures.

SET hash   An element which reduces the number of possible values using a hashing function such as the Secure Hashing Algorithm (SHA-1).

SET Idempotency   An attribute of a message which sees repetition yield a constant result.

SET message authentication   A process or usually sub-process that verifies that a message is received from the appropriate or legal sender.

SET message pair   Messages which implement the POS and certificate management in a SET implementation.

SET message wrapper   A top-level data structure which conveys information to message recipients.

SET order inquiry   A pair of set messages used to check the status of orders.

SET out-of-band   An activity that is not within the bounds of the SET recommendations, guidelines and standards.

SET PKCS (Public Key Cryptography Standards)   A set of public key cryptography standards used by SET which include:

1. RSA
2. Diffie-Hellman key agreements
3. Password based encryption
4. Extended certificate syntax
5. Cryptographic message syntax
6. Private-key information syntax
7. Certification request syntax.

(See Cryptography.)

SHA-1 (Secure Hashing Algorithm)   A mechanism for reducing the number of possible values.

Shannon's theorem   A theorem which can be applied to give the maximum data transfer limit over a given medium such as an access technology:

I $= F\log_2 (1 + S/N)$
F   = bandwidth
S/N = signal-to-noise ratio.

(See Access technology and Modem.)

Shell   1. A means of entering commands using Unix and other similar operating systems. A Unix shell can be considered as performing a similar task to the command line interpreter associated with DOS. 2. A term used to describe the framework of an expert system. The shell is occupied by a knowledge base that consists of IF . . . THEN rules that are used to solve entered problems. The knowledge (or rule) base is interpreted by an inference engine.

Shockwave   A streaming multimedia technology which uses AfterBurner compression. Its producers, Macromedia, also produce the popular Director and Authorware programs. Essentially, the technology is used to deploy Director movies over the Web, and can also be applied to applications that depend on the Lingo multimedia authoring language. Web browsers can be enabled using a Shockwave plug-in.

(See Lingo and Streaming.)*

Shopping basket   A metaphor used by e-commerce sites so that customers can accumulate products for purchase.

(See Shopping car.)

Shopping cart   An element of an e-commerce site which permits items to be collected and purchased at a virtual checkout. Typically items are written to the client as cookies and their information is read by the e-commerce site when the final purchase is committed and the transaction is made. Another method of implementing shopping carts involves the use of forms and hidden fields, and remedies situations where the cookie function on the browser is turned off, or when the browser does not support cookies. A number of shopping cart implementations are available free, and one may be found at www.eff.org. An alternative to using a shopping cart might be to create an order form that is embedded in an HTML page using an appropriate scripting language or you may prefer to reply on the forms and templates provided by a Web development tool.

S-HTTP   A means of seamlessly integrating encryption into HTTP. It was developed by Enterprise Integration Technologies and supports RSA, DES, triple DES and DESX.

(See Encryption.)

Signature   A means of securing transmitted matter which includes e-mail messages, and requires a digital ID which may be purchased from many sources.

SITPRO   Simpler Trade Procedures Board (UK).

Site Server   A Microsoft solution for enhancing, deploying and managing e-commerce Web sites.

SK8 ('Skate')   A multimedia authoring tool/environment developed by Apple Computer.

Skeleton   A server-side program which accepts methods along with their parameters, and performs the necessary state changes and invocations on relevant remote objects.

SLIP (Serial Line Internet Protocol)   A protocol often used for serial data transmission over media which include access technologies such as POTs.

(See PPP.)

Smalltalk   An OO programming language.

(See OOP.)

SmartCard   A credit-card size device that has an embedded processor chip which can store digital certificates and an e-purse which is a stored cash value for small purchases.

SMP (Symmetric Multi processing)   A system that has two or more processors, which do not operate independently with their own connected memory and I/O capabilities. Generally SMP systems are used as server variants. It is a system architecture comprising multiple processors that share an interconnecting bus and memory. Systems find application as servers, and such processor designs as the Intel Pentium Pro were optimised for SMP. SMP systems offer processor scalability, but not in the precise processing increments associated with MPP systems. Unlike MPP systems, limitless scalability is prohibited by the interconnecting bus bandwidth that is shared.

(See MPP and NUMA.)

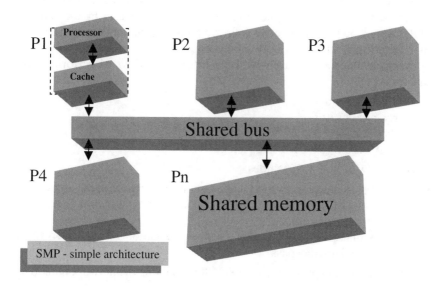

SMP - simple architecture

SMPTE   Society of Motion Picture and Television Engineers.

SMTP (Simple Mail Transport Protocol)   A protocol used to transmit e-mail messages over the Internet and across other compatible IP network.
(See TCP/IP.)

Sniffing   A term used to describe the use of a sniffer program to monitor data traffic to a network or server, in order to gain access information. For instance, it may be applied to gather illegal passwords and IDs for ISP accounts, and passwords to mail accounts, and to remote systems.
(See Firewall.)

269

Socket   An interface which offers a peer-to-peer endpoint, and has a name and an address. Datagram sockets interface with UDP; Stream sockets interface with the TCP protocol and Raw sockets interface with protocol levels which include the IP network layer. Berkeley sockets are the best known sockets for TCP/IP stack communications and were introduced in 1981. They have many variations including the Microsoft WinSock API which in a standardised TCP/IP implementation for Windows.

SOCKS   A secure proxy in a client/server environment where the server sees SOCKS as a client, and provides security, accountability, auditing, management, fault tolerance and alarms. An implementation includes a SOCKS server at the application layer and a SOCKS client library which is between the client's application and transport layers. In e-commerce SOCKS may be used as a network firewall, but is generally considered to be more than this, such as a networking middleware that enables enterprise networks to interface securely with the Internet. SOCKs v4 performs three functions:

- connection request
- proxy circuit setup
- application data relay
- authentication (SOCKS v5 only).

An overview of SOCKS includes:

- A client makes a request to SOCKS to communicate with the application server using the appropriate address, connection type (active or passive), and the user's identity.
- SOCKS makes a proxy circuit to the application server, over which application data may pass.

All application data passes through SOCKS, enabling the network data to be:

- filtered
- audited
- screened
- collected
- controlled.

SOCKS v5 includes:

- authentication
- authentication method negotiation that may include Username/ Password authentication (RFC1929) or Kerberos 5 based CSS-API authentication (RFC1961)
- message integrity and privacy
- UPD proxy to SOCKS V4.

(See Firewall.)

Software distribution   A method of delivering software to users. Software distribution may be by downloading from the Internet. Other distribution media include floppy disk, CD-ROM and DVD-ROM. The first commercial CD-ROM software distribution disc from a major producer was Microsoft Office. Farallon Computing released lesser known programs on CD-ROM prior to this, as did Microsoft itself. PC Sig released the world's first shareware compilation on CD-ROM in the USA. Used as a distribution medium, DVD-ROM presents vendors with new opportunities; spare storage space may be used for program demonstrations, program documentation, training material and advertising using DVD (MPEG-2) video. Currently most leading software producers distribute their programs on CD-ROM, but a swing to DVD-ROM is imminent.
(See CD-ROM and DVD.)

Software key   A method for unlocking encrypted data. It allows the customer to unlock the products purchased contained on a CD-ROM.

Sony Vaio   A popular family of notebook PCs from the Sony Corporation. Each include the iLink connector which is a synonym for Firewire or IEEE1394.

Sound card   A plug-in card which permits wave audio recording, multi-voice sound synthesis and speech synthesis.

SoundBlaster   A range of sound cards produced by Creative Technology.

SPAM   A form of unsolicited e-mail; the Internet equivalent of junk mail. The originators of such e-mail are termed spammers, and messages from known spammers may be filtered using appropriate software.

Speech recognition   A technique by which a computer is able to recognise speech and perform tasks. Modestly specified speech recognition programs recognise a modest number of words. Commercial examples include Creative VoiceAssist and Microsoft VoicePilot (included in Microsoft Windows Sound System), both of which provide a means for operating Windows and Windows applications using voice commands. More advanced speech recognition systems are voice-independent, dictation systems, such as IBM ViaVoice, and competing, successful products from Dragon Systems.

Speech synthesis   A process of generating recognisable speech using digital data. Currently, most speech synthesis programs operate by combining a predefined set of phonemes. Such programs are sometimes called text-to-speech convertors. Commercial examples include Creative TextAssist which reads text, and ProofReader (supplied with Microsoft Windows Sound System) that read monetary and numeric data. TextAssist is useful for proof reading long documents in Windows applications. ProofReader is aimed at reading data entered in real-time. Both tools serve to increase productivity. Other commercial speech synthesis programs include Texto'Le that may be embedded into documents as an OLE object. Occasionally the vocabulary of speech synthesis programs may be increased using a pre-defined set of phonemes, or sometimes it is necessary to add wave audio files.

Spider   *(See Search engine and Crawler.)*

Split shipment   An instance where an order cannot be shipped fully, but must be shipped in part at various stages.

Sprite   A screen image confined to a limited number of pixels, often used as 'characters' in computer games, and pointers in GUIs. They are highly mobile and may be defined by hardware or software.

SPX/IPX A network protocol.

Square mile   A financial centre in the city of London.

SQL (Standard Query Language)   A non-procedural language that is used to manipulate data stored in a relational DBMS. Like other procedural languages that include Prolog, it does not have a rigidly defined series of operations to perform a function. Some thirty commands are included in the SQL specification, of which a recent version is SQL-92. However, third-parties have extended it to semi-proprietary variants. the language permits:

- the creation of table structures
- the entry, correction and deletion of data
- databases to be queried, to satisfy perhaps data requests.

The SQL syntax is easily learnt and understood, as it depends heavily on English words and phrases. For example, creating a database requires the statement:

```
"CREATE DATABASE datawarehouse
```

Further reading: Data. C. J. *A Guide to the SQL Standard*, Addison Wesley, 1987. This text describes the original SQL standard.

(See C++, Datawarehouse, Java* and OOP.)

SRAM (Static Random Access Memory) A volatile form of electronic memory that is not constantly refreshed. It therefore consumes less power.

SSL protocol (Secure Sockets Layer protocol) A secure channel or protocol which is supported by the TCP transport protocol. It includes the higher level SSL Handshake protocol which authenticates the client and server devices, and allows them to decide upon an encryption algorithm and keys before data reception or transmission commences. Its ability to allow high level protocols to sit on top of it is perceived as an advantage. Used alone SSL is not perceived as a complete security solution, though it does present one significant security perimeter in the eyes of many security analysts. It ensures a secure connection by authentication of a peer's connection and uses integrity checks and hashing functions, to secure the channel between applications. It was designed to prevent:

- information forgery
- eavesdropping or sniffing
- data changes.

Private or symmetric key is the basis of the SSL's cryptography, and authenticates a peer's identity using asymmetric cryptography.
SLL's flaws are documented widely and include:

- When a browser connects with an SSL server, it receives a copy of its public key wrapped in a certificate which the browser sanctions by checking the signature. The flow here is that the browser has not the means to authenticate the signature, since no verification is performed up the hierarchy because many certificates used by SSL are root certificates.
- It consumes client and server processing resources.
- It has operational difficulties with proxies and filters.
- It has operational difficulties with existing cryptography tokens.
- Its key management tends to be expensive.
- Expertese to build maintain an operate secure systems is in short supply.
- It creates network traffic when handshaking.
- The migration path from nonpublic key infrastructures is arduous.
- It requires Certificate Authority with appropriate policies.
- Its communication data does not compress and therefore steals network bandwidth.
- It is subject to certain international import restrictions.

(See RSA* and cryptography.)

273

SSL handshake

Client Browser

SSL Web server

1 client hello

2 server hello

3 client master key

4 client finish

5 server verify

6 server finish

SSL Web Server   A web server which supports the Secure Sockets Layer protocol.
(See SET and SSL protocol.)

SSL-enabled Web Server   *(See SSL Web Server.)*

Stack   A contiguous series of memory locations utilised as a storage area. It is a LIFO (Last In First Out) system, in that the order in which items are dispensed opposes that in which they were deposited. A stack is sometimes called a push-down store. It can be used to store the return addresses from subroutines.

Start button   A button that provides single-click access to the main menu system in Windows 95/98/NT. By default it appears at the bottom left of the screen and is anchored to the Task bar which underlines all applications. The menus that result from the Start button may be navigated by dragging the mouse, and highlighted menu items may be run by clicking them once. The Start button and Task bar were introduced into the Windows 95 design in order to replace the Program Manager of Windows 3.x.

Store and forward agent   An object or event generator which uses an intermediate object to relay notification of events to objects or event listeners that have expressed an interest in hearing them.

Streaming   1. *Streaming audio*: a method of playing audio while the audio stream is being downloaded. Streaming audio plug-ins are available for popular browsers such as Netscape Navigator. Such plug-ins are useful for tuning into radio broadcasting services on the Web. 2. *Streaming video*: a method of playing video while the video stream is being downloaded. Streaming video plug-ins are available for Netscape Navigator, while equivalent ActiveX controls operate with Microsoft Internet Explorer.
(See ASF and Microsoft NetShow.)

Streaming media   A means of distributing audio, video and multimedia in real-time over the Web or similar TCP/IP network such as an intranet.

Strong cryptosystem   A cryptosystem that is considered safe from attacks, and is difficult to crack using known techniques.
(See Asymmetric*, Brute Force*, Cryptosystem RSA*, Dictionary attack, Public key encryption and SET*.)

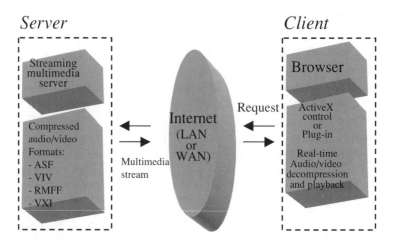

Streaming multimedia

Structured programming   A programming model which consists of procedures or subroutines, and has no GOTO commands in order to direct program execution unconditionally. All modern high-level languages can be assumed to comply with structure programming. One of the first implementations was structured BASIC, which was launched in 1982 by Acorn Computer. It was integrated into its Acorn BBC microcomputer design in the form of a ROM-based BASIC interpreter. One of the earliest structured programming languages was Algol which evolved into Pascal. *(See BBC BASIC.)*

Stub   A proxy object which is stored locally, is usually downloaded, and provides an interface with a remote object or service.

Stylesheet   An entity which imposes a presentation style on content that may include objects, text strings, graphics, UI components and hyperlinks, and is synonymous with template.

> **External stylesheet**   A template/document/file containing style information which may link with one of a number of HTML documents, permitting a site to be restyled by editing one file. They may be linked to a HTML document using the form:
>
> ```
> <HEAD>
> <LINK REL=STYLESHEET HREF="style.csss" TYPE="text/css">
> </HEAD>
> ```

Embedded style A style attached to one specific document using the form:

```
<HEAD>
<STYLE TYPE="text/css">
<!--
P {text-indent: 14 pt}
-->
</STYLE>
</HEAD>
```

Inline style An attached style that affects one element and is specified in the start tag as a value of the <STYLE attribute:

```
<P STYLE="text-indent: 10pt">Indented paragraph</P>
```

Imported stylesheet A style sheet that can be imported to (combined with) another sheet, combining:

- main sheets which apply to the whole site
- partial sheets which apply to specific documents.

Form

```
<LINK REL=STYLESHEET HREF="main.css" TYPE="text/css">
<STYLE TYPE="text=css">
<!--
@import url (http://www.botto.com/fast.css);
@import url (http://www.botto.com/fast.css);
.... other statements
-->
</STYLE>
```

Alternate Stylesheet A stylesheet used to define an *alternate* style to those declared as *persistent* and/or *preferred*. The persistent style is the default style and may be overridden by the alternate style.

Stylus A pen input device used to interact with, and write to, a computer or appliance. The first stylus was the light pen which was yielded by the US Defense SAGE project, an early warning radar system based upon digital graphics technology. A stylus might be used as a pen with a graphics tablet or bit pad. The stylus is used widely in pen computing with everything from notebook computers to PDAs. In pen computing the user simply writes directly on the screen, and data entry using normal long hand is valid.

Subnet A method of using an IP address so that a greater number of networks may be addressed. IP addresses are designed to accommodate networks which may have between 253 and several million hosts. In many instances, organisations wish to address a number of networks using a class

C address. By creating subnets using their IP address, they may link the separate networks using a router. Subnets are created by dividing the last octet of an IP address. The division involves reserving the most significant bits of the octet to provide addressing information for subnets. This may yield one of the following configurations:

- 2 subnets, each with 62 hosts
- 6 subnets, each with 30 hosts
- 14 subnets, each with 14 hosts
- 30 subnets, each with 6 hosts
- 62 subnets, each with 2 hosts.

(See IP address.)

Subnotebook   A portable computer which is smaller and lighter than a conventional A4-size notebook computers.

(See Notebook.)

Substitution   A cryptography technique that sees characters replaced by other characters.

(See Asymmetric*, Brute Force*, Cryptosystem, Dictionary attack, Encryption algorithm, Public key encryption, RSA*, SET* and Transposition.)

Subsystem   A physical element of a PC. Subsystems include graphics card, video capture cards, hard disks and sound cards.

(See Graphics card, Hard disk and Sound card.)

Sun Microelectronics   A division of Sun Microsystems, and manufacturer of chips which are optimised for the Java programming language, including:

- PicoJava chipset, which is used in cellular phones, and computer peripherals
- MicroJava processor, which is used in network devices, telecommunications hardware and consumer games
- UltraJava, which is optimised for use in 3-D graphics and multimedia-related computing, much like Intel's MMX Technology.

(See Java* and MMX.)

Superclass   A class of objects that has subclasses, which may inherit its attributes and behaviour.

Supercomputer   An MPP architecture that is based on a network of parallel processors.

(See MPP.)

Supply chain   A course or evolution which begins with raw materials and ends with the sale of a finished product or service. It includes entities such as buyers, manufacturers, distributors, suppliers and consumers. It is an e-commerce company's set of functions which may be internal or external, and allows the value chain to make or produce products and deliver services to customers. A supply chain includes information, communications and processes that bind the link between the supplier and customer.
(See Supply Chain Management.)

Supply Chain Management (SCM)   A set of processes and sub-processes which attempt to implement and optimise the functions, connected entities, and interacting elements that are in a supply chain. It addresses a number of key business areas and may be assumed to improve:

- enterprise performance
- corporate growth
- customer service
- order management
- demand planning
- warehouse distribution
- partnerships
- Y2K compliance
- Cash-to-cash cycle
- supplier/supply base management.

Supply Chain Management's key processes, techniques, networks, channels and infrastructures include:

- information networks
- EDI
- Internet/Web
- Distribution Resources Planning (DRP)
- distributed warehousing
- drop ship
- multi-sourcing
- integrated ERP
- interprise
- supplier scheduling
- virtual corporation.

(See Supply chain.)

Surf   An alternative and popular term for browsing the Internet.

SWIFT   (Society for Worldwide Interbank Financial telecommunications.)

SWING   *(See Java Swing.)*

Switched network   A telecommunications network that uses switches to route calls from one telephone to the next. It is also a switch metrix may be used to allow intercommunication between connected terminals.

Symantec   A large international software publishing company.

Symbolic constant   A symbolic constant has a name, and is assigned an unchanging value. It may be used just like an integer constant. Symbolic constants improve program maintenance and updating; a single change may be made to a symbolic constant, which might be used throughout a program. A symbolic constant multiplier may be assigned the value 10 using the C++ code:

```
#define multiplier 10
```
or
```
const unsigned short int multiplier = 10
```

Symmetric cryptography   A cryptosystem where the processes of encryption and decryption each require the use of a single key. Unless the recipient of the encrypted data already knows the key, it may be left to the sender to transmit its details over a secure channel.

Symmetric cryptosystem operation   A series of processes and sub-processes that:

- converts plaintext into ciphertext using a cipher or encryption algorithm
- returns ciphertext to plaintext using a decryption algorithm.

Using a symmetric key and the transposition technique, the processes include:

Encryption   Send the key, such as UNLOCK for example, to the recipient using a secure channel. Arrange the key in a columnar fashion with numerals indicating their alphabetical sequence:

U	6
N	4
L	3
O	5
C	1
K	2

Arrange the plaintext, such as ATTACK VESSEL in columns as shown below:

U	6	A	V
N	4	T	E
L	3	T	S
O	5	A	S
C	1	C	E
K	2	K	L

Create the ciphertext by writing the row values in sequence dictated by the numerical value, i.e:

CE   KL   TS   TE   AS   AV

Send the ciphertext to the recipient where a secure channel is optional.

Decryption   Again the key characters are assigned numerals indicating their alphabetical sequence:

U   6
N   4
L   3
O   5
C   1
K   2

The decryption algorithm takes the ciphertext, and based on the numerical value it creates the plaintext:

U   6   A   V
N   4   T   E
L   3   T   S
O   5   A   S
C   1   C   E
K   2   K   L

(See Asymmetric*, Brute Force*, Ciphertext, Cryptosystem, Dictionary attack, Encryption algorithm, Plaintext, Public key encryption, RSA*, SET* and Transposition.)

Symmetric key cryptography   A cryptosystem that uses the same key to encrypt and decrypt messages.

T

T1   An AT&T designation for a digital link with a bandwidth of 1.544 Mbps.
(See ATM, Frame relay and ISDN.)

T2   An AT&T designation for a digital link with a bandwidth of 6.312 Mbps.
(See ATM, Frame relay and ISDN.)

T3   An AT&T designation for a digital link with a bandwidth of 44.736 Mbps.

T50   An ITU-T designation for ASCII.

T90   An ITU-T designation for image coding that is used by Group 4 facsimile. This uses an ISDN 64 Kbps bearer channel.

Tape streamer   A magnetic tape storage device used to back up hard disk data as a contingency measure against data loss or data corruption resulting from system failure or an interruption of the power supply. Data recovery simply involves copying the contents of the tape streamer to a functioning hard disk.

TAPI (Telephony Application Programming Interface)   A Microsoft and Intel specification for Windows-based telephony, if converts PC data into telephony data. TAPI lets PCs:

- receive ANI (Automatic Number Identification) information
- generate, process and transfer calls
- outdial from a directory.

TAPI provides developers with a standard set of functions to interface various telecommunications equipment.

Task bar   A status bar used in Windows 98/NT that underlines all applications. It bears the Start button and illustrates all open applications that may be minimised or maximised. By default the Task bar also illustrates the time of day. The Windows 95/98/NT user interface centres around the Task bar that provides buttons to select open applications, and it anchors the Start button that invokes the Start menu. The Start menu bears options that lead to programs as well as to submenus. Once invoked, the menu system may be navigated by dragging the mouse rather than by clicking on its menu items. Programs are opened through a single mouse click.
(See Windows.)

TCP/IP (Transmission Control Protocol/Internet Protocol)   A standard network protocol used to transmit or route data from one IP address to the next. Protocols which use TCP/IP include:

• HRRP (HyperText Transfer Protocol)
• HTTPS (HyperText Transfer Protocol Secure) which integrates cryptography and forms the basis of a secure connection and secure site.
• SMTP (Simple Mail Transfer Protocol)
• FTP (File Transfer Protocol)

A standard set of protocols used in packet switched networks. Unix servers provide numerous commands and daemons that relate to TCP/IP. It consists also of standard and non-standard files, utilities, and daemons. It interprets a standard set of commands. TCP/IP originated from DARPA and ARPANET, and is one of the most established internationally agreed standard protocols. Occasionally, however, it includes proprietary files and programs through specific implementations that include that of Santa Cruz Operation (SCO). *(See ATM and Frame relay.)*

TCP/IP Daemons   A daemon is a program or process dedicated to perform what is usually a singular given function, such as sending mail. TCP/IP daemons include those added by third-parties including SCO. The Daemons include:

• DNS (Domain Name Server), which is used to provide IP address for given host names
• SYSLOG (System Logger), which stores messages pertaining to various operational events including status, detected errors, and debugging
• SNMP, which is an implementation of the Simple Network Management Protocol, and is capable of receiving information from such compatible agents
• INETD (Super Server), which monitors TCP/IP ports of incoming messages
• BOOTP, which implements an Internet Boot Protocol server
• ROUTE, which manages Internet routing tables, and is invoked when booted; the netstat command is used to print the routing tables, among other details, the resulting listing shows gateways to networks
• RARP (Reverse Address Resolution Protocol), which is able to provide a 32 bit IP address in response to a 48 bit Ethernet address

- LINE PRINTER, which accepts incoming print jobs and queues them for remote printing
- SLINK, which links STREAMS modules and is included within Unix implementations that use STREAMS-TCP/IP
- LDSOCKET, which initialises the System V STREAMS TCP/IP Berkeley interface.

Configuration   Interfaced devices are configured in terms of IP address, netmask, and operational status using the command:

ifconfig

Configuration files include:

- /ETC/HOSTS, which provides a loopup table for finding IP addresses for host names
- ETC/ETHERS, which provides a means of converting IP addresses into Ethernet hardware addresses. An alternative conversion method is provided by ARP (Address Resolution Protocol)
- /ETC/NETWORKS, which provides a lookup table for IP addresses and their respective network names
- /ETC/PROTOCOLS, which provides a list of DARPA Internet protocols
- /ETC/SERVICES, which lists services that are currently available to the host
- /ETC/INETD/CONF, which monitors a specified port, and invokes daemons when required.

Network access files   Access files include:

- /ETC/HOSTS.EQUIV, which contains a list of trusted hosts, and is significant to system security. Each entry is trusted, in that users access their accounts without a password
- RHOSTS, which lists system and user names; users are permitted to log in using any name in the file /ETC/PASSWORD.

(See IP address, Firewall and Unix.)

TDM (Time Division Multiplexing)   A technique by which several different signals may be transmitted concurrently over the same physical link.

Television shopping   An application of television broadcasting where the user purchases items which are usually shown and sometimes demonstrated on screen.

Template   An entity that determines the presentation of a document including its page layout, typestyles, fonts and other content, which may include text, fields and tables.

Telnet   A connectivity mechanism that permits a client system with Internet access to operate a remote computer. The screen images shown on the remote system are also seen on the remote user's client system.

Telstra   A large Australian telecommunications company.

Terminal   A system which is interfaced with a system (such as a mainframe computer). Typically it is dumb, meaning that it has no application logic or data, only the mere presentation element of an application.

TFT   *(See Display.)*

Thin client   A system within a client/server architecture (such as that of the Web) which features:
- presentation, which is typically in the form of a Web browser
- a portion of the application logic.

Many systems connected to the Web may be described as thin clients. Thin clients require less hardware resources, and are therefore cheaper to deploy than fat clients.

(See Application, Client/server, Fat client and NC.)

Third-generation language   A high-level language such as Java, Pascal, BASIC, C and C++.

(See C++, Java and Visual Basic.)

Thumb   An instance of thumbprint.

Thumbprint   A hash value that generates or verifies digital signatures.

TIFF (Tag Image File Format)   An image file format maintained by the Adobe Developers Association (ADA).

<TITLE>   An HTML tag that encloses the Web page title that is used as meta data by popular search engines when retrieving Web documents, displaying it as the document's title. Such data is collected by search engines periodically, but may remain transparent to some if your ISP uses a robots.txt file to stop Web robots from indexing Web pages. It is possible to determine if a server has a robots.txt file by entering the Web page's URL (including its domain name and domain category) and including robots.txt as a suffix:

- *http://www.FrancisBotto.com/robots.txt*

Sending Web page URLs to search engines may cause them to be categorised as available via additional search words and phrases, other than those contained in the Web pages themselves.

(See HTML, <META>, Search engine and Web page description.)

TMA (Telecommunications Managers Association)   A body whose membership is composed largely of telecommunications managers. Each year there is a TMA convention featuring state-of-the-art communications systems, techniques and standards.

Token ring   An IBM-developed network protocol and specification, officially named IEEE802/5.
(See LAN.)

Toolbar   An array of buttons which provide single-click access to features and/or applications.

For example, the default Windows 98/2000 Toolbar which is on the right of the Start button, offers single-clock access to the:
- Internet Explorer Browser
- Outlook Express
- Desktop
- Active channels.

Quick Launch toolbar

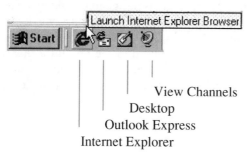

View Channels
Desktop
Outlook Express
Internet Explorer

By right-clicking the Windows 98/2000 Taskbar, and then selecting Toolbars, it is possible to select alternatives to that of the default, Quick Launch implementation. For instance, the Control Panel icons may be placed on the Taskbar as illustrated below:

(See Active Desktop, Windows and Windows Desktop.)

287

TookBook   A multimedia authoring tool for the PC, produced by Asymetrix Corporation. Recognised as the brainchild of Microsoft's co-founder Paul Allen, and as one of the first generic multimedia authoring tools, ToolBook is one of those products that has earned a much-deserved place in contemporary computing history. Its early implementations were used to create some of the first multimedia CD-ROM titles, which include Microsoft's Multimedia Beethoven: The Ninth Symphony. Since these memorable beginnings Asymetrix's ToolBook has evolved into a formidable family of products aimed at the creation of CBT (Computer Based Training) courses, of which ToolBook II Assistant is the latest addition. Other members of the product range include ToolBook II Instructor, ToolBook II Librarian, and Designer's Edge for ToolBook II. ToolBook II Assistant version 6.0 may be used to create multimedia programs, which may be distributed using CD-ROM, floppy disk, intranets, and over the Internet. Aimed squarely at trainers, teachers, instructional designers and other similar professionals, it requires not even rudimentary programming skills. It does not possess the Asymetrix OpenScript programming language that has become synonymous with ToolBook. This is a welcomed departure for Asymetrix and allows ToolBook to compete with tools like Authorware Professional, which has long since been regarded as an environment that does not require programming. Those with programming skills might be better served by ToolBook II Instructor, which also includes the OpenScript programming language. This gives programmers better control over resulting ToolBook applications by allowing them to define the behaviour of objects more accurately. ToolBook II Librarian is designed to help manage courseware deployed over the Internet and on corporate intranets by providing administrators with feedback regarding student progress. Designer's Edge for ToolBook II is a productivity tool used in the pre-authoring stages of development, and provides a walkthrough environment for developers, taking them from analysis to evaluation during the instructional design process.

(See Authorware Professional.)

Top-down analysis   A design approach which begins at a high level, and progresses to low-level component parts.

(See Bottom-up analysis.)

Touchpad   An x-y input device consisting of a small touch-sensitive pad or surface. It is the chosen device for notebook systems.

TP (Transaction processing) monitor   *(See Server.)*

TP-heavy server   A server that runs TP monitors.
(See Server.)

TP-lite server   A server that provides a portion of all the action required by full transaction processing (TP) monitors. Typically it will be able to commit changes to, and roll-back, changes made to operational data that is stored in an appropriate database variant. It may be devoid of:

- transaction coordination of multiple programs
- resource management.

(See Server and Transaction.)

Trackball   An input device that is integrated in older notebook and sub-notebook designs. Physically it is a ball joint. The ball may be rotated using fingers, so providing a means of manipulating a screen pointer or cursor in *X* and *Y* directions.

Transaction   A term used to describe the data exchange and data changes which occur as the result of an interaction. The interaction might be the submission of an order form using a client browser. A transaction server is allocated the task of transaction processing (TP), and often invokes the application logic necessary to perform database interactions and manipulations. The process(es) invoked directly or indirectly by the client are collectively referred to as the transaction. Transaction servers may include UI logic, driving the client UI, relegating the client device to little more than a dumb terminal. Typically mainframe based transaction systems might adhere to this model. Alternatively, the UI logic, or presentation may be distributed tot he client. The server consists of a TP monitor that performs transaction management and resource management. Transaction management ensures the so-called ACID properties of transactions. These include Atomicity, Consistency, Isolation and Durability. ACID property compliance is achieved through the two-phase commit protocol. *(See ACID, Jini* and Two-phase commit.)* Resource management is intended to optimise the use of resources which include memory, mass storage and processing. It may also be involved with load balancing between resources and between the software processes, which may be threads.

Transaction coordinator   *(See Two-phase commit protocol.)*

Transaction management   *(See Server.)*

Transaction processing ACID properties   Atomicity, Consistency, Isolation and Durability (ACID) properties define the real-world requirements for transaction processing (TP) which are supported by Jini:

- Atomicity ensures that each transaction is a single workload unit. If any subaction fails, the entire transaction is halted, and rolled back
- Consistency ensures that the system is left in a stable state. If this is not possible the system is rolled back to the pre-transaction state
- Isolation ensures that system state changes invoked by one running transaction do not influence another running transaction. The changes must only affect other transactions, when they result from completed transactions
- Durability guarantees the system state changes of a transaction are involatile, and impervious to total or partial system failures.

Transposition   A cryptography technique that rearranges streams of characters.
(See Asymmetric*, Brute Force*, Cryptosystem, Dictionary attack, Public key encryption, RSA* and SET*.)

Tree of Trust   A hierarchy specified by SET used for the management of Digital Certificates including:
- maintenance
- issuance
- currency.
(See SET.)

Triple DES   An encryption technique based on a variation of the DES encryption technique. One variation sees three DES encryptions using three different keys.
(See DES.)

Try block   A try block is a section of code which is responsible for exception handling. Both Java and C++ support try blocks.

TV shopping   *(See Television Shopping)*

Trusted Third Party (TTP)   A means of verifying the identity of Internet users.

TrustWise   A UK VeriSign equivalent.

Two-phase commit   A method used in transaction processing which ensures ACID properties. It coordinates the changes made to system resources which result from transactions. It tests for their successful implementation, in which case they are committed. If not, and any one fails, they are all rolled back. The transaction coordinator is key to the two-phase commit protocol. This queries all subordinates to verify that they are ready to commit. If the subordinates have other subordinates, these must also be queried. When all subordinates are ready to commit, the transaction coordinator records the information to protect it against any interruption that might be caused by a system failure. Having received information of the readiness to commit, the transaction coordinator sends a commit command to its subordinates, and they do the same. Once the transaction coordinator has received confirmations from all subordinates, the client may be sent a transaction complete message.

(See ACID and Server.)

Two-tier client/server   *(See 2-tier.)*

typedef   1) A C++ keyword that declares a name for a type and not for a variable:

```
typedef char * pchar;
```

2) A C++ command, which permits mnemonics to be assigned to the statements used to define variables. The following statements assigns the word xxxx to the unsigned short int statement:

```
#include <filename>
typedef unsigned short int xxxx;

int main ( )
{
xxxx coordinate;
// define coordinate as an unsigned short integer
variable
}
```

U

U A chrominance component in a video signal that comprises colour information.

UART (Universal Asynchronous Receive Transmit) An electronic device used for serial communications.

UDP (User Datagram Protocol) A protocol which is used widely in streaming audio and video. Macromedia Shockwave Director 6.0 is among a number of leading streaming server technologies that use UDP. It does not feature the reliability of TCP, and is therefore appropriate for streaming media where intensive error detection and correction is less important. Dropped packets, which are those that do not reach their destination, are acceptable in streaming media. UDP therefore, optimises performance and makes better use of available bandwidth because it does not insist on the retransmission of erroneous packets. *(See ASF and Streaming*.)* A low-level protocol, unlike Hypertext Transfer Protocol (HTTP) that is considered an high-level protocol. UDP may be exploited by multimedia streaming technologies, including ASF (Advanced Streaming Format). ASF is a container format that offers compression and protocol independence.

UI (user interface) A software module or program through which users interact with one or more applications.
(See GUI, OO user interface, Visual Basic and Windows.)

UltraJava A chipset from Sun Microsystems which is optimised for the Java programming language. Like Intel MMX Technology, it is application-specific, thus optimised for 3-D graphics and multimedia-related computing, including MPEG video playback. UltraJava is licensed to NEC, Samsung Electronics, LG Semicon, and Mitsubishi.
(See Java, MMX and Sun Microelectronics.)*

UMTS Universal Mobile Telephone Service A mobile network providing global roaming provided by orbiting satellites which may integrate BTSs (Base transmitter Stations) and BTCs (Base Switching Centres). To create this type of network as many as 840 satellites may orbit at altitudes between 780 km and 1414 km to minimize signal transmission latency. There are 840 satellites that make up Teledesic whose consortium is led by Bill Gates. Other mobile satellite services include Motorola's Iridium (66 satellites), Loran's/Qualcom's Globalstar (48 satellites) and TRW-Matra's Odyssey (10 satellites). These satellite mobile telephone systems offer data rates of 4.8 Kbps to 9.6 Kbps but have the potential to deliver wireless higher rates through other communications standards. They operate in the K-band (10.9-36 GHz) and L-band (1.6-2.1 GHz), and provide a basis for UMTSs. This means that a Jini device might 'roam' between terrestrial GSM-type services and satellite mobile telephone networks depending upon geographical location or at the speed or travel. Aeronautical and maritime telecommunications were catalysts in the development and deployment of satellite mobile telephone services with the first maritime satellite launched in 1976. Called AMRISAT it consisted of three geostationary satellites and was used by the US Navy. This later evolved into the INMARISAT (International Maritime Satellite Organization), which provide public telecommunications services to airliners.

Undo A feature provided by almost all fully specified programs. It simply cancels the last editing operation.

Uniprocessor system A system design based on a single processor. Such serial systems might be referred to as von Neumann implementations. *(See MPP, NUMA and SMP.)*

Universal resource locator *(See URL.)*

Unix A multitasking, multi-user operating system originally developed at Bell Laboratories for the creation of interdepartmental reports. It has since evolved into numerous commercial variants including XENIX. Typically Unix OS variants feature the X-Windows GUI. *(See X-Windows.)*

Unix grep filter A filter that allows you to search files for specified text strings.

Uploading A process of transferring files from a client system to a server. Usually the transfer takes place using the FTP protocol.

294

UPnP Universal Plug and Play A technology introduced in 1999 by Microsoft as a response to SunSoft's Jini technology. It features the same discovery protocol technique used to locate registered services on networks.
(See Jini.)

UPS (Uninterruptable Power Supply) A device which prevents data loss following power supply failure or deviation.

URL (Universal Resource Locator) An address of a service or Web site or Web page, which may be used by the Web browser to open specific sites and pages. For, example, the Web page www.altavista.digital.com is a URL, and can be opened to show the Altavista search engine home page. Additionally, the browser permits such URLs to be stored in directory that might be called Favorites, or something similar. The user can then open frequently visited sites and pages, through one or two mouse clicks, depending on the browser used. The underlying HTTP protocol implements a client/server connection for each URL which is opened by the client Browser. It transmits and receives data, and carries the subsequent contents of an opened URL. Typically, when a URL is opened, the first procedure involves finding the requested site or page on the Web. Having made an appropriate connection, the browser waits for a reply, and then downloads the ensuing page data. Eventually, the HTTP breaks the connection with the remote server, where the requested site or page resides. This break may be carried out manually by selecting the Stop button or a similarly named button.
(See HTTP and IP address.)

USB (Universal Serial Bus) A serial interface for connecting peripheral devices.

Usenet A source of subject-oriented notes that are posted to servers; each subject is a newsgroup that can be joined and even formed. The initial Usenet protocol was Unix-to-Unix Copy (UUCP), but this was superseded by Network News Transfer Protocol (NNTP), and all modern browsers provide Usenet support.

User authentication A process of identifying the user of a system or program.
- The most common user authentication technique is based on tokens, such as ID names, passwords and PIN numbers.

- User authentication can also be implemented using biometric data, which may be a fingerprint, thumbprint, or retina image.
(See Encryption, Firewall and Security.)

User block data A CD-ROM Mode 1 block contains 2048 bytes of user data.
(See CD-ROM.)

User communication A rarely used term that describes the user's interaction with a system or application.

User communication device A rarely used term which described an input device such as mouse, touchpad, trackball, or touch screen.

V

V.1 A standard covering power levels for telephone networks.

B.21 A standard modem speed capable of transmitting and receiving data at 300 bps.

V.32 A standard modem speed capable of transmitting and receiving data at 9600 bps.

V.32turbo A upgrade to the V.32bis standard introduced by AT&T.

V.42 An international error correction standard for modem-based communications. MNP2-4 (Microcom Networking Protocol) and LAPM (Link Access Procedure M) provide error correction.

V.90 An official designation for the 56.6 Kbps modem standard. 56.6 Kbps = 56 600 bps.

VAB (Value Added Bank) A financial institution able to transmit electronic data between multiple trading partners.

VAT (Value Added Tax) A tax added to many purchases in the UK and is currently set at 17.5%. It requires VAT registered businesses to complete quarterly returns which presents the difference between the amount of VAT charged and that which has been expended. The business has to pay the difference or reclaim it if the business has paid more VAT than it received.

Validating credit card numbers A process of authorising a credit card transaction using a merchant bank. The numbers may be validated by processing their checksum digits, because all the credit card companies adhere to a *mod 10* check digit algorithm.

VBScript A scripting language that is a subset of Visual Basic, and may be used to deliver functionality gains to applications. VBScript may be used to enhance Web pages through the addition of:

- event-driven objects
- ActiveX controls
- interactive content
- Java applets.

VBScript does not harness:

- OOP methodologies (1998)
- DLL calls (1998)

The VBScript syntax is similar to that of Visual Basic, and includes statements for loops, events, procedures and functions.

VBScript For . . . Next loop A means of repeating statements based on a true or false condition

```
For pointer = first To last [Step step]
' statements
' statements
Next
```

VBScript While . . . Wend loop

```
While condition
'statements
'statements
Wend
```

VBScript procedures VBScript has Sub and Function procedures, and the latter should be used to return values, (in accordance with definition of a function).

VBScript The Sub procedure has the following form:

```
Sub Subroutine_Name ([parameter])
'statements
End Sub
```

VBScript function A function procedure is of the form:

```
Function FunctionName ([parameter])
'statements;
End Function
```

(See Visual Basic.)

VBXtras An object factory which specialises in Visual Basic controls and add-ons.

(See www.vbxtras.con.)

Vendor Express   A US Treasury program for making federal government vendor and commercial payments. It uses the CCD+, CTX and CTP formats.

VeriSign   A US source and supplier of digital certificates.

Vertical market   A specialist or niche market. Until the late 1980s multimedia was considered a vertical market.

VGA (Video Graphics Array)   An IBM PC graphics controller standard released in mid-1987 by IBM as part of its PS/2 range. Like all add-ins for PCs, graphic controllers (adapter cards) plug directly into expansion slots. *(See Graphics card.)*

ViaVoice   An IBM speech recognition program for desktop computers. Speech recognition has been high on IBM's agenda for over 25 years, and is part of an ongoing multi-million dollar research and development program that yielded the VoiceType family of products. This high level of interest indicates that speech recognition has great potential IBM's research program has also led indirectly to some impressive offshoots, including the DragonDictate program from speech recognition specialists Dragon Systems, which was founded by husband and wife James and Janet Baker, whose combined experience included research at IBM. DragonDictate competes directly with the VoiceType packages, and with IBM's latest offering as well as ViaVoice. The mention speech recognition programs differ from voice-dependent programs like the Microsoft Windows Sound System which requires the user to train it to recognise each and every word.

Video capture card   A card that can be used to capture and sometimes compress motion video, converting it into digital form. The majority of video capture cards sold are aimed at the production of video for the Windows environment, and are often supplied with the full implementation of Video for Windows. Manufacturers of mainstream video capture cards include Creative Labs, Fast Electronics, Intel, VideoLogic and Spea.

Video capture file   A capture file is set up prior to video capture to optimise the rate at which digitised video can be written to hard disk. This improves the quality level of captured video. If necessary, the target hard disk should be defragmented so that video data is written to a contiguous series of blocks thus optimising the target hard disk performance. The specified size of the capture file should be large enough to accommodate the video sequence that is to be captured and stored. Though the capture program will usually enlarge it automatically, the possibility of complete frames being omitted or dropped during video capture is increased, as is the possibility that the capture file will become fragmented.

(See Video capture.)

Video CD (or White Book)   A standard for storing MPEG1 video on single density CD variant. It can be assumed to store approximately 74 minutes of MPEG-1 video. Discs are interchangeable between appropriately specified PCs and appliances. It can be assumed that a Video CD, or a White Book disc, can be used to store around 74 minutes of MPEG-1 video, the quality of which may be equated to an analogue VHS video recording. A key advantage of Video CD over analogue VHS video cassette is that there is no incompatibility between PAL and NTSC recordings, thus eradicating the need for separate NTSC and PAL versions as is currently the case with VHS cassette video distribution.

(See MPEG*.)

Video editing   A process of editing a video file. Digital video files can be edited using programs such as VidEdit, Adobe Premier, and Asymetrix Digital Video Producer. Typical video editing operations include:

- copying frames from one point to another in a sequence
- moving/cutting frames from one point to another in a sequence
- copying frames from one sequence to another
- moving frames from one sequence to another
- deleting unwanted frames from a video sequence
- titling video sequences
- cropping video frames
- altering the playback speed in terms of frames per second
- fading colours
- tinting colours
- changing colours.

Video for Windows   A video standard. Video for Windows (VfW) permits video playback, capture and editing. Microsoft Video for Windows which includes the VidCap video capture program, VidEdit video editing program, BitEdit 8 bit graphics editor, and PalEdit 8 bit colour palette editor. VidEdit provides a gateway to several video compression schemes, the variety of which depends upon the video card you have. Compression algorithms such as Intel Indeo, Microsoft RLE (Run Length Encoding) and Microsoft Video 1 can help reduce video file sizes by varying amounts. The size and quality of resultant video files may be controlled using compressors through the adjustment of compression settings, about which more shall be

said later. The resultant video can be added to applications through OLE (Object Linking and Embedding). It supports the AVI (Audio Video Inter-leaved) format and features a number of compressors including Microsoft 1, Microsoft RLE and Intel Indeo.
(See JPEG and MPEG.)

Video-on-demand (Vod)   An e-commerce implementation that permits customers to view selected purchased movies.

Video playback fps   The playback frame rate of a video sequence.

Video playback frame resolution   The frame resolution of a video sequence.

Videoconferencing   A process by which users in remote locations communicate in real time both visually and verbally. Systems may be divided into the categories of:
- desktop videoconferencing using conventional desktop or notebook computers
- conference room videoconferencing, which typically include appropriately large displays.

Desktop videoconferencing systems include a camera, microphone, video compression/decompression hardware/software, and an interface device that connects the system to an access technology. The interface device might be:
- a conventional modem used over a connect with an ISP or intranet server, and thereafter use an Internet-based videoconferencing solution such as CU See-Me
- a cable modem, which might provide high-speed internet access via cable
- an ISDN interface, which provides connection to the Internet or appropriate IP network
- a Network Interface Card (NIC), which connects to a LAN
- a wireless interface, which provides connection over GSM or other mobile communications network.

Access technologies for videoconferencing include PSTN, ISDN, ADSL, cable, GSM, ATM, T1 frame relay, and proprietary wireless technologies. Point-to-point videoconferencing involves communication between two sites, while multi-point videoconferencing involves interaction between more than two sites. The latter might require a chairperson to conduct proceedings. Also the collective system might be voice activated, switching sites into a broadcasting state when the respective participant begins speaking. Vendors of videoconferencing solutions include Intel, PictureTel, Insoft and Creative Technology. Internationally agreed standards relating to videoconferencing include H.320 and T.120. The former was introduced in 1990 and provides guidelines to vendors and implementers that yield appropriate levels of compatibility.

(See ATM, ISDN, T1 and Video*.)

Videotex   A service used to publish text and graphics over the PSTN. It emerged from the BT Research Laboratories in the 1970s, and was launched in the form of Prestel in 1979. Videotex uses alpha-mosaic text and graphics. The display is based on character blocks, which require 7 or 8 bits, and produced from a look-up table or from a character generator. A videotex frame consists of a matrix of such characters, consisting of 24 rows of 40 characters. Typically the frame requires 960 bytes, and may be transmitted in around 6.5 seconds over PSTN. Using faster ISDN access technology, the transmission time is reduced.

ISDN D channel

Transmission time $=(960 \times 8)/16\,000$
$=480\,\text{mS}$

ISDN B channel

Transmission time $=(960 \times 8)/64\,000$
$=120\,\text{mS}$

(See DCT and MPEG*.)

Virtual processor   A processor which is implemented in software. It may sometimes be referred to as a virtual machine. It is design approach used by such programming languages as Java, so as they may be system- and OS-independent. They can, therefore, be applied as applets in heterogeneous environments such as the Web.

Virtual reality   *(See VR.)*

Virtual shopping   An activity where the consumer purchases items from intangible stores that are usually on the World Wide Web.

Virtual Shopping Cart   *(See Shopping Cart.)*

Virtual store   An intangible store that exists on the World Wide Web.

Virtual Web server   A Web server which is not physically implemented, rather it may exist with a number of other such virtual Web servers on the same site. Virtual Web servers can be created by using Microsoft IIS and they may have a:

- domain
- TCP/IP address
- root directory.

Whether or not a Web server is virtual, it is transparent to the user. *(See Microsoft, IIS, TCP/IP and Web server.)*

Virtual window shopping An Internet equivalent to window shopping, which is a leisurely activity for many.
(See On-line*.)

Virus An entity which causes a program to function incorrectly and might result in the loss or corruption of data.

VisiBroker for C++ An ORB for Borland that forms the basis for middleware implementations.

VisiBroker for Java An ORB that forms the basis for middleware implementations.

Visual Basic A programming language. The most popular implementation is the Microsoft Visual Basic programming tool which may be used to tackle a variety of different programming projects, including the development of:

- ActiveX controls
- client/server applications
- mainstream business applications
- utilities
- multimedia-related programs such as media players
- Leisure programs.

Microsoft Visual Basic forms part of its Visual Studio package, and is also available in standalone form. (1998) editions of Microsoft Visual Basic are:

- The Standard Edition, which may be used to build 16 bit and 32 bit applications. The standard edition does not support ODBC databases or Visual SourceSafe.
- The Professional Edition, which adds to the Standard Edition's facilities through such features as ODBC compliance.
- The Enterprise Edition, which includes the features of the Standard and Professional Editions, and also integrates Visual SourceSafe.
- The Control Edition, which is intended for building ActiveX Controls.

(See ODBC and Visual SourceSafe.)

Visual C++ A Microsoft C++ programming environment, which may be used to create

- DLLS
- ActiveX controls
- 16 bit and 32 bit applications

(See C++.)

Visual FoxPro A Microsoft OOP database management system for creating enterprise solutions. It is supplied with the Microsoft Visual Studio.

Visual InterDev A Microsoft development tool which is used for creating Web and intranet applications. It can be used to:

- access ODBC databases
- script client and server Web pages
- edit content files
- manage multiuser Web projects.

The files of an InterDev application are stored on the Web server. Files are accessed with Visual InterDev, using a local project file that points to the server and to the relevant Web. InterDev lends itself to the team collaboration environment because multiple developers can work simultaneously with files (on the Web server or in a Web). The Web project includes the Web files on the server, and the client-side, local project files. A Web Project File is available for the creation of project files which point to relevant Webs and Web servers. Visual InterDev is also supplied with the multimedia production tools:

- Image Composer, which offers a sprite-based drawing environment. Each imported image becomes a sprite. A number of effects and filters are available. Support is provided for plug-ins from Adobe and Kai. It supports BMP, GIF and TIF formats.
- Music Producer is used to create MIDI sequences.
- Media Manager empowers Windows Explorer to view media files.

(See MIDI, Multimedia Production and Wave audio.)

Visual Java++ A Microsoft development environment for writing, compiling and debugging Java applications and applets. Visual J++ may be used to integrate JDK packages into Java programs, and to create multi-threaded Internet and intranet applications.

(See Java*, JavaScript, and JDK.)

Visual programming A programming technique where the programmer simply draws usually standard components on screen and then attaches code to them. The code segments may be written in a line-by-line fashion or selected from a library. Many multimedia authoring tools and modern development tools employ visual programming techniques at various levels. *(See Visual Basic.)*

Visual SourceSafe   A useful Microsoft solution which lends itself to the team collaboration environment. Once installed, this restricts editable files to individual, authorised developers.

Visual Studio (Enterprise Edition)   A comprehensive suite of Microsoft development tools, which includes:

- Visual J++
- Visual C++
- Visual Basic
- Visual InterDev
- Visual FoxPro.

It also includes numerous tools, extensive documentation and the Microsoft Developer Network (MSDN) on CD-ROM.
(See ActiveX*, C++, Java*, and Visual Basic.)

VLAN (Virtual Local Area Network)   A network where computers may not be connected to the same physical LAN; rather they are connected on different networks, and in remote locations. They may be configured using software, and are immune to the physical location of the networked systems.
(See Ethernet, LAN and VPN.)

VLB (Versa Local Bus)   A standard local bus, which supports compatible peripherals such as hard disk controllers, I/O cards and graphics cards. It is internationally agreed and backed by VESA (Video and Electronics Standards Association). It is used widely on PC designs, and gives better performance than IBM's original ISA (Industry Standard Architecture) expansion bus developed for the PC AT (Advanced Technology) in the early 1980s.

VOD server   A server that provides streams of video.
(See Server*.)

VOD service provider   A company engaged in providing video on demand.

VOD usage habits   A profile of users' habits when using VOD services indicating the most popular movies and the most popular viewing hours.

Voice recognition   *(See Speech recognition and ViaVoice.)*

Vortal   A portal targeting a vertical market.

VPL Inc. (Virtual Programming Language Inc.)   A company founded in 1985 by Jaron Lanier, with the purpose of serving the VR market. Its products include the DataGlove and the EyePhone HMD. Other early products include RB1 (Reality Built for 1), a single-user VR system. Its specification was raised to RB2 (reality Built for 2), which could interface two users.
(See VR.)

VPN (Virtual Private Network)   A network which may be built using Internet technologies, as opposed to private lines. VPNs may be LAN-to-LAN, or even extranets, which include remote users that may be business partners or even customers.

VR (Virtual Reality)   A non-linear medium that can extend to the concurrent communication of interactive 3-D images, sound and numerous different variables that include 3-D movements and manipulations. Its key property is that of a theoretically infinite bandwidth. Users' extracted movements typically include body, limb and digit movements, but can span from intricate muscular contractions to intimate vessel expansions and retractions and surface movements of the skin to eye movements. Trends point to a yet more sensitive interface able to read every movement down to the blink of an eye, the enlarging of a pupil, and even the displacement of a human hair. A verbatim image of the interfaced user is foreseeable. Jaron Lanier lays claim to having coined the term. Users themselves may also be the recipients of 3-D movements, most notably in simulation applications. Subtler manipulations may also be experienced. Variables, that are uni-directional include user coordinates, pulse rate, heart beat rate, blood pressure and capacity. Variables that may be bi-directional in nature include temperature and moisture. Other more specialised variables include pressure, flow, air flow, acidity, luminance, potential, mass, velocity/speed, acceleration, and directionality. Computer generated 3-D images comprise full or partial virtual environments, as well as perhaps complete or partial replications of interfaced users. The attainable sophistication of the overall graphical environment is a function of the driving graphics engine, the software, and particularly transformation algorithms. Features which determine complex virtual environments include requirements for high-speed graphic transformations, large sets of coordinates, high-resolution images, large numbers of independent 3-D graphic objects, complex 3-D objects with changeable behaviours, and high levels of chrominance. Voice commands can replace and/or complement tangible and even virtual mechanisms for interaction and navigation. 3-D sound rendering also may be included to maintain the perspectives of virtual sound sources. The tangible VR platform provides the necessary mechanisms for navigation, browsing, interaction, stimulation of sensory channels, and monitoring variables. At the core of a standalone VR systems is at least one appropriately specified computer that might typically range from a single-processor-based variant, to a multiple microprocessor-based system based on a single shared data bus, to a complex supercomputer architecture including multiple processors (such as transputers as used by Division (Bristol, England) working in concurrence. The graphics performance of the collective virtual engine and accompanying graphics engine/controller is key to determining overall complexity and effectiveness of supported applications. Obvious VR applications can be revealed, or discovered, by considering instances when interactive 3-D graphics/environments have to be communicated and experienced. The experience may be intimate, vague or detached, where the user need not be fully immersed, in which case the HMD may be exchanged for something less intimate, or even a two-dimensional display. Current applications include architectural visualisation, scientific and engineering visualisation, civil and military simulators, surrogate travel, surgery (telepresence), point-of-information using realistic computer-generated images or video overlay. Distant future applications include virtual conferencing, three dimensional multimedia authoring tools, and the simulation of ergonomically effective working environments yielding the virtual desktop. The visualisation tool market for desktop computers has mushroomed in recent years giving professionals of various different kinds the ability to experience, and experiment with structures, in three dimensions. The resultant acceleration of understanding renders visualisation a useful instrument for learning. The absorption of 3-D movements at various different levels, and their replication in remote, and even multiple sites is termed telepresence. Related applications include instances where human operatives may be subject to hostile elements in the remote environment; human operatives cannot physically exist due to the large or small scale of the remote environment; the cost of physically implanting human operatives in the remote environment is reduced through telepresence; a single human operative must have a concurrent presence in multiple remote environments; or the presence of human operatives must be shifted quickly between different multiple remote environments. Current real-world applications include remote surgery and keyhole surgery, while a plethora of others wait in the wings ranging from deep-sea diving to the remote realisation of military roles. Conceivably telepresence will one day extend to VR-conferencing providing full interaction between participating users; conference members or even a complete workforce could be congregated from multiple locations. An almost mandatory stage in the development of a multimedia application is the development of a storyboard, that may also include the various implanted links that support its non-linear paths. This preliminary design stage may be carried out using the multimedia authoring tool itself, which is the case with Asymetrix ToolBook and many others. This stage provides a prototype structure for testing the partial or complete interactive design.

Multimedia based on a complex hypertext model that features a fine level of granularity can be difficult to storyboard in two dimensions; a single page, window or screen that forms part of a frame-based multimedia application may contain a number of micro features that provide navigational controls. The micro features may include active words/phrases, image fragments, micons (motion icons) all of which will require the implantation of links. Modern authoring tools offer visual programming techniques where you first draw screen objects such as buttons and then attach program scripts to them so defining their behaviour. Modern tools also provide a number of commonly used, readily-made scripts that may be used to handle events such as mouse clicks. Even if the authoring tool provides a means of drawing the links using a graphical model of the application the underlying hypertext structure can remain difficult to overview. This is largely because the conventional computer monitor is restrictive and Creditcards a tunnel vision that significantly lengthens the design stage. Now consider a 3-D multimedia authoring tool; a virtual environment ergonomically designed as a receptacle for the components of a multimedia application. It could be a room of any shape or size, a sphere, or simply free space without visible boundaries. Documents/frames with multiple media types could be pasted on virtual walls and surfaces, or suspended in free space. Mixed media documents could be cascaded or tiled as required, while the all-important links could be implanted graphically. Multimedia, hypermedia and hypertext authors familiar with two-dimensional environments will appreciate fully the advantages of a third dimension: both the story board and interactive design are implemented and overviewed more easily; while testing the interactive design and debugging is made easier.

Further reading: Sutherland, Ivan, 'A Head-Mounted Three-Dimensional Display', Harvard Computation Laboratory, *Proceedings Fall Joint Computer Conference*, Thompson Books, 1968.
Larijani Casey, L. *The Virtual Reality Primer*, McGraw-Hill, 1993.

VRML ('Vermul') (Virtual Reality Modeling Language)   A file format, and a language for creating and describing objects or nodes and their behaviour. VRML extended the Open Inventor specification to include cone, cube and cylinder primitives, along with methods for embedding hyperlinks. Applications of VRML include:

- multimedia presentations and titles
- leisure software
- virtual reality
- Web pages.

Objects may be:

- static 3-D images
- static 2-D images
- audio
- multimedia
- embedded with hyperlinks.

VRML authoring tools or generators are widely available.

VRML nodes   Node properties have:

- a name that is dedicated to the class
- parameters that offer an object's definition and have fields that contain dimensions etc.

VRML events   The nods are event driven, and receive and send messages such as:

    eventIn

which typically changes a property of the node.

    EventOut

which sends a message from an object that might have undergone change due to an interaction with a message. Nodes interact using messages passed via ROUTE that interconnects `eventOut` and an `eventIN` processes.

VRML ISO/IEC 14772   An official designation for the internationally agreed VRML specification.

V standards   A set of recommendations that covers voice and data telephone. Popular V standards cover the following full-duplex modem speeds:

V.22	1200 bps
V.22 bis	2400 bps
V.32	9600 bps
V.32 bis	14 400 bps
V.34	28 800 bps
V.90	56 600 bps

(See Access technology and Modem.)

Vulnerabilities   A listing of comparative flaws in a network's defences against illegal access.

(See Firewall and Security.)

W3C (The World Wide Web Consortium)   An organisation dedicated to the standardisation of Internet related technologies such as HTML.

Wall Street   The financial centre of New York City.

WAN (Wide Area Network)   A network of computers and interconnected LANs. Typically a WAN is spread over a greater area than a LAN.

WAP (Wireless Application Protocol)   An open, global specification that lets wireless devices access and interact with on-line information and services. The WAP Forum has over 200 members and has developed a standard technology for digital mobile phones and other wireless terminals. *(See http://www.wapforum.org/)*

WAV   A Microsoft standard file format for storing wave audio data. It can be used to store 8 bit and 16 bit wave audio at sample rates of 11.025 kHz, 22.050 kHz and 44.1 kHz. WAV files are compatible with all fully specified multimedia presentation programs and multimedia authoring tools. They are also compatible with all modern Windows wave audio recorders and editors including Sound Recorder, Creative Wave Studio and QuickRecorder. *(See ASF, MPEG*, Streaming* and Wave audio.)*

Wave audio   A term often used to describe digital audio recordings, usually made using an analogue signal provided by a source device. Such wave audio may be distributed in real time over the Internet using streaming server technologies, or it may be distributed using CD- and DVD-based variants. It may provide content for CD-ROM, DVD or Web applications. Generally it can be distributed and played back using any medium that is capable of sustaining an average data transfer rate that is appropriate to the recorded wave audio quality level. Principal parameters which drive the quality of wave audio recorded using PCM (Pulse Code Modulation) include the sampling frequency and the sample size. The wave audio quality levels that can be achieved are a function of the wave audio recording software and the sound facility on the recording system. MPC-2/3-compliant sound cards can be used to record and play wave audio in mono and in stereo at sampling rates of 11.025 kHz, 22.05 kHz and 44.1 kHz, using 8 bit or 16 bit samples. Used with appropriate software, highly specified sound cards offer higher sampling frequencies and larger sample sizes. They may make DAT-quality wave audio possible that equates to 16 bit samples recorded at a frequency of 48 kHz. Simple calculations imply that one minute of uncompressed CD-quality wave audio, which amounts to 10.08 Mb (10321.92 kByte), requires a DSM capable of providing an average data transfer rate of around 172.032 kByte/s. Approximate file sizes when recording one minute of 8 bit stereo wave audio at different sampling rates are as follows:

110.25 kHz	1.25 Mb
22.050 kHz	2.52 Mb
44.1 kHz	5.04 Mb
48 kHz	5.49 Mb

Approximate file sizes when recording one minute of 16 bit stereo wave audio at different sampling rates are as follows:

11.025 kHz	2.52 Mb
22.050 kHz	5.04 Mb
44.1 kHz	10.08 Mb
48 kHz	10.98 Mb

The memory capacity consumed by a sequence is a function of quality. If it is necessary to calculate the exact memory/date capacity consumed, then the following simple formula may be applied:

```
Memory capacity required (bits) = Sequence duration
(secs) × Sampling rate (Hz) × bits per sample
```

For example, if an 8 bit sound digitiser with a sample rate of 11 kHz were used to digitise a 15 second sequence, then:

```
Data capacity required (bits)
    = 15 × 11 000 × 8
    = 1 320 000 bits
    = 165 000 bytes
    = 161.13 kByte
```

Memory or disk data capacity required naturally increases linearly with increased sample rates.

(See Streaming.)

Web A global hypertext-based structure that may be navigated and browsed. It provides links to information sources and services that are termed Web sites. Tim Berners-Lee is accredited with the Web's invention, and his initial work was carried out when he was a computer scientist at the Centre for Nuclear Research (CERN) in Switzerland. Web is based on the hypertext model for information storage and retrieval. URLs are key to permitting the implantation of hypertext links and navigation schemes on the Web. It was released in 1992 by CERN when the initial model was static. Its origins are in hypertext, hypermedia and multimedia models and concepts.
(See Berners-Lee, Tim, W3C and Web*.)

Web cam A Web site which features real-time video broadcasting from one or more locations. The screen updates or the frame playback speeds, vary according to the site implementation and may be quoted as frames per second, frames per minute, or even frames per hour. Generally Web cams provide images of locations and people from around the world and serve as entertainment, while more serious applications include CCTV-type applications, remote viewing of child care centres etc. Web cams generally provide non-linear broadcasting, while video-conferencing provides bi-directional communications.
(See MPEG*.)

Web mail An e-mail service deployed using Web technologies, it supports global roaming as it may be accessed from a Web browser irrespective of geographic location.

Web page A page that may be accessed via the Web. A Web page may include links to other pages, 2-D and 3-D graphics, sound bites, video, an e-mail address and various forms for user feedback. Its underlying code or flue is HTML, which may be used for formatting as well as for holding together such components as ActiveX controls.
(See ActiveX* and Web*.)

Web page description A stream of 200 characters that exists after the <BODY> tag on a Web page, and is retrieved by search engines as a description of the document.
(See HTML.)

Web page title A Web page title is enclosed by HTML <TITLE> tags. It is used as metadata by popular search engines when retrieving Web documents and is displayed as the document's title.
(See HTML, Search engine and Web page description.)

Web phone *(See Internet telephony.)*

Web proxy An agent which may be perceived as existing between the browser and the Internet or intranet. Typically they are used for caching Web pages in order to improve performance, hence the term *caching proxy*. *(See Security proxy.)*

Web security A method of securing Web applications and their associated data from illegal unauthorised use. Securing Web applications and their data typically involves:

- implementing a firewall, which restricts access to selected Web applications and data
- using client-side security features of Windows NT, and security programs like Virtual Key
- restricting access to server-side data and components, which might include CGI scripts and ISAPI filters
- monitoring system logs
- restricting user's rights to upload files to server-side directories, to minimise the possibility of virus infections
- adhering to SET guidelines
- designing a security regime, where users require membership of the complete site or to selected components
- requiring site members to change their passwords
- granting users guest rights, where they may be peruse demo Web applications and data.

(See Encryption, Firewall, Security and SET.)

Web server An architecture which maintains the connection between the server-side processing and data with that of the client-side. The mainstay of one or more Web applications, the Web server may also implement interactions between users and server-side databases. User interaction via the browser might be processed on the client-side or on the server-side. ActiveX controls might form a basis for such client-side processing. The Web server interpret user requests, and implement specified tasks, such as:

- serving HTML pages, which are interpreted by the browser
- downloading files
- downloading Java applets
- downloading ActiveX controls
- interacting with server-side databases.

Web servers include the Microsoft Personal Web Server, which can be used for prototyping and for proving conceptual designs. With Microsoft IIS, Windows NT is used as the Web server's operating system.
(See IIS and MCIS.)

Web server security   A set of issues which relate to security data traffic between servers and clients so that legal usage is maintained.
(See Firewall and Security.)*

Web site   1. A physical server (or collection of such servers) and software that supports the server-side applications and data of Web applications. Users may connect with the physical or virtual Web servers contained therein, using Web addresses such as www.server.com.au. Server-side components of Web applications are numerous, including:

- software server components
- ActiveX controls
- Java applets
- Perl scripts

2. A software solution which serves clients with a Web application. The application contains a page, or number of pages, and has a Web address (i.e. www.testsite.com.). Such sites can be created with numerous software packages. Microsoft Publisher 98, for instance, has numerous useful wizards which guide you through the design of Web sites. The site's interactive and media content will reside physically on the Web server, and be distributed across:

- HTML code
- Scripting languages such as JavaScript and VBScript
- ActiveX controls
- Java applets.

(See Active Desktop, ASP, Server, Virtual Web server and Web server.)

Web TV   1. A Web site used in television broadcasting capacity. 2. An Internet access appliance that connects with a television. It can take the form of an STB (set-top box.)
(See Streaming and Video.)*

Web-based company   A company that uses the Web as its marketing and selling channel. Historically, such e-commerce Web sites require CGI scripts and programs in order to implement processing logic. Typically forms posted from the browser are validated in terms of credit card details

and so on, and if accepted the customer's order is placed in the database and processed by the vendor at an appropriate point in operations.
(See ASP, CGI, Perl and Transaction.)

WebBot   A name given to components included with Microsoft FrontPage. They each have a specific functionality:

- *Comment* is used to at Web documentation that is only visible at design time
- *Confirmation* echoes entered user data
- *Include* replaces the contents of a Web page with another
- *Scheduled Include* echoes the Include WebBot functionality, except it may be scheduled for a future date
- *Scheduled Image* echoes the functionality of the Scheduled Include WebBot, except it includes an image rather than Web page contents
- *Search Component* provides Web Site search facilities
- *Table of Contents* generates a Web's outline, together with its hyperlinks
- *TimeStamp* is used to display the date and time the Web page was last updated.

(See Active*, FrontPage, Java* and Plug-in.)

Webcasting   A process by which a Web server serves clients or users with specific data or files. The user merely specifies what is required. Webcasting software includes Intermind Communicator and PointCast. Such a process exists within the *push* model.
(See Application* and Client/server*.)

Webmaster   An individual who manages and maintains a Web site. His/her duties are numerous and include updating Web pages, adding new content, removing old content, overlooking integrated security features and policies.

What-if   A term commonly applied to hypothesising in a computer environment. Using fully specified relational databases, it is possible to play What-if by querying stored information. The querying process involves using either standard SQL such as ANSI-92 SQL, OQL (Object-oriented Query Language) or a proprietary querying language or feature such as Borland's QBE (Query By Example). Querying may be used to set up hypothetical situations such as increasing a product price, for instance. The consequences may be viewed almost immediately.
(See Data warehouse and OLAP.)

White Book *(See Video CD.)*

Wildcard A shorthand for search strings. For example, Van Gogh AND Amsterdam may be exchanged for Van *gh AND ?msterdam where '*' represents any series of characters and '?' replaces any single character.

WIM (WAP Identity Model) A security mechanism for WAP.

WIMP (Windows, Icons, Mouse and Pop-up menus) A traditional term for the GUI environment such as OS/2 Warp and Windows.

Winamp An MP3 wave audio file player. *(See MP3.)*

Windows An industry-standard graphical user interface (GUI), operating system and environment which has been a core software technology since circa 1990. Windows is the chosen client-side operating system for almost all client/server applications (including the World Wide Web). Its roots are entrenched in research carried out at the Xerox Palo Alto Research Center (PARC), and in the first commercial multitasking GUI implemented by Apple Computer for inclusion in the Apple Macintosh which was launched in 1984. Windows is the realisation of Bill Gates' early vision of the computer as a universal and invaluable support mechanism. Wherever you may be, close by there is almost always a running copy of Windows, but it is not the nightmarish scenario of George Orwell's novel *1984* where workers are slaves to machines; far from it, because Windows 98 actually frees users. The most notable freedoms it gives are those of browsing the Internet, and permitting users to make purchases through e-commerce Web sites. Users may also publish documents on the large unregulated World Wide Web and communicate in real time. Equally, Windows can be used to run day-to-day applications which include word processors and spreadsheets and even voice-operated dictation systems such as IBM ViaVoice. Windows is quite literally a single gateway, through which everything is accessible. Combined with its underlying and surrounding technologies, its impact greatly surpasses that of any other operating system. For some time Microsoft has sought to make transparent the boundary that separates the Windows Desktop from the Internet. Windows 98 achieved this through the Active Desktop, where Active Channels provide single-click access to Web sites. Windows 98 has much that is required to exploit all is target platforms and software applications, and the technologies that surround us. Windows 98 is an operating system which has evolved over a number of years to become a feature-rich environment. It is increasingly difficult to cite omissions from

Maximise and
Minimise button   Restore button   Close button

Control menu button

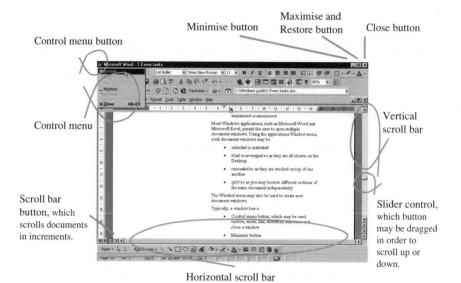

Control menu

Vertical
scroll bar

Scroll bar
button, which
scrolls documents
in increments.

Slider control,
which button
may be dragged
in order to
scroll up or
down.

Horizontal scroll bar

new versions, and Windows 98 is no exception. The obvious absent features and applications are the result of continuing pressure to steer Microsoft away from monopolistic practices. Included in Windows 98 is an impressive array of features, and where you begin and end with them, rather depends on what you want to do. Equally, features that are important to one user, may not be to another user. Generally, however, key features of Windows 98 include:

- Windows Explorer, which permits you to browse files, manage files and disks, open applications, and to do a host of other operations.
- Windows Desktop, upon which are: Program icons, Active Channels, and the Task bar that also has toolbars.
- Active Desktop, which integrates the World Wide Web more tightly with the Windows Desktop. So-called Active Channels can be placed on the Desktop, and provide single-click access to Web sites and the dynamic reception of information. You may also add Active Channels of your own.
- Start button, which provides single-click access to Start menus. These are used to open documents, and to open applications.
- Taskbar, which anchors the Start button, and shows the time of day, and buttons that are used to activate open applications. it also has icons which are used to access various background applications such as Internet and network connections. There are also toolbars that provide single-click access to selected applications and features.

- Dial-up Networking (DUN), which provides access to remote networks and to ISPs.
- Internet connectivity and email features, including the software required to connect with Compuserve, and to other ISPs.
- File Allocation Table32 (FAT32) filing system, which is an advancement of the FAT16 implementation.

(See FAT32.)

The founding father of the Windows concept is Douglas Engelbart, whose work was built upon an Xerox PARC (Palo Alto Research Center). Microsoft's Bill Gates, and Apple Computer's Steve Jobs, learned of the modern Windows implementations that were developed at PARC. This yielded the graphical user environment (GUI or 'gooey'), which was included in the Apple Macintosh launched in mid-1984. The success of the 'Apple Max' led Microsoft to develop a competing GUI in the form of Windows. Work on Microsoft Windows began in earnest with Scott MacGregor from the PARC windows initiative playing a key role. However, the early releases of Windows had little impact in a world where the PC software market was dominated largely by text-based DOS applications. Windows was finally accepted as the *de facto* PC environment in the late 1980s when version 3.0 was released. The Microsoft Windows continuum approximates:

- *Windows 3.0*, which supported 16 bit instructions only, and featured the Program Manager which was used to organise applications and to launch them. It also featured the File Manager later renamed the Windows Explorer through the launch of Windows 95. It did not integrate any multimedia support, because Microsoft had yet to specify the Multimedia PC-1 (MPC-1). At this time, PCs were little more than text-based appliances that offered fairly crude graphics.
- *Microsoft's Multimedia Extensions* were launched in 1990, and could be added to Windows 3.0. These included the Media Player used to play audio, MIDI and video files. As such the Windows PC had become a multimedia-enabled appliance. However, it continued to be devoid of network connectivity features, and was very much a standalone implementation.
- *Windows 3.1* integrated the Multimedia extensions as standard.
- *Windows 3.11* for Workgroups included support for creating peer-to-peer Local Area Networks (LANs), in which connected computers could share their resources with other connected systems.
- *Windows NT (New Technology)* supported 32 bit instructions, and was aimed at the corporate market. Its key strength is improved robustness when compared with Windows 3.1/3.11 and Windows 95/98.

319

- *Windows 95* saw the introduction of the Start menu and Taskbar that replaced the Program Manager as a means of opening applications. It also supported 32 bit instructions and was aimed at home and small office users. Networking features found in Windows 3.11 for Workgroups were also integrated in the design.
- *Windows 98* included new features such as the Active Desktop.

(See GUI.)

Windows 2000 A version of Windows.

(See Windows.)

Windows CE (Compact Edition) A version of Windows intended for portable and consumer devices.

(See Windows.)

Windows Desktop A metaphor used by Windows, providing numerous features including:

- Start button which may be used to open applications and documents
- Taskbar, which anchors the Start button and shows the date, as well as other important icons

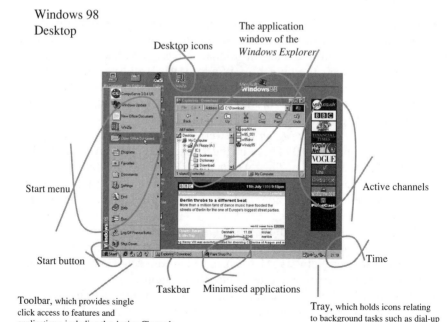

Windows 98
Desktop

Desktop icons

The application
window of the
Windows Explorer

Start menu

Active channels

Start button

Time

Toolbar, which provides single
click access to features and
applications, including the Active Channels.

Taskbar   Minimised applications

Tray, which holds icons relating
to background tasks such as dial-up
networking connections.

- Program icons, which may be double-clicked so as to open applications
- Buttons for open applications, which are displayed on the Taskbar
- Time, which when double-clicked invokes the Date/Time Properties
- Channel bar, which provide single-click access to Web sites and information services.

The Taskbar also serves to display numerous icons, such as those associated with connections to networks and to the Internet.

(See Windows.)

Windows Explorer   *(See Explorer.)*

Windows for Workgroups   *(See Windows.)*

Windows Help system   A Windows Help system uses Hypertext-based navigation.

Windows Media Player A Windows progam, which is able to play audio, video and MIDI.

Windows NT Registry   A configurable set of parameters, which allow Windows NT to optimise resources for applications. The registry is stored in an initialisation (INI) file, and is also used to register components that might be:

- ActiveX
- OLE
- DCOM
- COM.

The *regsvr32* program is used to register such components.

Windows NT Server   A Microsoft 32 bit operating system, which includes the functionality of Windows NT Workstation and an additional array of server-orientated features. *(Refer to the Microsoft Web site.)*

Windows NT Workstation   A Microsoft 32 bit operating system which has a graphical front-end. Windows NT Workstation is a complex OS and suite of integrated applications, and includes:

- Windows Explorer, which is used to browse local and remote files, open files, and launch programs
- Start menu, which permits applications to be launched
- Desktop, upon which icons reside
- NotePad, which is a simple word processor

- Network connectivity functions
- Internet connectivity functions, but has no browser (1998)
- e-mail functions

Windows Sound Recorder   A Windows program able to record wave audio.

Winsock   A Windows Application Programming Interface (API) which provides input/output operations for Web applications. Its implementation takes a form of a DLL (Dynamic Link Library), and is an evolution of the Berkeley Unix sockets, which provide interprocess communications both locally and over networks.

WINS (Warehouse Information Network Standard.)

WinZip   A batch file compression/decompression utility, which may be used for archiving, transmitting digital matter over narrow-bandwidth network and access technologies such as analogue modems.

Wizard   A software feature, which guides the users through the steps required to perform a specific task. The task might be the addition of computer hardware or programs.

WML (Wireless Markup Language)   An industry standard for developing applications that are deployed over wireless communication networks. The WAP Forum, originally founded by Ericsson, Motorola, Nokia and Unwired Planet, designed WML for users of devices that have:

- small displays and limited input devices
- limited memory and processing resources
- narrowband network connection.

WML includes four major functional areas:

- text presentation and layout
- deck/card metaphor
- intercard navigation and linking
- string parameterisation and state management

Word   A Microsoft word processor that is an industry standard.

Workflow management   A broad term used to define the coordination of processes necessary to implement a given task, or given set of tasks.

WorldPay   An electronic credit card clearance solution.

Wozniak, Steve A technologist and co-founder of Apple Computer, and responsible for the design of the early Apple microcomputer.
(See Apple Computer.)

Wrapper
1) A data entity that is a prelude to a program's main data.
2) A program that primes another program so that it may run correctly.
3) A VRL prefix such as http:// or ftp://.
4) A data entity that may include header and trailer, and used in data transmission. It may restrict viewing the data to intended recipients.

Wrappering A process used to migrate a conventional program structure to that of an object. The program is renovated in terms of the addition of an object interface. Thereafter it may be stimulated as any other object.
(See Object*.)

WWW *(See Web.)*

www/netcraft.co.uk/ A Web site which can be visited to gain information about Web servers.

World Wide Web Consortium (W3C) A publisher of specifications of Web technologies which include: HTTP, HTML and CGI. Further information can be obtained at www.w3.org.

WYSIWYG (What-you-see-is-what-you-get) A term applied to a program which is capable of generating on screen exactly what will be printed.

X

X3 An ANSI committee dedicated to Information Processing Systems.

X9 An ANSI committee dedicated to Financial Services.

X12 An ANSI designation and committee dedicated to EDI.

X.25 A standard set of protocols for packet-switched networks which was introduced by the CCITT, but now comes under ITU-T. It covers the protocols between DTE (data terminal equipment) and DCE (data circuit terminating equipment). X.25 were developed in the 1970s, when data transfer rate requirements were slow in comparison to today's. High-speed data transmission using the X.25 protocol is possible, but increasingly modern communications networks integrate frame relay. The X.25 error-correction is accommodated using a scalable acknowledgement window, which may typically include seven packets. This means that the sending device must wait for an acknowledgement for each group of seven packets. The maximum packet size is defined as 256 bytes, so the transmitting device may send $n \times 256$ bytes of data before receiving an acknowledgement that verifies data reception. The error correction that is integrated into X.25 is robust because earlier networks were unreliable. Today's digital networks are much more reliable; thus there is an opportunity to develop more efficient protocols. These need not include the intensive error detection and correction of previous packet-switched protocols. Frame relay is one such relatively contemporary protocol designed for modern communications networks.
(See ATM, Frame relay and ISDN.)

X.509 An internationally agreed standard for digital certificates designated by the CCITT. SET specifies a modified X.509 implementation for payment cards.
(See SET.)

XA 1. A standard protocol which is used to coordinate transactions. 2. A shorthand term for CD-ROM XA (Compact Disc – Read-Only Memory eXtended Architecture). Published by Microsoft, Philips and Sony in march 1988, XA permits a near-CD-I title to be delivered using a conventional desktop computer with installed CD-ROM drive and XA decoder. Initially it appeared for the PC and was seen as a response to Intels' DVI (Digital Video Interactive) digital video compression. It brought CD-I level B and level C audio quality to the PC. Level B audio is equivalent to a high-quality stereo FM broadcast transmitted under optimum conditions. An entire CD-I disc gives a maximum of four hours B-Level stereo playback. Technically level B audio is an 8 bit recording digitised at a sampling frequency of 37.7 kHz. Level C audio equates to an AM radio broadcast transmitted under optimum conditions. A whole disc could yield over 16 hours playing time. It is also termed mid-fi quality. It equates to a 4 bit ADPCM wave audio recording sampled at 37.7 kHz.
(See CD-ROM and DVD.)

Xanadu A unified repository of literature and information, invented by Theodore Nelson. It was conceived before the Web and abstracts much of the thinking embedded in the work of Vannevar Bush, and his momentous article, 'As We May Think.' Conceptually, Xanadu was the Web. If Vannevar Bush and Ted Nelson were responsible for putting forward the concept of the Web, then Tim Berners-Lee must be considered its architect.
(See Web*.)

XDSL (Digital Subscriber Line) An digital access technology which provides sufficient bandwidth for multiple virtual lines over a single physical telephone connection to accommodate for example, concurrent Internet access and voice/fax communications. Supporting data transfer rates that approach 2 Mbps. XDSL applications include video on demand interactive video and data communications, and since it can use twisted pair (or telephone lines as its medium its deployment is cost-effective.
(See Access technology and ADSL.)

XENIX A Unix variant which was developed by Microsoft.

Xeon A shorthand term for the Pentium II Xeon processor, originally aimed at workstations and servers.

Xerox PARC (Palo Alto Research Center) *(See PARC.)*

XingCFD A software product from Xing (Arroyo Grande, USA) capable of compressing video according to the MPEG-1 compression algorithm.

Used without an MPEG-1 player it is able to play MPEG video without sound.

XingSound   A software product from Xing (Arroyo Grande, US) useful for compressing wave audio according to the MPEG-1 audio compression standard. It can record and compress audio from an analogue source in real time. It can also be used to perform standard editing operations on MPEG-1 wave audio files, including cut, copy and paste.

Xing Technology Corporation   A company engaged in the development of MPEG encoding and editing products, and audio and video compression in general. It is headquartered in Arroyo Grande, USA. Products include the XingCD which may be used to compress video according to MPEG-1 compression algorithm, and XingSound which may be used to produce and edit MPEG-1 audio streams.
(See MPEG*, Streaming* and Video.)

XML (eXtended Markup Language)   A language that may be used to communicate information in various media including the World Wide Web. It structurally approximates HTML and was designed by a group sponsored by the W3C.

XMS (eXtended Memory Specification)   A software specification which provides access beyond the 1 Mbyte boundary of PC architecture machines. Access to extended memory is provided by an appropriate driver in the CONFIG.SYS file that may be assumed to be HIMEM/SYS.

XNET   A interprocessor communications scheme used by the MasPar MP-1 SIMD processor. It addresses processors as a two-dimensional network topology.
(See MPP.)

X/OS   A Unix variant developed by Olivetti.

XPATH (XML Path Language)   A common syntax and semantics for functionality shared between Xpointer and XSL Transformations (XSLT), and is used to provide addressing to XML documents which it models as a tree of nodes. Xpath expressions may yield an object type that may be:

- node-set (or set of nodes)
- boolean (true or false)
- number (that is a floating-point number)
- string (or sequence of UCS characters).

(See XPointer.)

XPOINTER A language expression that gives specific references to XML document content. An XPointer expression may search a document's structure based on criteria that include properties such as element types, attribute values, character content, and sequence. Xpointers can:

- address into XML documents
- be used over the Internet
- be integrated in URLs.

(See XML.)

Xpress A shorthand name for the QuarkXpress desktop publishing package.

XSL (eXtensible Stylesheet Language) A language used to create stylesheets that describe XML data files in terms of the style, page format and pagination, for electronic media such as Windows and browsers or printed matter. An XSL *stylesheet processor* generates XML source from the XML document and the XSL stylesheet by:

- tree transformation that constructs a result tree using the XML source tree
- formatting to produce a formatted presentation using the result tree.

XSL is based on Cascading Style Sheets (CSS2) and on the Document Style Semantics and Specification Language (DSSSL), and has many of CSS formatting objects.

XSLT (eXtensible Stylesheet Language Transformations) A part of the CSL language that transforms XML documents into other XML documents. The XSL Transformations (XSLT) Version 1.0 was published in October 1999 as a W3C Proposed Recommendation. XSLT accommodates XSL-related transformation types which are expressed as a well-formed XML document that complies with Namespaces in XML Recommendation. A transformation describes rules for transforming a source tree into a result tree and is achieved by associating patterns with templates as follows:

- patterns are matched against source tree elements.
- templates are instantiated to build the result tree.

(See XSL.)

X standards A series of evolving recommendations covering data networks. Among the most significant X standard is X.25.

XT A shorthand term used to describe the IBM PC XT. And early desktop computer design produced in the very early 1980s. Its specification is now defunct.

X Window   A GUI system often used with almost all Unix OSs, and was developed by at Massachusetts Institute of Technology (MIT), which surrendered it to the public domain. X Window System implementations include Motif and OpenLook.

X-Y input device   An input device which measure input movement in two dimensions only.

Y

Y 1. A horizontal dimension of a coordinate in a two- or three-dimensional vector coordinate representation. The value may be absolute, measured from the origin $[0, 0]$ or relative such as $[X_0 + X_1, Y_0 + Y_1]$. A 2-D computer image or animation might be stored and generated using absolute or relative coordinates that include X (horizontal) and Y (vertical) dimensions. Authentic 2-D animations depend upon matrix multiplication where sets of coordinates are multiplied by a transformation matrix. 2-D vectors $[X, Y]$ might be exchanged for homogeneous vector coordinates $[X, Y, H]$. The homogeneous dimension (H) is added to accommodate a three-row transformation matrix, so increasing the number of possible 2-D transformations. *(See 3-D.)* 2. A luminance component of video signal.

Y2K (A Year 2000) A term used to describe the year 2000. The lead up to the end of the millennium saw numerous IT systems being renovated to accommodate the need for date stamping using the year 2000 and its increments. Many non-compliant Y2K IT systems were created decades ago, when little consideration was given to the future.

Yahoo A Web site featuring multiple information sources, services and search engine facilities.

Y-axis A horizontal axis on a graph or drawing.

Y-dimension A horizontal measurement that might be absolute or relative, in a 2-D or 3-D coordinate.
(See 2-D and 3-D.)

Yield A measure of the amount which an investment generates, such as ordinary shares.

331

Yellow Alarm An alarm state which forms part of the T1 circuit specification. *(See T1.)* The Yellow Alarm is activated by:
- the receipt of a Red Alarm signal
- severe burst traffic.

Yellow page service A directory service for a Web site or suite of services running on a network or server.

YMODEM A protocol which supports data transfer using 1024 byte blocks, and is also referred to as XMODEM 1K.

YMODEM G A protocol which transmits a complete file before an acknowledge signal is received. It is intended for modem devices that have built-in error detection and correction.

Z

Z 1. A dimension of depth in a 3-D image or animation. A 3-D computer image or animation stored and generated using absolute or relative co-ordinates that include *X* (horizontal), *Y* (vertical) and *Z* (depth) dimensions. It might be:

- an absolute measurement from the origin
- a relative measurement from another coordinate.

2. A measurement of impedance. Connected electronic devices typically have an input and output impedance. By matching these using the maximum power transfer theorem, an optimum electronic/electrical connection may be made. 3. The dimension (n) in which a processor exists in an MPP network configured as a cube or hypercube.

Z80 An ANSI Committee dedicated to ophthalmics.

ZAP A process of eradicating date or applications from a system.

Zero beat A state where two frequencies are the same.

ZIF socket (Zero Insertion Force socket) A type of socket commonly found on motherboards that permits the safe and easy removal and replacement of processors. The socket is fitted with a lever which is used to lock the processor in place and to release it. ZIF sockets are also available for DIL (Dual In-Line) devices such as ROM (Read-Only Memory) chips.

ZIP 1. A file format from PKWare that used for batch file compression. WinZip is an application that may be used to zip and unzip such compressed files. 2. A removable storage device manufactured by Iomega. Its removable discs store 100 Mbyte of data.

Zoom A feature on many graphics and video editing programs that permits the user to enlarge a frame or image. All Windows applications feature such a control which may typically be invoked form the View menu. The user may be presented with Zoom-in values, such as 75%, 100%, 125%, 150% etc, or a value may be specified. Alternatively scale ratios may be selected such as 2:1, 3:1, 4:1 et cetera that may be used to zoom in and out.

Zoom options   A control that presents the user with the ability to zoom in and out, of an application workspace or window. All Windows applications feature such a control that may typically be invoked form the View menu. The user may be presented with Zoom-in values, such as 75%, 100%, 125%, 150% et cetera, or a value may be specified. Alternatively scale ratios may be selected such as 2:1, 3:1, 4:1 etc., which may be used to zoom in and out.